Unit 4

design and produce multimedia products

Unit 22

creating sound using ICT

Unit 23

creating video

D1494634

Ruksana Patel
Anne Kelsall
Graham Manson
Steve Cushing

Consultant: Keith Parry

OCR level 2 Nationals ict

Payne-Gallway is an imprint of Pearson Education Limited, a company incorporated in England and Wales, having its registered office at Edinburgh Gate, Harlow, Essex, CM20 2JE. Registered company number: 872828

www.payne-gallway

First published 2007

12 11 10 09 08
10 9 8 7 6 5 4 3 2

British Library Cataloguing in Publication Data is available from the British Library on request.

ISBN 978 1 905292 13 4

Edited by Alex Sharpe
Designed by Kamae Design
Produced and typeset by Sparks www.sparks.co.uk
Cover photo/illustration © Steve Shott
Printed and bound in China through Phoenix Offset

Acknowledgements
The author would like to thank Penny Hill and Abdul Patel for working through the book and activities, for providing invaluable feedback and for their support. Thank you to Keith Parry for reading the first drafts. Thank you to my family Abdul, Fayaz and Fozia Roked for their patience, encouragement and support. Thank you to Nadezda Poole and Thomas Winter at Harcourt, for their input and support which has improved the quality of the book. Thank you to Professor Peter Mumby at the University of Exeter for permission to use the video clips from the ReefVid website (http://www.reefvid.org). Thank you to Brian Byrne at the University of Birmingham for his help with the sound and video clips and to Chris Jowsey for his help with the video clips.

The images, video clips and sound clips provided as downloadable resources on the Payne-Gallway website are made available with permission from Professor Peter Mumby, Chris Jowsey and the ReefVid website (http://www.reefvid.org).

Microsoft product screenshots reprinted with permission from Microsoft Corporation.

Websites
The websites used in this book were correct and up-to-date at the time of publication. It is essential for tutors to preview each website before using it in class so as to ensure that the URL is still accurate, relevant and appropriate. We suggest that tutors bookmark useful websites and consider enabling students to access them through the school/college intranet.

Ordering Information
Payne-Gallway, FREEPOST (OF1771),
PO Box 381, Oxford OX2 8BR
Tel: 01865 888070
Fax: 01865 314029
Email: orders@payne-gallway.co.uk

Contents

Series Introduction

Introduction

This book is one of a series of books that has been designed to guide you in your work for the OCR Level 2 Nationals in ICT. Each book covers two or three units and explains the skills and concepts that are needed for each. It also sets out in detail how to create a portfolio to achieve a **Pass**, **Merit** or **Distinction** for each assessment objective.

Design and produce multimedia products, *Creating sound using ICT* and *Creating video* cover the assessment objectives as set out in Units 4, 22 and 23 of the specification.

How to use this book

This book is divided into three sections which guide you through each Assessment Objective as set out by OCR in the specifications for Units 4, 22 and 23. Every chapter helps you to understand how you would build evidence for your portfolio through a clear Scenario, helpful Tips and structured Activities, using step-by-step instructions. At every stage clear guidance is given as to the level of evidence required for a **Pass**, **Merit** or **Distinction** so that you are able to plan you own progress effectively.

Work through the chapters in sequence. Read all the explanations and work through the sections explaining the skills. Carry out each activity making sure you save all files as you complete the activities.

To help you, example forms are provided in the **Units4,22&23StudentResources** folder which can be downloaded from the OCR Nationals in ICT (Units 4, 22 & 23) Student Resources page on the Payne-Gallway website (**www.payne-gallway.co.uk**).

Use the forms as they are or adapt them as you wish. For some objectives, more than one example of a form is provided. You should view all the examples and select the one which you think is most appropriate. You may wish to ask your teacher or tutor for guidance too.

Save the forms that you are going to use into your user area, then remove the read-only properties: right-click on the file (a shortcut menu displays) → Click **Properties** (a dialogue box (window) displays) → Click in the box for **Read-only** to remove the tick (or square) → Click **Apply** → Click **OK**.

Symbols used in this book

→ means that a new instruction follows or an option from a menu or sub-menu should be selected.

Example: **Edit** → **Copy** means click **Edit** on the menu bar, then click **Copy**.

The practice assignment

This assignment is provided to help you practise the skills required for the units in this book.

The project scenario:

You have been asked to design, create and test an interactive multimedia presentation promoting adventure holidays for teenage girls and boys aged 12–17. This presentation will be given on a CD-ROM to visitors attending a holiday roadshow. The CD-ROM will also include an audio clip and a video clip promoting one of the aspects of the adventure holidays. The audio and video clip can be included in the multimedia presentation but should also be provided as separate clips on the CD-ROM.

The adventure holidays are organised for parties of about 20 teenagers, supervised by three tour guides. The company offers a variety of activity holidays to Europe during the spring and summer school holidays. Bookings need to be made six months in advance with a minimum of a 10 per cent deposit. Subsequent instalments are paid on request with the final sum payable two weeks before the departure date.

The cost of the trip includes accommodation but participants are required to organise their own travel insurance. Special clothing for activities can be hired at each location, however teenagers should bring rainproof jackets and waterproof shoes.

Portfolio builder

Your work for each unit should be presented as a portfolio. This will include paper copies of your work and could also include an electronic copy of your interactive presentation on a floppy disk/memory stick/CD-ROM. Keep your portfolio organised from the start – label all your work clearly and organise all your printouts logically. It is helpful to create separate sections, e.g. using file dividers, for each assessment objective. For example, there are five assessment objectives in Unit 4, so you could have five sections as follows:

1 Review
2 Design
3 Source
4 Create
5 Test

All your printouts must display your name. It is also good practice to include a filename and the date. You could insert a footer in every document in which you type your name and use an automatic filename and an automatic date.

UNIT 4

Design and Produce Multimedia Products

In this unit you will cover the following...

- AO1 **Review several existing multimedia products**
- AO2 **Design a multimedia product**
- AO3 **Source and store suitable multimedia elements**
- AO4 **Create the multimedia product**
- AO5 **Seek feedback and suggest improvements**

Introduction to Unit 4

Overview

In this unit, you will first review at least three existing multimedia products. These may include websites, CD-ROMs, DVD-ROMs, educational and other games or multimedia presentations. You will identify the aims and purpose of each product, the intended audience, and the good and not so good features. You will comment on how well the aims of each product are met and suggest possible improvements.

Next you will start to think about a multimedia product that you will be creating. You will decide the purpose and audience for your multimedia product, produce plans of the product, including details of how each page/screen will be linked, and details of what each page/screen will contain.

The next step will be to find appropriate content for your multimedia product (e.g. text, images, sounds, animations and video clips). Some of the content to be used in your multimedia product may have been created when working on other units or in other subject areas. You must keep a record of the filenames and other details (e.g. copyright information) for each element you will use, and also accurate details of where you have found the materials (e.g. the website or network location of files to be used).

Next you will create the multimedia product. It must include opportunities for users to interact with the product (e.g. by clicking on buttons or hyperlinks to move between different screens or sections of the product).

Finally you need to evaluate your product and suggest possible improvements and how these could be carried out. The evaluation should include both your own self-evaluation, and also feedback from others in the form of interviews, questionnaires or checklists.

Key term

Multimedia

Multimedia, as the name implies, is the integration of multiple forms of media. A multimedia product includes any combination of different media: text, graphics, animation, audio, video or other special effects. For example, a presentation with text and/or graphics that includes a video and/or audio clip is considered to be a 'multimedia presentation'. Educational software or recreational computer games that include sound, animation and text are referred to as 'multimedia software'. A website that includes a combination of text, animation and audio or video is considered to be an 'interactive website'.

The project

You may be set a topic or brief by your centre or you may choose a topic of your own. If you choose to follow a topic of your own, you must ensure that your project allows you to meet all of the assessment objectives and the grading grid for this unit.

In order to practise the skills required for this unit, in this book you will work through a sample project similar to the one you will use for your assessment. The sample project scenario for this unit is provided in the Introduction to this book.

Software

This unit is written for Microsoft PowerPoint 2003. It can be used with other versions of PowerPoint although some screenshots and methods may not exactly match these versions.

Other software such as Macromedia Flash or MatchWare Mediator is also appropriate for this unit.

CHAPTER 1

Assessment Objective 1

Review Several Existing Multimedia Products

Overview

In this chapter, you will need to review at least three different, existing multimedia products. You will then use the knowledge and skills gained during your reviews when planning and designing your own multimedia product.

You will learn how to recognise the target audience and the products' aims. You will try to decide whether or not the aims were met and if not, why not. You will identify the good and not so good features of each product. You will also suggest possible improvements that could be made to each multimedia product.

There are two reasons why you need to look critically at existing multimedia products:

- To help you see what makes a good product so that you may get some design hints for your own product.
- To help you see the weaker features of a product so that you avoid making similar mistakes when you create your own.

Review forms

To help you record your reviews, example review forms can be downloaded from the Student Resources page on the Payne-Gallway website: **www.payne-gallway.co.uk**. The forms are contained in the **Unit4StudentResources** folder, in the subfolder **Unit4Forms**. The review forms are provided in Microsoft Word format. You can print the forms and handwrite your comments or type information in the Word file.

How this assessment objective will be assessed...

The grade you are awarded for this assessment objective will depend on the amount of detail you include in your review of each multimedia product.

As a minimum, you must list and give an explanation of the good and not so good features of each of the three different products. For a **Merit** grade, your explanation of these features should be detailed, and for a **Distinction** grade, this explanation must be thorough.

If you also identify the aims of the multimedia products and you suggest possible improvements, you can achieve a **Merit** grade.

If you include more detail in your review of each product, such as identifying the target audience and suggesting a range of valid improvements that could help the product meet its aims, you can achieve a **Distinction** grade.

Key terms

You will come across the words 'thorough' and 'detailed' frequently in this qualification. 'Detailed' is usually a descriptor used for **Merit** or **Distinction** grading and 'thorough' is usually a descriptor used for **Distinction** grading. In this qualification, a 'thorough' explanation should include more detail than a 'detailed' explanation.

Detailed

A detailed explanation or detailed plan is one that is developed with care and in minute detail. It should contain enough detail for someone else to be able to clearly understand what is intended.

Thorough

A thorough explanation is one that is methodical and comprehensively complete. It is extremely careful and accurate and includes all the necessary information.

Skills to use...

You will need to:

- **select** appropriate multimedia products to review
- identify the intended **audience**
- identify the **aims** of each multimedia product
- **recognise** the features used and comment on the good **features** and not so good features
- assess whether or not the **aims are met**
- suggest **possible improvements** for the multimedia products reviewed.

How to achieve...

Pass requirements

P1 You will list and give an explanation of the good and not so good features of three different multimedia products.

Merit requirements

M1 You will identify the aim(s) of the multimedia product.

M2 You will give a detailed explanation of the good and not so good features of at least three multimedia products.

M3 You will suggest possible improvements for the products reviewed.

Distinction requirements

D1 You will identify the aim(s) and the audience of the multimedia product.

D2 You will give a thorough explanation of the good and not so good features of at least three multimedia products.

D3 You will suggest a range of valid improvements to help the product meet its aims.

Key term

Non-linear

A style of displaying parts of a product in a way that is not chronological. Instead of advancing the pages or screens in a product in sequence, the user can click on navigational controls (e.g. images, buttons, text) that link the various sections in the product. The user can therefore access any part of the product at any time.

What is an interactive multimedia product?

An interactive multimedia product is one where the content can be viewed in a **non-linear** way. The product brings together combinations of images/graphics, audio, video and text into a single product allowing the user to move from one part of the product to another, and to activate parts of the product, using buttons, hyperlinks or other methods.

The product will have a navigation structure allowing the viewer to choose the topics he/she wants to go to by clicking and choosing. The product requires active participation by the user. All the elements of multimedia, like sound or animation, are used to convey information effectively.

The information is accessed through a specialised computer program. Some examples of multimedia products and how they are accessed are given below:

- **Interactive multimedia websites**

Websites are accessed through a web browser (e.g. Internet Explorer, Netscape, Firefox).

- **Online and CD-ROM/DVD-ROM presentations**

A presentation may be a slide show presentation, but this is not the only type of presentation: a website is also a presentation.

Presentations may be accessed through presentation software (e.g. Microsoft PowerPoint) or may be set up to be viewed without the software.

- **Educational or recreational computer games**

Educational computer games are usually designed to run on particular types of computer (e.g. PCs or Mac computers). The software needed to run these is usually 'packed' within the game or may need particular software to be installed on the computer.

Recreational computer games can be designed for use on specific platforms or on specialist hardware (e.g. Sony PlayStation, Nintendo Wii, Microsoft Xbox).

The hardware and software specifications required are usually stated on the product.

- **Commercials/advertisements on CD-ROM/DVD-ROM**

In the same way as computer games these may designed to run on particular types of computer (e.g. PCs or Macs) and may need particular hardware and/or software (e.g. commercial advertisements for new films and quizzes may be included on film DVDs which would need to be viewed on a DVD player or computer with a DVD drive). Often, however, as the aim is to advertise the product to the widest market possible, commercial advertisements on CD/DVD-ROM are frequently designed to run on all types of computer and are usually not reliant on any particular software.

1. Select appropriate multimedia products to review

Your teacher or tutor may provide you with a list of multimedia products to review or may allow you to make your own choices. Either way, you must review at least **three different multimedia products**. For example you may select a computer game, an interactive website and a multimedia presentation. It is acceptable, though not recommended, to select three different multimedia products of the same type, for example, three different interactive websites or three different interactive presentations.

Documentation for reviewing multimedia product

To record details of the multimedia products you will review, you may use or adapt the example form titled **AO1_ReviewMultimediaProduct** provided with this book or any other recording documents provided by your teacher or tutor. If you are using the provided example, you should use a separate form for each product you review.

TIP

When choosing your three multimedia products to review:

The idea is not to look for a 'near perfect' product, so avoid spending too much time choosing which products to review.

Try to avoid choosing very large products with lots of pages/screens.

Activity 1: Select multimedia products to review...

In this activity you will:

- decide which three multimedia products to review
- start to record specific details about each product using a separate document for each product.

Use the provided example forms titled **AO1_ReviewMultimediaProduct** (use one form for each multimedia product). In the Activity 1 section of each form, you will need to complete the two boxes titled **Type of product** and **Brief detail about product**.

➔ Have a discussion with your teacher or tutor about which multimedia products would be suitable for you to review. Find out if your teacher or tutor has already identified appropriate products for you to review or has a list of products from which you can choose three.

➔ If you need to make your own choices, find out what facilities (e.g. hardware, software, Internet access) will be available to you. This is important because if you are reviewing an interactive multimedia website for example, you will need Internet access and a sound card on your computer, as well as software (e.g. Real Player, Windows Media Player) that will allow you to hear sound and to see video clips. You will also need headphones or speakers connected to your computer.

- If you need to find your own products to review, here are some ideas to help you:
  - Search for interactive multimedia websites, or, try some of these:
    http://www.gspsoftware.co.uk
    http://www.metoffice.gov.uk
    http://www.bbc.co.uk
    http://www.bbc.co.uk/wales/education/index.shtml
    http://www.bbc.co.uk/travelnews
    http://www.howstuffworks.com
    http://www.miniclip.com/games
    http://stickcricket.com
    http://www.sticksportsfootball.com
  - Visit your school or college library or Open Learning Centre (if you have one). Ask if they have copies of educational CD/DVD-ROMs.
  - Ask your school/college library, teacher/tutor or friends for copies of film DVDs that contain interactive elements. For example some of the Harry Potter DVDs include interactive elements (e.g. out-takes, interviews, quizzes, etc.).
  - Search the Web for 'interactive presentations' or ask at your school/college for copies of interactive presentations.
  - Look for newspapers and magazines which include free copies of games or presentations on CD.
- Using a separate form for each product, enter the type of product.
- Give brief details about the product, for example if you are reviewing a website, enter the website address.
- Save each form separately. You will update them later.

2. Identify the intended audience

Key terms

Audience

The group or type of people that the product has been designed to appeal to most. A website dedicated to a particular football team is likely to appeal to supporters of that team, but not to people supporting their rivals! A presentation about a rap artist may appeal to people of a certain age group who like that type of music, but may not be of any interest to an older person who dislikes rap music.

Target audience

An important concept that describes a group in the community selected as being the most appropriate for a particular advertising campaign. The target audience is usually defined by the characteristics of the group that a product is aimed at. A target audience might be as wide as 'adults aged 25 to 40' or as narrow as 'teenage female violinists'.

Identifying the audience

Some general products appeal to a very wide range of people (e.g. a fizzy drink available in most shops and supermarkets) – they are purchased by many different groups of people. They have a very wide target audience, therefore the advertising of such a product needs to be quite general. Other products appeal to a narrow group of people (e.g. long-length skirts for taller than average women), therefore the promotion of such products would need to appeal to this narrow target audience.

When you describe the audience for any multimedia product try to be as specific and as precise as possible. For example you could think about things like:

- **age group** – products may be aimed at people of a certain age (e.g. teenagers)
- **gender** – a product may be aimed at either males or females
- **education** (level/background) – a product may be aimed at people in a particular profession (e.g. medical postgraduates). A target group's level of education could influence how and what they buy
- **family size** –a commercial presentation for larger cars (e.g. people carriers) may be aimed at larger families
- **income level** – this factor is about the affordability of a product and what the product says about the wealth and income of the person (e.g. skiing holidays)
- **geographic location** – a local newsletter is aimed at a small group of people living in a particular suburb or town.

The examples above are just a few of the different groupings that can be applied to target audiences. The groupings can be used on their own but they can also be combined or used with other factors, for example a target audience for a website promoting security alarm systems could be single females living in Birmingham city centre. It does not matter if other groups of people use the website and order the security systems because the target audience is the group that the product is aimed at, not necessarily who buys the product.

Activity 2: Identify the intended audience...

In this activity you will:

- first complete a short practice exercise in which you will identify the target audience for each description
- then begin your review of each of your three chosen products
- use the forms saved in Activity 1 to record details of the target audience for each of your chosen multimedia products
- need to complete the Activity 2 **Target Audience** section on each of the three forms.

➔ For each brief description below, decide who the target audience is and state whether you think that target audience is narrow or wide.

  - Burgers from a fast food chain.
  - Ready prepared kosher meals.
  - An interactive CD-ROM about how to build aeroplane models.
  - A famous boy band's monthly magazine.
  - Cricket bats.

➔ For each of your chosen multimedia products, spend some time becoming familiar with each product. Navigate the different pages/slides/screens, all the time thinking about who you think the product has been created for.

- On your **AO1_ReviewMultimediaProduct** form for each product, in the **Target audience** section, enter a description of who you think the intended audience is. Try to make your description as specific and precise as possible. Refer back to the section 'Identifying the audience' on page 9 to help you.
- Save the updated forms.

3. Identify the aims of a multimedia product

Key terms

Aim

This is simply the purpose of the product – why the product has been produced.

Identifying the aims

The products you review will be designed for a particular audience (see Section 2 on pages 8 and 9) and for a particular purpose. Some examples of the purpose of multimedia products are given below:

- **To provide information** – a website may aim to provide information about particular hobbies or interests. An educational CD-ROM/DVD-ROM is designed to provide information in an engaging manner. A number of elements of interactivity are usually added to keep the interest of the user.
- **To attract attention** – a multimedia presentation in, for example, a car showroom, a reception area, an entrance hall, etc. is designed to attract the attention of people entering or passing through the area. Such a presentation needs to be eye-catching and dynamic so that people are encouraged to stop and look. The addition of interactive elements such as hyperlinks will help to engage the user.
- **To persuade the target audience to purchase a product** – the aim of the multimedia product is to generate as many sales as possible. Every positive aspect of the product being advertised will be glorified and all possible benefits to the target audience will be emphasised.
- **To persuade the target audience to join something** – parents visiting a school or college open evening may be shown a multimedia presentation. It may include photographs of happy students doing interesting things in lessons, the school orchestra, students using computers to do their work, etc. The aim of the presentation may be to persuade parents that the school is a good place and that their children will be happy if they choose to go there! It may give lots of factual information about examination results and successful past students. It is unlikely to show the corners of the school where there may be graffiti or litter. It will aim to give a very good impression and will be trying to persuade the viewer to send their child to the school/college – not to put them off!
- **To entertain or engage the user** – a recreational computer game is designed to entertain the user so that they will keep playing the game. Different levels of achievement are usually used to engage the user and entice them to want to continue playing in order to progress to the next level. Some games are designed to be played by more than one person – the player may be able to link to other players using the Internet – and take part in contests or collaboration with others.
- **To change behaviour** – for example anti-drink driving or anti-smoking campaigns.
- **To teach/train/educate to specific learning objectives** – for example educational CD-ROMs.

When you review your multimedia products, think about the purpose of each multimedia product – the product's aims.

Activity 3: Identify the aim(s)...

In this activity you will:

- spend some time reviewing each of your chosen multimedia products in turn
- continue to use the forms saved in Activity 2 to record details of the aims for each of your chosen multimedia products
- need to complete the Activity 3 **Aims of product** section in each of the three forms.

➔ Open your saved forms **AO1_ReviewMultimediaProduct** and remind yourself of who the target audience is.

➔ Continue your review of each multimedia product, working on each product in turn. Navigate the different pages/slides/screens. This time consider why the product was created. Ask yourself: What is the purpose of this product? Why was this product produced?

➔ On your form **AO1_ReviewMultimediaProduct** for each product, in the **Aims of product** section, enter details of what you think the product's aims are.

➔ Save your updated forms.

4. Identify the good and not so good features of a multimedia product

Multimedia products will usually have a number of different features. When reviewing each product, you should:

1. identify what features have been used
2. then decide how appropriate and effective each feature is
3. provide an explanation about the good features (positive features/aspects)
4. provide an explanation of the not so good (negative) aspects of each feature in turn.

You will need to recognise what features are good and when features have been used inappropriately or ineffectively. You will find this easier to do in stages, for example firstly identify the images used and then make some comments about the images. Next, consider the text provided, etc.

The table below lists some points you could think about for the images used in a multimedia product. 'Images' include all pictures (e.g. photographs, clipart, image buttons, drawn or computer graphics, animations, etc.).

Feature	Factors to consider regarding images and animations
Images	• How appropriate are the number of images for the type of product and for the target audience? • How do images attract the viewer's attention? Are images distracting? • How well do the images relate to the text? • What is the quality of images? How clear is any text on images? Is the text clearly readable? • Are images positioned appropriately on each page in relation to other content? • How quickly do images load? • Have rollover images been used? If so, are they effective? • Have flashing images been used? Would these be appropriate for anyone with visual difficulties? • Have animations been used? Are these positioned appropriately? • How are animations relevant to the product content and target audience? • Have pop-ups been used? Are these appropriate or are they annoying?

Key term

Rollover

An action or event that takes place when the mouse passes over a specific image or section of text in a multimedia product, for example, on a web page a different image displays when the mouse moves over an existing image, or a different image displays depending on the direction the mouse is moved (up, down, left, right).

Commenting on the good and not so good features of images

Some example comments that could be used when you are providing an explanation about the good and not so good features of images used in an interactive multimedia product are given below.

Examples of positive (good) comments that you could make about images and animations in a multimedia product:

The images were of very good quality and were all appropriate to the text; they added purpose to the text.

Image sizes were all appropriate for the page size and layout. Good use was made of the space to the right of text. Images did not overlap any text.

The image used as a background behind the text as a watermark looked very professional and was very effective as the image related well to the text and made the presentation look interesting.

The animation used on the home page was very effective. It moved smoothly across the screen and added interest to the website. It made me keen to see the rest of the website.

The animation of the person skiing through the slopes was very lifelike – it made me want to try it myself. This was a good technique which should encourage people to want to try skiing.

Examples of negative (not so good) comments that you could make about images and animations in a multimedia product:

Too many pictures were used and these did not relate to the product being advertised. They looked as if they were just put there to add colour to the page.

Most images were too big in comparison with the size of the page. The captions on the images were difficult to read. The images took a long time to display on the pages.

The images were not always positioned appropriately on the page making the page look untidy. On several pages, two or three images were placed next to each other with very little text to explain what the images were about.

The animation on every page was irrelevant to the content and distracting. It was difficult to concentrate on the content because of the frog constantly jumping up and down.

Activity 4: Identify the images used and comment on the good and not so good aspects of these...

In this activity you:

- should spend some time reviewing each page/slide/screen of your chosen multimedia products in turn. Your aim is to comment on all the images, including buttons, animations, graphics, etc. used in each multimedia product
- will use the forms you saved in Activity 3 to comment about the images used in each of your chosen multimedia products
- will need to complete the Activity 4 section in each of the three forms.

➔ Open your saved form **AO1_ReviewMultimediaProduct1** and remind yourself of who the target audience is for your first product. This is necessary because you need to comment on whether the images are appropriate for the intended target audience (not whether *you* think the images are appropriate!).

➔ Go through each page/slide/screen of your first multimedia product and identify all the different types of images used: photographs, image buttons, animations, graphics, etc.

➔ On your form **AO1_ReviewMultimediaProduct1**, in the Activity 4 section, comment about the good and/or not so good aspects of all the different types of images. If a feature has not been used (e.g. there are no buttons), you could comment about whether this is appropriate to the product or not.

➔ Now review your second and third multimedia products and fill in the relevant sections of your review forms.

➔ Save your updated forms.

TIP

For a Merit grade, your explanations should be detailed. For a Distinction grade, your explanations should be thorough. To make your explanations more detailed, you could discuss the images on each page/slide/screen separately. On your forms AO1_ReviewMultimediaProduct, in the row for each feature, enter a subheading for each page/slide/screen as shown in the example on page 14 for the review of an interactive presentation. Alternatively, take a screen print of each page/slide/screen and discuss each page separately. Refer to pages 74–76 in Chapter 4 if you need to learn how to produce screen prints.

Images and animations		
Feature	**Good features**	**Not so good features**
Photographs, clipart	**Slide 1** **Slide 2**	**Slide 1** **Slide 2**

Example of Activity 4 table on ***AO1_ReviewMultimediaProduct*** *form.*

Continuing the review – considering the use of colour, text and information

The table below lists some points you could think about regarding colour, text and information used in a multimedia product. You should also try to think of additional factors to consider regarding colour, text and information, for example you could make comments about the template used.

Feature	**Factors to consider regarding use of colour, text and information**
Use of colour	• How appropriate are text and background colours? Are text colours clearly legible against the background image and/or colour? • How do text, link, hyperlink, visited link colours and background colours complement each other? • Is the use of different colours appropriate? Are there too many or too few colours? • How effective are the colours used on different pages/slides/screens in the product?
Text	• How appropriate is the amount of text on each page/slide/screen? For example, is there too much or too little text? • How appropriate is the text layout on each page/slide/screen? • How easy is it to read the text? For example, is the text style (font type, font size) appropriate?
Information	• How appropriate is the amount of information provided? For example, is there too much information to absorb? Is there too little information? • How relevant is all the information? • How appropriate is the level of language and tone for the target audience? • How does the information provided enhance the instruction/delivery of the subject matter? (Applicable to certain types of product, e.g. educational CD/DVD-ROMs, educational websites, presentations.) • How accurate, factually and technically, is the content? The following point will apply more to educational CD/DVD-ROMs and games: • How easy to understand are learning activities? Do activities cover any stated learning objectives?

Explaining the good and not so good features of colour, text and information

Some example comments that could be used when you are providing an explanation about the good and not so good features of colours, text and information in an interactive multimedia product are given below.

Examples of positive (good) comments that you could make about colour:

The text, link and background colours were clear and easy to read and complemented each other well.

The text colour was effective against the background colour and made the page look very striking and professional.

Examples of negative (not so good) comments that you could make about colour:

The pale text colour was difficult to read against the pale background colour. Once the links were visited the linked text colour was almost illegible.

Red text against a green background is difficult for some people to read. This is not considered appropriate and should have been avoided.

Activity 5: Consider the use of colour, text and information and comment on the good and not so good aspects of these...

In this activity you:

- should continue reviewing each page/slide/screen of your chosen multimedia products in turn
- should comment on the use of colours, the text on each screen and the information provided
- will continue to use the forms saved in Activity 4
- will need to complete the Activity 5 section in each of the three forms.

➔ Go through each page/slide/screen of your first multimedia product and review how different colours have been used. Consider the different factors relating to text and consider the factors relating to the information on each page/slide/screen.

➔ On your form **AO1_ReviewMultimediaProduct1**, in the Activity 5 section, comment about the good and/or not so good aspects of each of these three features.

➔ Remember that your explanations should be detailed to attain higher grades. To achieve this, you could make comments about each page/slide/screen separately.

➔ Now review your second and third multimedia product, and fill in the Activity 5 section on each review form.

➔ Save your updated forms.

Review the use of sound and video features and the ease of navigation

The table on page 16 lists some points you could think of about any sound and video clips and navigation used in a multimedia product.

Feature	Factors to consider regarding sound, video and navigation
Video	• How relevant are video clip(s) to the product and target audience? • How easily visible are any link(s) to the video clips? Is it clear to users how to load the video clip? • How quickly does the video clip load? • How appropriate is the length of any embedded video clips? • What is the film quality? • How appropriate is the use of associated sound/music/voice? • If applicable, does the video clip contain the appropriate playing buttons (e.g. pause, rewind, forward, stop)?
Sound	• How relevant is sound to the product and target audience? • If sound is playing continuously, how easily are users able to adjust the volume or switch off the sound? If sound is used continuously, is this appropriate? • Are any links to the sound clips clearly visible? Is it clear to users how to load the sound clip? • How clear is sound clarity? Is the sound volume of different clips consistent or are there large variations in volume? • How appropriate are the lengths of any sound clips? • How well do sounds synchronise with video clips? • What is the impact of the sound clip on the listener? • How appropriate and effective is any narration?
Navigation	• How clear is the navigation? Is interactivity used appropriately and effectively? • How clearly visible are links to all other pages/sections of the product? Are buttons/links available for the user to return to a previous page or go back to previously visited pages/slides/screens? • Are all hyperlinks clearly visible? Do hyperlinks remain visible whilst the user is navigating the product? • How quickly do links load? • Is the use of anchors (e.g. named anchor, return to top) appropriate? If anchors have not been used (e.g. on long pages), should these have been included? • How quickly do linked items (e.g. web pages/slides/objects) load?

Explaining the good and not so good features of sound and video

Some example comments that could be used when you are providing an explanation about the good and not so good features of sound and video in a multimedia product are given below.

Examples of positive (good) comments that you could make about sound and video:

The spoken instructions at the beginning of each section were very useful because it meant that the user did not have to read lots of text.

The background music as you reached the end of the game added to the tension and was very effective.

The video clip was fun, interesting and really held the attention from start to finish. The length was just right.

Examples of negative (not so good) comments that you could make about sound and video:

The continuous narration was distracting and made it difficult to concentrate when reading the content.

The sound was badly recorded – there was a crackling noise in the background and the speaker's voice echoed making it impossible to understand what was being said.

The video quality was poor, the sound was barely audible and did not synchronise well with the images.

Activity 6: Review and comment on the use of sound and video and the ease of navigation...

In this activity you:

- should continue reviewing each of your chosen multimedia products in turn
- should comment on the use of sound, video and navigation in each product
- will continue using the forms saved in Activity 5
- will need to complete the Activity 6 section in each of the three forms.

➔ Review the use of sound and video clips, and effects in each of your three multimedia products. To achieve higher grades, ensure your explanations are detailed.

➔ On your forms **AO1_ReviewMultimediaProduct**, in the Activity 6 section of each form, comment about the good and/or not so good aspects of sound and video.

➔ Review and comment on how easy and quick it is to move from one page/slide/screen to another (i.e. the navigation).

➔ Save your updated forms.

Factors to consider for products on CD/DVD-ROM

If you are reviewing products on a CD or DVD, you should comment on the ease of use and the user interface. Here are some points to consider:

- How easy is it to install and run the product?
- Does the product allow the user to bookmark pages/sections to return to? (E.g. can the user continue to work from where they left off?)

Here are some additional factors to consider for educational products:

- Is the course designed in such a way that ensures users will learn?
- Are learning activities student-friendly and interesting?

Key term

Bookmark

A marker or address that identifies a document or a specific place in a product to enable a user to return to that place or address later. When viewing web pages using a web browser, a bookmark is a saved link to a web page. To go back to a particular web page quickly, a bookmark is created for the page. Bookmark is the term used by Netscape; Favorites is the Internet Explorer term.

Final review of the product as a whole

Once you have commented on individual features, you will be quite familiar with the entire product. You should then make some comments on the product as a whole. Here are some points to consider:

- How suitable is the type of product? For example, is the use of a presentation appropriate or would a website or CD-ROM have been more appropriate?
- What is the overall effectiveness of the number and type of multimedia elements used?
- How effective is the product? Does it meet its aims? Is it suitable for the target audience?
- Does the product include an overview that describes its purpose and who will benefit from it?
- Are there any introductory tips on how to successfully use the product?
- Is the content laid out in a logical manner? Is the sequence of information presented appropriate?

TIP

When reviewing a multimedia product, think about:

Who? = the target audience.
What? = the aims.
Where? = is the product easily accessible by the target audience?
How? = how effective is the type of multimedia product?

Activity 7: Comment on the good and not so good features of the multimedia product as a whole...

In this activity you will undertake a final review of the whole product.

- Comment on the effectiveness and appropriateness on the product as a whole.
- Complete the Activity 7 section of each **AO1_ReviewMultimediaProduct** form.
- Proofread, then save your completed review forms.

5. Decide if the aims have been met and, if so, how they were met

Once you have identified the intended audience, identified and stated the aims, and commented on the good and not so good features, you should then be able to assess whether the aims were or were not met and, if they were met, how they were met.

You may be tempted to base your decision about whether or not the aims were met by the overall impression you have gained about the multimedia product. But remember that the product may not be aimed at you! Therefore **you** may not necessarily find the product appealing or interesting – this does not mean that the product has not met its aims.

To help you to make your assessment about the aims objectively, you are advised to comment on each aim in turn. By considering each aim separately, you will find it easier to identify how each individual aim has been met.

You may find it helpful to list each aim, state whether or not you think the aim was met, provide a brief explanation for your decision, then state how you think the aim was met. To identify how each aim was met, refer to your list of good and not so good features. If an appropriate number and variety of features were used, this will usually mean that the use of these features has helped to meet that particular aim.

Refer to the notes you have already made about the intended target audience, the aims, and the good and not so good features that you have already identified. You will then be able to judge whether the aims you identified were met.

If you have noted a good combination of interactive elements in the product and have identified more good features than not so good ones, and the general impact of the product is effective, it is likely that the multimedia product has met its aims. However, if the balance of not so good features is greater than the good features, it is possible that the aims of the multimedia product have not been met.

Activity 8: Comment on how the aims are met and explain why any aims are not met...

In this activity you will comment on whether the aims are met.

- Refer to your review forms and the guidelines in Section 5 on pages 18 and 19.
- For each multimedia product that you reviewed, comment on whether or not you think the aims have been met.
- If you think the aims have been met, give reasons as to how they have been met.
- If you think the aims have not been met, give reasons why you think they have not been met.
- Add these comments in the Activity 8 section of your **AO1_ReviewMultimediaProduct** forms for each product.

6. Suggest improvements to a multimedia product

For a **Merit** grade, you need to suggest possible improvements to the products you reviewed and for a **Distinction** grade, you should suggest a range of valid improvements to help the product meet its aims. A product may meet its aims but could still be improved, you should suggest these improvements as well.

TIP

Once you have progressed through the unit and developed your own skills in designing a multimedia product (Assessment Objective 2), sourcing suitable multimedia elements (Assessment Objective 3), creating a multimedia product (Assessment Objective 4) and seeking feedback from others (Assessment Objective 5), you may find you have more ideas and are therefore able to add to your suggested improvements.

Suggesting improvements

Your goal here should be to suggest improvements that are appropriate for the type of product you reviewed (e.g. interactive multimedia website, educational CD-ROM, etc.) and relevant and appropriate for the intended target audience. Remember you are not necessarily the target audience, therefore if the product is not aimed at your age group, it may not be appropriate for you to identify clever, 'jazzy' features that you would like to see or that you would use! Your intention should be to try to enhance that particular product for that particular audience.

Two useful techniques are:

- List each feature that you identified as being not so good, then make suggestions on how to improve that feature.
- Refer to the features you identified and list any features that were not originally included in the product that you think should be included and would help to improve the product.

Where possible, back up your suggestions with examples.

Feature	**Not so good comment** and **suggested improvement**
Use of colour	**Product: Commercial advertisement on DVD-ROM** **Not so good feature identified**: Although the target audience was teenagers, the advertisement looked like it was intended for very young children because too many bright and garish colours were used. The colours clashed with each other and with the pictures – the user might want to turn off the screen. **Suggested improvement**: Avoid the use of too many different, bright colours – simple is often the most effective. White text on a black background would have worked better than grey text on a white background and would have coordinated very well with the images of the fireworks which all had black backgrounds.
Images	**Product: Interactive presentation** **Not so good feature identified**: The quality of the images was poor when the screen was displayed in full size. The images became very pixellated and the captions could not be read. **Suggested improvement**: The original image sizes should be a little bigger on the page and better images with a higher resolution should be used so that when the page is maximised the image quality is not spoilt.

Feature	**Not so good comment** and **suggested improvement**
Navigation	**Product: Interactive multimedia website** **Not so good feature identified**: It was difficult to go back to the contents page or previous page because the link buttons were at the very bottom of the page and the pages were long. **Suggested improvement**: To make the website easier to navigate, a navigation table could be created with named buttons and alternative text linking every page to all other pages. This navigation table should be placed at the top centre of the screen or the top left of the screen so it is clearly visible when a new page is loaded.
Overall review of product	**Product: Educational computer game** **Lack of a feature identified:** There was too much text on every page with very few images, this made the product dull. **Suggested improvement**: The amount of text on every screen should be considerably reduced, and an interesting, relevant image could be added alongside the text to liven up the text. Animations could be added to keep the attention of the user. Instead of providing user instructions in the form of a long page of instructions, a video or audio clip could also be used explaining the instructions for the next task.

TIP

Some example of suggested improvements based only on the not so good features identified for different types of multimedia product are shown in the table above. It is not intended to be a complete review or a complete list of suggested improvements. You should refer to the features you have identified as being not so good or features that could have been included and suggest possible improvements for these features.

Activity 9: Suggest possible improvements...

In this activity you will suggest improvements that could help to improve the product. For a [illegible] you must suggest at least one possible improvement, more than one for a **Merit** and a range of valid improvements for a **Distinction**.

- Refer to your review forms. Referring to not so good features you identified, suggest possible improvements for each product that would help to meet its aims.
- To achieve a **Distinction**, you must suggest a range of valid improvements.
- Use the provided **AO1_SuggestedImprovementsProduct** forms to suggest improvements for each product separately. You could copy and paste (or write) the not so good features that you have already identified in your review forms into these forms.

Portfolio builder

By reading and understanding the guidelines in this chapter, and working through the activities, you have learned how to review multimedia products and how to record your review notes. You should now be ready to start working on your own portfolio.

For your own portfolio, you will need to review at least *three* different, existing multimedia products of any of the following types: interactive multimedia websites, educational and recreational computer games, online presentations or presentations on CD or DVD, commercial advertisements on CD-ROM or DVD-ROM.

You do not need to find the multimedia products yourself: your teacher/tutor or someone else in your centre may provide you with appropriate products. You should try to review three *different* types of multimedia products (e.g. a computer game, an interactive website and an interactive multimedia presentation).

You may use the review forms provided with this book to record your reviews for your portfolio.

Before you begin, you should read the 'How this assessment objective will be assessed…' and 'How to achieve…' sections at the beginning of this chapter. Discuss with your teacher or tutor what grade he/she would advise you to aim for.

For each multimedia product you review, you should:

- identify and record the intended audience
- identify and record the good and not so good features. To do so, you should refer to the **Factors to consider** tables in this chapter and discuss the different features separately, then refer to the section about reviewing the product as a whole
- identify and record the aims. You should comment on how each aim is met and if they are not met, comment on why you think they were not met
- suggest possible improvements for the multimedia products reviewed.

CHAPTER 2

Assessment Objective 2

Design a Multimedia Product

Overview

In this chapter you will learn how to design a multimedia product. An explanation of multimedia products and examples was covered in Chapter 1 (page 6). From your work for Assessment Objective 1, you should now realise that a multimedia product is produced for a particular purpose and is aimed at a particular target audience.

Before you start to create your own multimedia product, you will need to spend some time planning it and producing documentation to show your planning process. The product you will plan in this chapter will be based on the project scenario given in the Introduction to this book.

You will learn how to define the purpose and audience for your multimedia product; plan the product by drawing up a site map or plan; create a suitable house style for the product; design the navigation system to enable users to move effectively through different parts of the product; and create a storyboard or flowchart as appropriate for your product. These elements can be referred to as the 'design documentation' for the multimedia product.

Planning is very important and will help to ensure that the product you produce meets its aims and is appropriate for the target audience. The planning features you use (e.g. site map or plan, and storyboard or flowchart should be appropriate for the type of product you are going to create).

How this assessment objective will be assessed...

- You will need to produce design documents for a multimedia product that you will then create for Assessment Objective 4.
- The grading for this assessment objective will be based on the amount of detail in your description of the purpose and audience for your product.
- You will also need to provide a plan, house style and navigation system for your product. Grading will depend on the amount of detail included in your plan, the appropriateness of your house style guidelines and how effective your navigation system is.
- If you also provide a storyboard showing all elements of your product, you can achieve a higher grade.
- To achieve a **Merit** grade, your designs should have a clear structure; if your designs are well-structured, you could achieve a **Distinction**.

Skills to use...

You will need to:

- determine the **purpose** of the product and decide who your intended **audience** is
- decide what the most appropriate **type** of product is for your intended audience and purpose (e.g. for a female audience aged 50–60, would an interactive computer game be an appropriate product?)
- produce an appropriate **plan** of the product (e.g. a site map of a website or a plan for an interactive presentation)
- decide on an appropriate **house style** for the type of product you are going to create and for your target audience and create house style sheet guidelines
- work out a clear **navigation** system for all pages/slides of the product
- sketch a storyboard and/or flowchart showing a visual overview of the plan for your product.

How to achieve...

Pass requirements

P1 You will give the purpose and audience for the product.

P2 You will produce a basic plan, house style and navigation system.

P3 You will provide a simple storyboard covering the main elements.

P4 Your designs may lack structure.

Merit requirements

M1 You will give the purpose and audience for the product.

M2 You will produce a detailed plan, house style and navigation system.

M3 You will provide a storyboard covering the main elements.

M4 Your designs should have a clear structure.

Distinction requirements

D1 You are thorough in your description of purpose and audience for the product.

D2 You will produce a detailed plan, appropriate house style and effective navigation system.

D3 You will provide a storyboard covering all elements.

D4 Your designs are well-structured.

1. Define your purpose and audience

You identified the purpose (aims) of existing multimedia products in Chapter 1. In this chapter, you will decide the aim of the product you are going to design. You will need to decide who you are going to create your multimedia product for (i.e. decide who your intended target audience is). To do so, you will also be determining the purpose of the product (i.e. determine what the intention of producing the product is).

Before you proceed, ensure that you are familiar with the following sections covered in Chapter 1: 'Identify the intended audience' and 'Identify the aims of a multimedia product'. You need to use the skills you learned during your reviews of existing products to define and explain the purpose and describe the intended audience for your own product. To achieve a higher grade, your description of the purpose and audience should be thorough.

Describing the purpose of your multimedia product

Your description of the purpose of your multimedia product must make it clear *what your product is intended to do*. You may write short, clear statement(s) or, for added clarity, you may choose to display a subheading titled 'Purpose of multimedia product'. Your purpose is your *expected outcome*, the *overall goal or objective* of your multimedia product. The purpose should guide your plans.

Describing the audience

Describe the *group(s)* of people that your multimedia product is *intended* to *appeal to*. Remember your target audience can be narrow or wide and that you may combine two categories (e.g. single mothers living in Dudley).

You may want to explain how you intend to appeal to that target audience by including examples of the language you will use or what images you will include.

If your intended target audience is wide, you could describe the main target audience group and explain who the secondary audience might be.

Presenting the information for your purpose and audience

You may use any appropriate style to present the information about your purpose and audience – you must show evidence that you have completed this stage of the design documentation.

Here are some suggestions for presenting this information with examples:

Three subheadings with a description or list of factual statements under each subheading, for example:

Subheadings with statements for multimedia website aimed at pupils thinking of taking a gap year

Purpose

- To provide information about different types of holidays available.
- To provide information about the role of our company.
- To provide information about the requirements for participants.
- To provide information about the methods of travel, clothing, travel partners, etc.
- To produce a website that attracts the attention of the target audience.
- To persuade as many of the target audience as possible to use our company when taking their gap year.

Target audience

- Pupils in school and school leavers, girls and boys, aged 16–18.

An overview in the form of an advertisement for your product – this could be the basis of your home page or opening slide of a multimedia presentation, for example:

1. Advertisement or opening page for multimedia website promoting adventure holidays

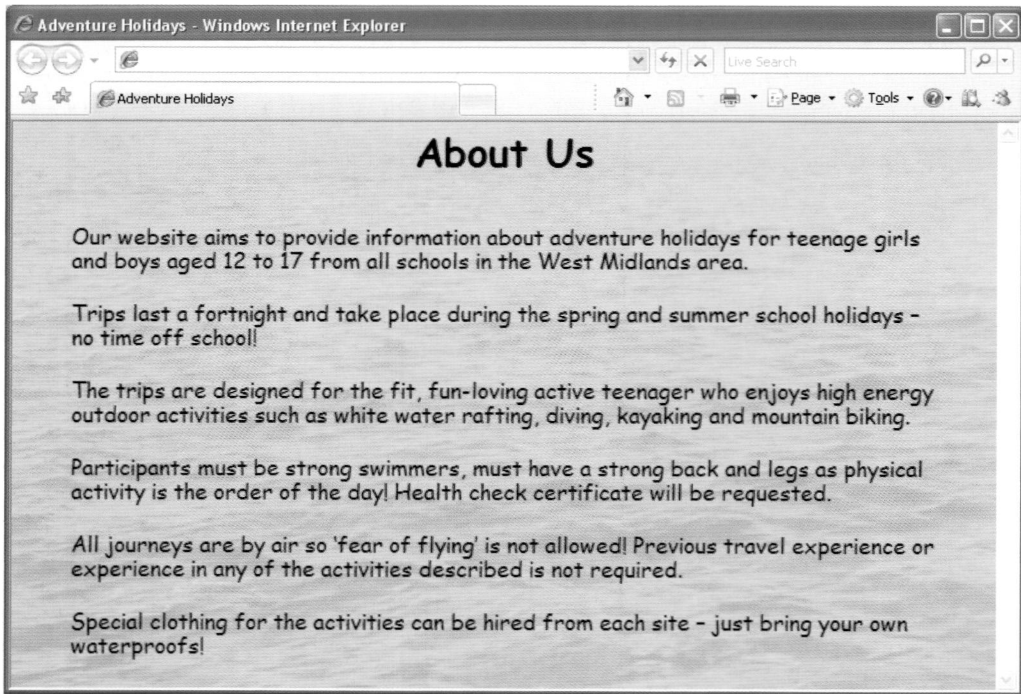

Figure 2.1: *Example of purpose on the home page of a website.*

2. Opening screen for multimedia presentation promoting adventure holidays

Adventure Holidays

- For teenagers in the West Midlands
- Spring and summer holiday trips for a fortnight
- White water rafting, diving, kayaking and mountain biking
- Health check certificate required
- Journeys are by air
- Special clothing not required

Figure 2.2: *Example of purpose on the opening slide of a multimedia presentation.*

A table showing the purpose and audience, for example:

Table that can be inserted on a website, flyer or presentation providing information for pupils wanting to take a gap year

Item	Description
Purpose	To persuade students to take a gap year. To promote the opportunities available for school leavers. To provide information about the requirements and travel arrangements for gap year students. To persuade the target audience to plan a gap year with our company. To engage the viewer by including videos of previous students' adventures and experiences.
Target audience	Students, male and female, aged 16–17.

TIP

The examples given are not intended to be definitive. They are simply presenting some ideas to get you started. You may be able to think of alternative or additional descriptions for your purpose and audience.

Activity 10: Describe purpose and audience...

In this activity you will describe the purpose and audience for the multimedia product you intend to create.

- Refer to the Project Scenario in the Introduction to this book.
- As part of your planning and designing process, create a new document and describe the **purpose** and intended **target audience** for the adventure holiday company's interactive presentation. Give as much detail as possible about the purpose and target audience.
- You may present the information in any format.
- When describing your purpose and audience, you could think about the following:
    - Do the participants need to belong to a particular club or school?
    - What activities are on offer?
    - Should the participants have any tests (e.g. do they need a medical certificate certifying they are in good health)?
    - Should participants have a certain level of fitness (e.g. be able to walk five miles a day)?
    - Are there any special requirements (e.g. be able to carry a backpack weighing a certain weight for a certain number of hours a day)?
    - Will participants be flying? Should they have previous travel experience?
    - Will participants need to provide their own transport to and from the departure airport?
    - Will participants need to be able to provide their own special clothing and footwear (e.g. fully waterproof garments)?
    - Will special meals be catered for or not?
- Save the document (or if handwriting, file your page).

2. Select the type of product to create

Types of interactive multimedia product

Examples of interactive multimedia products you could create for your portfolio are:

- an interactive multimedia website
- an interactive multimedia presentation – this could be an online presentation, one to be included on a CD/DVD-ROM or a presentation that could be used at an information point/kiosk (using touch screens as you may have seen in shopping centres or at exhibitions)
- an educational computer game
- a recreational computer game
- a commercial advertisement (this could be a website or a presentation).

As part of your planning, you will need to decide what type of multimedia product will best suit your intended audience and purpose and what resources you have available or can obtain. For example, you cannot produce a commercial advertisement on a DVD-ROM if you have limited or no skills in producing videos, you have no access to DVD-burning software or you do not have the budget to buy DVD-ROMs.

Spend some time deciding what type of multimedia product will best suit you, your purpose, and your target audience because once you start designing your product you do not want to find you have to start again.

TIP

Ask your teacher or tutor for advice – he/she may want you to create a specific type of product for this unit. If you have created a website for Unit 2, your teacher/tutor may prefer you to create, for example, an interactive presentation for this unit to allow you to broaden your skills.

Resources available

When considering the resources available to you, think about the following:

- The software, software version and facilities you have access to (e.g. software applications, Internet access).
- The hardware you have access to (e.g. sound card, graphics card, CD-ROM/DVD-ROM drive or player).
- Your own knowledge and skills.
- The skills/expertise of the people who could help and advise you (e.g. your teachers/tutors and other staff at your school/college).
- Your budget.

Appropriateness of product

When considering the most appropriate type of product to create, think about the following:

- Your target audience.
- The type of product most likely to appeal to your target audience.
- The skills of your target audience.
- The resources that are likely to be available to your target audience.
- Where your product is most likely to get the most attention. For example if your target audience is retired pensioners, they are less likely to have computers and computer skills so a 'jazzy' multimedia website with 'funky' videos and 'rap music' clips may not appeal to them!

Activity 11: Decide what multimedia product you should create...

In this activity you will make a decision about the multimedia product you will produce.

- Refer to your notes from Activity 10 in which you described the purpose and target audience for your multimedia product.
- Have a discussion with your teacher/tutor about his/her recommendations (if any) for the type of product that you should create. Refer to the Project Scenario in the Introduction to this book.
- Find out what hardware and software you will be able to use.
- Find out what other resources you will have access to.
- Decide what types of product that you are capable of producing (or can learn how to produce).

- Think about the most suitable type of product for your target audience and one that will allow you to fulfil your stated purpose and the requirements of the given project scenario.
- Finally, decide what multimedia product you are going to create!
- Write down the reasons for making this choice and why you think it will best meet the needs of your audience.

3. Plan your multimedia product

Planning is vital before producing a multimedia product. At this early stage of your planning, you will need to:

- decide the type of plan that you will use
- decide the type of structure
- decide how many pages/slides you will include and how many sections you will have in your product
- make a note of all key dates.

Think of the plan as the initial stage where you note down your outline ideas. As you continue to produce your design documents, you may decide to make some changes to your plan. This is fine, but it is important to put down your initial plans in writing, even at this early stage.

Gathering ideas

Before you produce the plan for your multimedia product, it is helpful to view examples of other similar existing products, then use your imagination and creativity to design your own, incorporating the better features from the products you viewed. But be realistic, not overly ambitious, and bear in mind your time constraints.

Deciding the type of plan

The type of plan that is most appropriate for your product will depend of what the multimedia product is. So, at this stage of your planning, you will need to have decided what type of product you will create, so that you can decide on the most appropriate type of plan for that type of product. For example, the most appropriate plan for a website is a site map. For an interactive presentation, an outline of the initial ideas followed by a more detailed storyboard may be more appropriate.

Key term

Site map

An overview of the entire structure of a website, like a table of contents. It shows users the pages and scope of the site and how the site can be navigated. Site maps can be textual or, more commonly, visual. The site map makes it easier for a user to find information on a site without having to navigate through the site's many pages.

Types of structure for a multimedia product

There are two main types of structure that you could use for your non-linear multimedia product: *hierarchical* and *mesh*.

A *hierarchical* structure is one where the pages/slides are linked in sections. The product would have a main page (e.g. an overview of the website/presentation) with links that go down a hierarchy with general information to more specific information. For example, in an interactive multimedia presentation the opening slide would have links to title slides – which in turn will have links to slides in that section about the topic on the title slide. A *hierarchical* structure for a multimedia presentation might look like this.

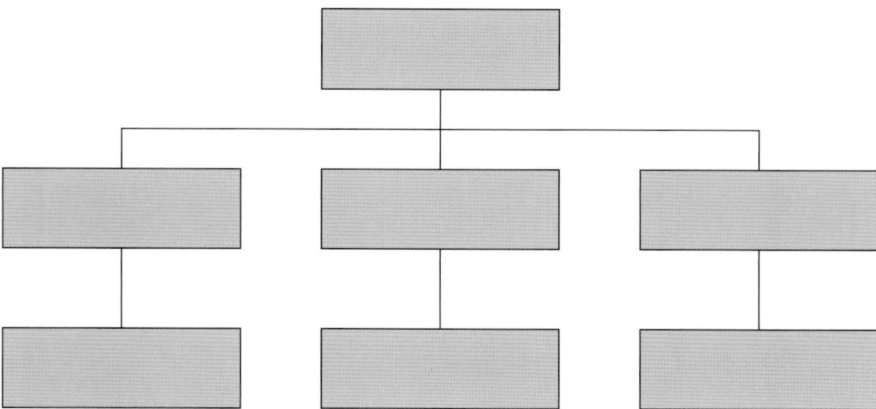

Figure 2.3: *Hierarchical structure.*

A *mesh* structure is one where each slide, screen or page is linked to all others and the user of the product is able to choose their own pathway through the product. A *mesh* structure for a multimedia product might look like this.

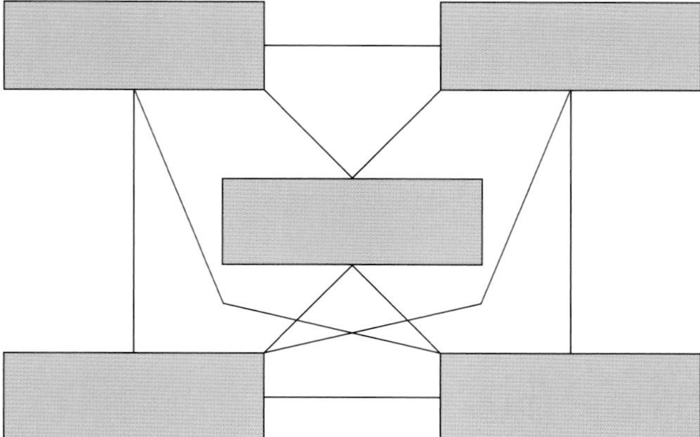

Figure 2.4: *Mesh structure.*

Planning the number of pages/slides and sections

You will need to decide how many pages/slides you will include in your multimedia product and the structure of the pages. Think about the following:

- Will you have an opening page/slide?
- Will you have separate pages/slides for different sections (e.g. title slides in a presentation)?
- Will you have a conclusion or final page?

Guidelines for producing your plan

Produce a plan of the overall structure of the product first. You could use any style for this plan, for example a table, a bulleted list or a sketch (a sketch could be hand drawn – you don't get any extra marks for using the computer, although you may do so if you wish).

Here is an example of an initial plan for an interactive, multimedia presentation:

Plan for interactive, multimedia presentation about activity holidays

- master slide using a design template
- design template showing sporting activities
- navigation table at bottom centre of master slide, navigation table will then be displayed on every slide in the presentation
- navigation table to have five buttons – one to link back to the introduction screen, one to link to the title slide for each country and one information button which will be linked to a booking form
- total of 16 slides
- introduction screen – overview of what presentation is about
- three title slides – one title slide for each country featured in the presentation
- three to five slides linked to each title slide giving more information about the activities in each country
- final blank slide at the end of the presentation.

- **Key dates:**
  1. design documentation to be completed by: [enter date here]
  2. text, images and multimedia elements to be collected by: [enter date here]
  3. presentation to be completed by: [enter date here]
  4. presentation to be checked by teacher/tutor on: [enter date here]
  5. seek feedback from test users on: [enter date here]
  6. collect feedback from test users on: [enter date here]
  7. evaluate own product on: [enter date here]
  8. suggest improvements by: [enter date here]

TIP

When producing your plan, aim to have a minimum of 10 to 12 slides in your presentation. There is no prescribed maximum, but try not to exceed 20 slides – you need to keep your presentation manageable for yourself and interesting to your audience. Quantity does not mean quality!

Activity 12: Produce a plan...

In this activity you will produce a plan detailing the overall structure of your multimedia presentation.

- Refer to the Project Scenario in the Introduction to this book.
- Refer to the design documents you produced in Activities 10 and 11 in which you described the purpose and audience for your product and decided on the type of product to produce.
- Decide what structure you will use in your presentation (e.g. hierarchical or mesh).
- Think about different ways you could present your plan (e.g. table, bulleted list, sketch).
- Produce your plan – ensure your plan shows how many slides you will have in your presentation and shows an indication of the layout (e.g. home page, title pages).
- Include all key dates in your plan.

4. Determine the house style

Key term

House style

This is a term used to describe a set of guidelines or conventions (rules) that organisations use to create and maintain a consistent look for the documents produced by anyone in that organisation. The guidelines may cover the overall layout and spacing, font type, font sizes, background, text and link colours, background and other images or logos, image sizes and file formats. Documents produced based on the house style guidelines will then all have a standard look and feel.

Why is house style important?

House style is important for any organisation. When people see any printed or multimedia items from that organisation it is important that they will quickly and readily recognise the organisation that has sent or created it. For example, a company that sells trainers will have a recognisable logo, suitable colours, and will always use the same font styles in their advertisements and other documents. If they record and show an advertisement on television, the same logo, colours and fonts are likely to be used. Each time the advertisement is seen, viewers will instantly recognise the company. In the same way, each time a person receives a letter or any other document from the company, they will see exactly who it is from as they will instantly recognise the style used in all of the things they produce.

Deciding your house style

As you are not working for an organisation you can create your own house style guidelines. However, remember that your house style guidelines should be suitable for your target audience and for the type of product.

- **Considering the target audience** – an interactive presentation for young children would benefit from the use of bright colours, 'fun' font types, larger text sizes, bright, colourful logos and images, interesting animations, background sound and engaging video clips. However, in an interactive presentation designed for a group of head teachers, bright colours, large text and distracting animations would be inappropriate.
- **Considering the type of product** – interactive, 'do-it-yourself' type tasks and quizzes with background music and animations flying across the screen may be appropriate in a computer game for children but not for a revision website for medical students.

What to include in your house style guidelines

You could present your house style guidelines as a bulleted or numbered list, as a diagram or in the form of tables.

Whatever format you choose, you should include details of the following design elements:

Page layout

- page/paper size
- orientation
- margins
- line spacing.

TIP

Make sure your entire product is consistent. Avoid using too many different page sizes or margins or different line spacing.

Fonts

- font name for headings, subheadings, body text, bulleted text, tables, etc.
- font size for headings, subheadings, body text, bulleted text, tables, etc.
- emphasis, e.g. bold, italic, underline, shadow.

TIP

Avoid using too many different font styles and sizes. As a general rule, no more than three different font styles should be used. Your product should look professional and be clear to read.

Don't use complicated fonts or handwriting style fonts as these can be difficult to read on-screen.

Serif fonts (e.g. Times New Roman, Garamond, Courier) are difficult to read on-screen; sans serif fonts (e.g. Arial, Helvetica, Verdana) are clearer to read and are recommended for text that will be read on-screen.

Underlining may signify hyperlinks: use a different colour, or bold or italic, to emphasise text if needed.

Colours

- background colour
- text colour
- linked text colour
- visited linked text colour
- active hyperlink colour.

TIP

Avoid using too many colours. Make sure your colours complement each other and are 'easy on the eye'. Use complementary colours, e.g. light text on a dark background and vice versa.

Remember the rhyme: 'Red and green should never be seen!'

Logos

- is a logo to be used and if so which one?
- logo size
- position.

Images

- size
- position
- file types
- text wrap
- sources.

TIP

Large image sizes in the centre of the screen imply importance. Resize images proportionally and position them appropriately.

Too many bright images, especially clipart, may distract your audience. Make sure your images relate to the text and don't overuse images.

Text layout

- alignment
- line spacing
- bullets and/or numbers
- tables.

TIP

Keep it simple, don't display too much text on a page/slide.

TEXT IN ALL CAPITALS IS DIFFICULT TO READ. Sentence case is easier to read.

Use numbers for lists with sequence; use bullets to show a list with no priority or hierarchy.

Make sure your layout is consistent; differences will draw attention and may imply importance.

Navigation

- details of navigation
- positioning of links
- what should be linked (e.g. text, buttons, images).

Multimedia elements

- what multimedia elements should be included
- where these should be sourced from
- where these should be positioned on the page/slide
- requirements for animation effects
- timings.

TIP

If inserting sounds, use these carefully and selectively as continuous or inappropriate sounds can be distracting to a viewer.

Don't overdo special effects (e.g. don't use too many different transitions, builds and effects in presentations). Remember the saying: 'Less is more'. A few carefully selected animations will be more effective than lots of different animations.

Copyright notice

- text for copyright notice
- where this should be positioned on the page.

Presenting the house style information

There is no prescribed way of presenting house style guidelines. You should try to display this information as clearly as possible. One way of presenting house style guidelines clearly is to use tables. Examples of 'House style guidelines for presentations' and 'House style guidelines for web pages' can be found in the **Unit4StudentResources** folder on the Payne-Gallway website:

Activity 13: Produce house style guidelines...

In this activity you will create a house style for your planned multimedia presentation.

- Refer to the Project Scenario in the Introduction to this book and all your design documents from Activities 10, 11 and 12.
- Decide what house style will be appropriate for your multimedia presentation.
- Create a house style sheet showing each of the design elements that you will use in your multimedia presentation.
- Make sure that the guidelines are all clear and relevant to the presentation you intend to create.
- Use your imagination; don't copy the examples given!

5. Plan a clear navigation system

Key term

Navigation system

A multimedia product of any type involves some sort of user interaction. This means that the user will need to be able to move from one part of the product to another. In the case of a multi-level computer game, for example, completing one level will enable the player to move to the next level.

In the case of a multimedia presentation, the user is likely to use buttons and/or hyperlinks to move between slides or to access other features. For example, the user may need to click on a button to start a video clip playing in a different program or to open a document displaying more information.

The navigation system for an interactive multimedia product must work in such a way that the user can move from one page or slide to another – and be able to move backwards and forwards through the product.

Careful thought must be put into the design of a navigation system. For example you may want to have a link on each page/slide to take the user to the home page or main menu – and from this page/slide you may want the user to be able to navigate to any other part of your product – or you may wish to restrict them to moving to just one point in the product. It may be suitable to create a button on a template page/slide which can be used throughout your product to take the user back to the main menu or home page. The user should be able to navigate back to a previous page or slide from wherever they are in a product.

A navigation bar could be created on a template or master page. If so, it will be in the same place on every page/slide of your product giving your finished product a professional 'look and feel'. The navigation bar can include words, short phrases or text as the links, or small images, image buttons or icons. If appropriate to the multimedia product, rollover images can also be used either in the navigation bar or on individual pages/slides (e.g. rollovers are effective on websites).

Remember, as stated in Section 4, navigation details could be included on the house style sheet. An example of a navigation system for a presentation is shown below.

NAVIGATION BUTTONS FOR A PRESENTATION

Navigation buttons to be placed at the bottom of the Slide Master and Title Master:

- **5 action buttons on one row, equal height, width may vary**
- **Buttons to be grouped and centre aligned, no border.**

Images to be formatted and linked as follows:

Image/text	Screen tip	Link to
'home' action button	back to Slide 1	Slide 1
France	about holidays in France	Title slide 1
Turkey	about holidays in Turkey	Title slide 2
Greece	about holidays in Greece	Title slide 3
'information' action button	booking form	bookingform.doc

Figure 2.6: *Example of navigation bar design for a multimedia presentation.*

6. Create a storyboard and/or flowchart

Key terms

Storyboard

A visual script for a multimedia product. It is a term 'borrowed' from film makers where the director and camera operator will need to 'see' the shots before they film them. It saves time and money for the producer and is widely used for films, commercials and animations.

A storyboard for a multimedia product shows a visual overview of the plan for your product and can show when automated actions are going to happen (e.g. animations, sound, video). As the name implies, a storyboard tells a story of the product as it will be viewed – it shows the main events that will occur. There are different types of storyboard (e.g. text-only storyboard, simple linear storyboard, graphical storyboard and hand-drawn storyboard.

Flowchart

A diagram consisting of symbols (such as rectangles or diamonds) and connecting lines and/or arrows that shows step-by-step progression through a procedure, process or system.

Planning a storyboard

A well-produced storyboard should display clearly the structure and content of the completed product. Spending time designing a storyboard for your multimedia product will make it easier for you when you start to create it. The storyboard should include details of the items that will be displayed on each slide or screen. The navigation buttons and/or hyperlinks should be shown, as well as where images will be placed, areas for text, positions of animations and video, and where sounds will be included.

As you need to produce a non-linear multimedia product, you are advised to produce a graphical storyboard. You should include as much detail as possible in your storyboard.

Creating a storyboard

Your storyboard can be hand-drawn or produced on the computer. You don't get any extra marks for one produced on a computer, so use whatever method you find easier and quicker.

If you are hand-drawing it, you could use a printed template and handwrite the details. Don't worry if you do not have good drawing skills – your storyboard is not going to be published, it is simply a sketch to show the placement of items on the different pages/screens of your multimedia product. In fact, you should not spend too much time producing an artistic storyboard – just draw suitable shapes to represent items on each page. Try to display the size of items correctly relative to text or other items on the page. A simple rule is that if a page/slide and item is going to go in the product, it must be shown on the storyboard.

An example of an overview storyboard is shown on page 40. It is also provided in .pdf format in the **Unit4Forms** folder.

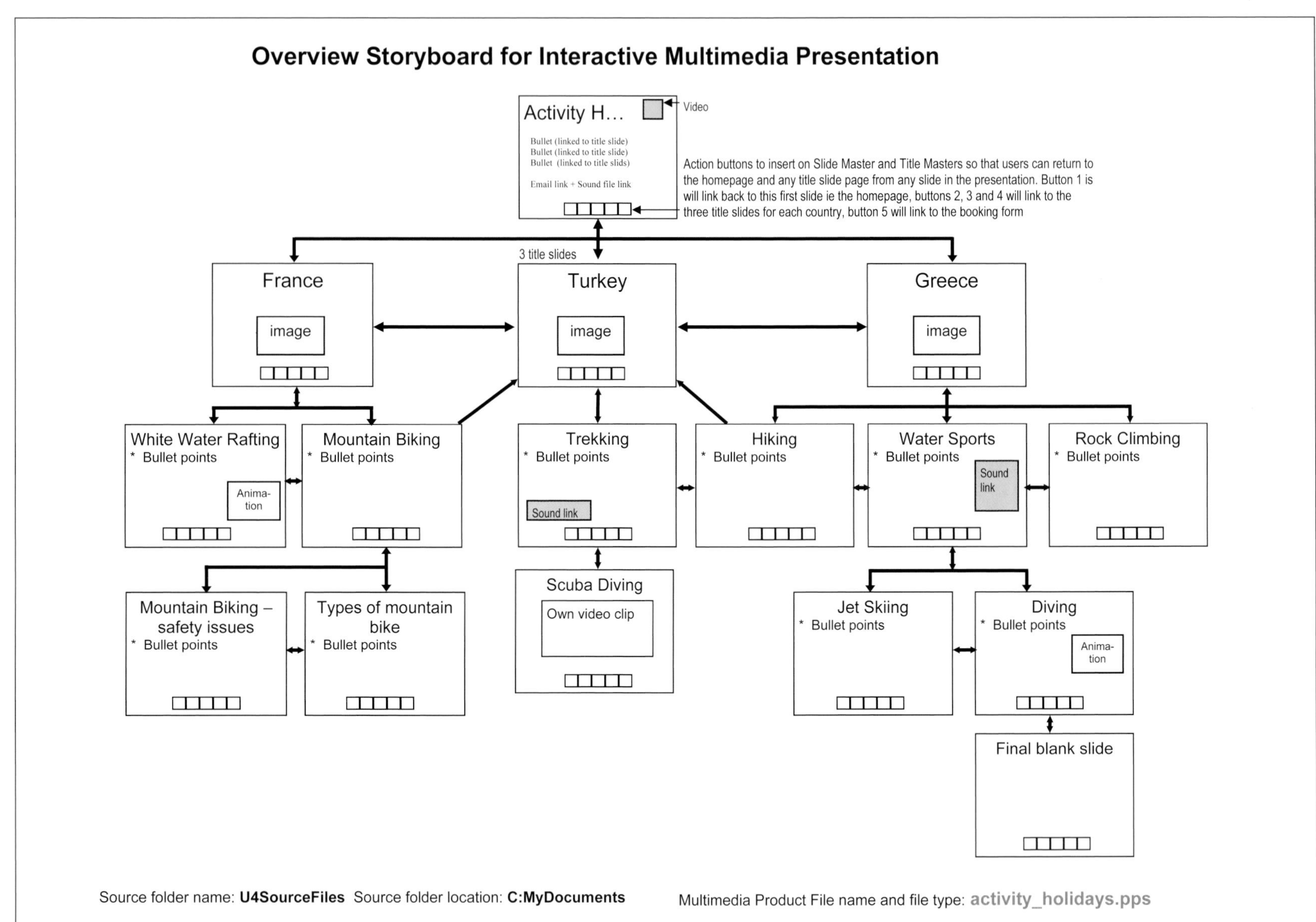

Figure 2.7: *An example of a storyboard*

What to include in your storyboard

Design

- Your storyboard should include sufficient detail for someone else to see what the final product will look like when finished. There should not be much difference between the design and content shown on the storyboard and the design and content of the completed product.

Number of pages/slides and sections

- Show how many pages/slides in total will be included in your product. If your product will have lots of pages, you should show how many sections there will be and how many pages/slides there will be in each section.
- Navigation – use arrows to show how the pages/slides or sections will be linked to each other.
- Display the pages in the orientation that you intend to use (you should have decided this when you created your house style sheet). For example, for a presentation your slides may be landscape but for a website your pages may be portrait.

Content on the pages/slides – text, images, navigation bar

- Show where the various sections of text (e.g. headings, body text, bullets, tables, etc.) will be placed. You do not need to enter all the text or even sentences, a few words with dots to show the remaining text will suffice. If you have not yet sourced your text or decided what will go on each screen, you could simply show what items will be placed where, e.g. 'heading' or 'heading here', and 'bullets here', etc.
- Draw a box to show where images, image buttons and icons will be placed. If you know the image names, write the names in the boxes.

Hyperlinks

- It is essential to show all links clearly.

You should show:

- the type of hyperlink (e.g. internal, external (to another document or to a URL), email link)
- the target (what the link will display when clicked)
- what you are linking (e.g. text, images, buttons, drawings, icons).

Multimedia elements – sound, video, animation

- Show on which pages/slides you will include any sound or audio clips or animations. Display the position on the page/slide where these items will be placed.
- If you intend to include narration, indicate this on your storyboard.

Transitions and timings

- If appropriate to the type of product, make a note on the storyboard of how pages/slides will appear. Include information about any custom effects/animations and timings (e.g. for presentations).

Key terms

Transition

The method used to change from one screen to another.

Timing

The duration that one page/slide will display on-screen if the product is set on automatic timings.

How to create a storyboard

1. If you are producing your plan on the computer, use text boxes or rectangular/square shapes to represent each page/slide. Use arrows to show how the pages/slides will be linked.
2. If you are intending to display background images or use design templates, indicate this clearly. You could also include this information on your house style sheet.
3. You may use a template provided by your teacher or tutor.
4. To help you create your storyboard, three different templates of a **storyboard** have been provided for you – **AO2_Storyboard** versions 1, 2 and 3. These templates can be downloaded from the Student Resources page on the Payne-Gallway website: **www.payne-gallway.co.uk**. The templates are contained in the **Unit4StudentResources** folder within the subfolder **Unit4Forms**. They are provided in Microsoft Word format. You can use each of them in a number of ways, for example:
   - you can print the template and add sketches and notes by hand. It does not matter if your drawings are rough – stick drawings are fine! You should not spend too much time producing an artistic storyboard – just draw suitable shapes to represent items on each page, however, make sure your handwriting is legible
   - you can use the template to produce your storyboard on the computer. You can type your notes in the text boxes then print the storyboard and draw sketches of the page/slide content to give a visual idea of the page/slide.

Use any method that you find easiest and quickest, but, whatever method you choose, note that it is worth spending time producing a clear storyboard for your multimedia product because it will help you when you start to create your product.

TIP

A useful test to determine the clarity of your storyboard is to see whether someone else would be able to use your storyboard to create exactly the product you had in mind. Remember your ideas must be documented clearly on paper, not in your head!

Activity 14: Plan a navigation system and create a storyboard...

In this activity you will:

- plan how different slides of your multimedia presentation will be linked
- plan how users will navigate the presentation
- create a storyboard showing the structure and outline content of your presentation.

You may use or adapt any one of the three storyboard templates provided with this book.

- Refer to the Project Scenario in the Introduction to this book.
- Refer to the plan you created in Activity 12.
- Produce a detailed storyboard showing the number of slides in your presentation.
- Show what items (text, images, buttons, etc.) you will place on each slide and the position and approximate size of all items on each slide.

- Show what multimedia elements (sound or video links) you will include and on which slide. Show the positioning of the links to these items.
- Show how all slides in your multimedia presentation will be linked.
- Decide what you will use as hyperlinks and how users will be able to move from one part of the presentation to another. Remember your presentation must be non-linear, so users should be able to go to any slide they want to view and back – they should not have to go from one slide to the next in a prescribed sequence.

Portfolio builder

By reading and understanding the guidelines in this chapter, and working through the activities, you will have learned how to plan and design an interactive multimedia product. You should now be ready to prepare your source files and produce your own planning documents for your portfolio.

It is very important that you spend time thinking about and planning your interactive multimedia product at this stage. You will probably be tempted to start creating it, but planning it and producing planning documentation is essential!

You will need your own project scenario. Before you can start working on your plans, you should discuss with your teacher or tutor what type of interactive multimedia product you could create and what it should be about (the purpose). At this stage, you should also think about who your intended audience will be so that you can produce a multimedia product that is suitable for that target group.

Before you begin documenting your plans, you should read the 'How this assessment objective will be assessed…' and 'How to achieve…' sections of this chapter. Discuss with your teacher or tutor what grade he/she would advise you to aim for.

Now begin creating your planning documents. Create a new document and describe clearly the purpose (aim) and audience of your interactive multimedia product. Include the key dates that you need to work to in your plan.

The next stage is to produce a plan that is appropriate for the type of product you have decided to create (e.g. a site map for a website or a storyboard/flowchart for an interactive presentation).

Decide an appropriate house style for the type of product and for your target audience and create a detailed house style sheet (e.g. font sizes, font types, etc.).

Think about a suitable navigation system and note this down. You could record navigation details on a separate document or include it on your house style sheet or storyboard/flowchart.

Produce a storyboard or flowchart showing a visual overview of the plan for your product. Show as much detail as possible on the storyboard. You can use or adapt one of the storyboards provided with this book. Remember to write down all your ideas – your plans should not be in your head!

When you have completed your plan and storyboard, ask your teacher/tutor to look at your plan, house style sheet, navigation details and storyboard/flowchart. Ask him/her whether he/she would be able to use your planning documents to create the interactive multimedia product you have planned.

Good luck!

Assessment Objective 3

Source and Store Suitable Multimedia Elements

Overview

In this chapter you will learn how to collect a range of multimedia elements for the multimedia product that you have designed. You will need to obtain suitable text, photographs, other graphics (e.g. drawings, clipart, sound and video clips and animations) and any other material that would be suitable for the product you will be creating. You will learn how to acknowledge the sources of any elements that you have not created yourself.

Record of Files form

To help you record the files you source, an example form titled **AO3_RecordOfFilesCollected** can be downloaded from the Student Resources page on the Payne-Gallway website: **www.payne-gallway.co.uk**. The form is contained in the **Unit4StudentResources** folder, in the subfolder **Unit4Forms**. The form is provided in Microsoft Word format. You can print the form and handwrite your comments or type details in the Word file.

How this assessment objective will be assessed...

You will need to source and store all the elements for the product that you have already planned and which you will create in the next chapter.

This assessment objective will be assessed by the range of multimedia products that you collect. As a minimum you will need to collect text, images (photographs, drawings, clipart) and sound files and acknowledge all your sources. If you also source other suitable elements as well, such as animation and video, and give accurate acknowledgement of all your sources, you can achieve a higher grade.

Skills to use...

You will need to:

- keep a **record** of all files that you will collect. Your record should show from where and when each file was obtained, whether copyright permission has been sought and what you intend to use the file for
- save all files into a folder
- collect or create appropriate **text**
- obtain or take appropriate **images** (e.g. photographs), other computer graphics (e.g. drawings) and clipart images
- collect appropriate sound and audio **clips** or you could use the sound and video files available within Microsoft PowerPoint
- find appropriate **animations**.

Once you have gathered all your files, you should create a backup of your files.

Sourcing files from other units

If you have completed or are intending to complete other related units, you may use the files you created or sourced in other units. Examples of files that could be used from other units are:

Unit 1 ICT skills for business: text files and images are collected or created in this unit.

Unit 2 Webpage creation: text files and images are collected or created in this unit.

Unit 3 Digital imaging – plan and produce computer graphics: graphic images are created and edited in this unit.

Unit 20 Creating animation for the WWW using ICT: an animation is created in this unit.

Unit 22 Creating sound using ICT: a sound file is created in this unit.

Unit 23 Creating video: a video clip is created in this unit.

Animated gifs and animations in Microsoft PowerPoint

You must be clear about the difference between an animation that you need to source in this assessment objective and an animation in Microsoft PowerPoint that you may add when you create your interactive multimedia product in Assessment Objective 4. They are two very different things.

If you are aiming for a **Merit** or **Distinction** grade for this assessment objective, you need to show evidence that you have sourced at least one animation.

Animation in this assessment objective means an animated image (i.e. an image that appears to be moving – often referred to as an animated gif). Animated gifs are frequently found on the Web, but animated images can also be found in other file formats (e.g. animations created in Macromedia Flash are saved in .fla format).

Animation in Microsoft PowerPoint is the way objects enter and/or exit a PowerPoint slide.

If you add an animation scheme or a custom animation in Microsoft PowerPoint to your presentation (e.g. Fade in, Appear and dim, On mouse click, etc.), you have **NOT** fulfilled the requirement to ***source*** an animation for Assessment Objective 3.

Note about downloading files in your centre

If network security policies in your centre prevent students downloading and saving certain types of files, you will need to ask your teacher/tutor to make arrangements for suitable files to be provided for you to use.

How to achieve...

Pass requirements

P1 You source and store multimedia elements including text, images and sound.

P2 Some acknowledgement of sources is given.

Merit requirements

M1 You source and store multimedia elements including text, images, sound and animation.

M2 Acknowledgement of most sources is given.

Distinction requirements

D1 You source and store multimedia elements including text, images, sound, video and animation.

D2 Accurate acknowledgement of all sources is given.

1. Keep a record of files and acknowledge sources

Before you begin collecting your files, you should be aware that it is important that you obtain permission to use all text, images, graphics, sound and video clips, and animations that you obtain from the Web or other sources. Most websites will have copyright information that you should read.

If you have been given permission to use items that you have found on the Web, you must keep copies of all correspondence. If a website states that materials are free from copyright restrictions for educational use, you should print this page for your records.

Copyright, Designs and Patents Act 1988: the rights and regulations protected by this Act are called intellectual property rights (IPR). They are designed to ensure the owner of the copyright is not commercially exploited, can keep control over their original work and can get a fair financial return for it.

You must reference your sources. You could use a referencing method based on the Harvard System of referencing as follows:

Websites: copy and paste the URL (website address) from the **Address bar** on to your record of files list, note the names of author(s) (if available), the date published to the Web (if available), the type of electronic format and the date you accessed the site.

Magazines and journals: note the names of author(s), the title of the article, the publication name, its issue date and number, and volume number (if relevant).

Books: write down the surname and initials of the author(s) or editor(s), the date of publication, the book title, the publisher's name and the edition and page number (if relevant).

Own materials: make a note of any files that you have created yourself (e.g. if you have typed text yourself or taken any photographs yourself).

Keeping a record of files and sources

Start keeping a record of all the files that you collect and plan to use as soon as you start collecting your resources and keep updating it as you go along. Don't leave it until the end to do it – you may not remember where you got certain files from or you may forget what you intended to use a file for. It will also be time consuming to revisit websites if you have to go back to find information.

You could use a table with the headings below to keep a record of your sources.

File name and type	Source (where you got it from)	Date collected	File content (what the file shows/includes)	Reference (e.g. URL, copyright information)	Intended use (where you will use it, e.g. slide number)

2. Save all files into a folder

Create a new folder using a suitable folder name (e.g. u4_files) in which you can save all the files that you intend to use for your multimedia product.

To create a folder in your user area: **File** → **New** → **Folder** → **Backspace** key to delete the given folder name → Type the new folder name you have chosen → **Enter**.

3. Collect text

Refer to your plan and storyboard you created in Chapter 2 to remind yourself how many slides you intend to have in your presentation and therefore how much text you will need. There is no need to gather more text than required.

Here are some ideas for obtaining text for your multimedia product:

- **Type your own text** – the advantage of this is that you include only the text that you need for your product. You will not need to edit any additional, unwanted, irrelevant or inappropriate text.
- **Use provided text** – your teacher or tutor may give you with the exact text you need for the product you will be creating or may provide you with general text from which you can select the text you need for your product. If you have a copy of the text in electronic format (e.g. as a Microsoft Word file or a text file) you could delete the unwanted sections and keep just the text you need, or copy and paste the text you want to use for your product into a new document.

- **Use previously used text** – you may have your own text from your work for other units in this course or other projects that you may have completed. You could copy and paste the text that is appropriate for your multimedia product from other files into a new document.
- **Search for copyright-free text on the Web** – for example, some American government websites allow text to be used without needing copyright permission, but, of course, this text would need to be appropriate for your product. If you use any text from websites, make sure you spell check the text using a UK English spellchecker (as some American spellings are different).
- **Search other websites** – check to see if there are contact details on a website. Ideally you should email and ask for permission to use information from the site and keep a record of all communication and of all permissions given. However, you can extract and adapt text from websites without having to seek permission, but you must not copy the text word for word!
- **Use a variety of sources** – carry out research from any resources that you have access to (e.g. books in libraries, websites, etc.) but you must keep a note of all your sources.

Preparing your text files

Once you have collected your text files you should:

- spell check and read through the text files and make any changes required
- save the files in an appropriate file format. For example, files saved in .txt format can be imported into most programs so this would be an appropriate format for any multimedia product you are going to produce. If you are creating a presentation, you are advised to save the files in Microsoft Word format (because Word can collect up to 24 items on its clipboard).

Activity 15: Prepare folders, source text files and keep a record...

In this activity you will:

- prepare your folder for your source files
- start your record of files
- collect or create your text files.

➔ Create a folder using a suitable filename in which you will save all your files for the multimedia product that you will be creating in Chapter 4.

➔ Start your 'Record of Files'. You may use or adapt the example provided with this book titled **AO3_RecordOfFilesCollected**.

➔ Refer to your plans and storyboard (that you produced in Chapter 3).

➔ Create or collect suitable text for your planned multimedia presentation.

➔ Save the text file(s) in a suitable file format in your folder. You may save all the text in one file or save the text for different slides in separate files.

➔ Enter details of your files in your form **AO3_RecordOfFilesCollected**. Save this document for use later.

4. Collect images (photographs, graphics, clipart, animations)

TIP

Refer to your plan and storyboard to see how many images you will need. There is no need to gather more images than required.

Your teacher or tutor may provide you with the exact images you need or with a selection of images from which you can choose appropriate ones for your product. Here are some ideas to help you if you need to source your own:

Collecting photographs

Here are some suggestions for how to collect photographs for your multimedia product:

- Take your own photographs using a digital camera or camera phone – think about the image quality. Make sure your camera is able to capture images at a suitable resolution. You could then save and transfer the photographs to your computer. Make sure you save them in a suitable file format – digital cameras usually capture images in a .jpg or .jpeg format which is a suitable format for inserting into most programs.
- If you have any suitable photographs in hard copy (paper) format, you can scan these in. Before scanning make sure you use appropriate scanning software, that you adjust or set the scanning resolution, and that you check the file size and file format.
- Ask your teacher/tutor or your school/college library if they hold CD or DVD photo-libraries with images that are either copyright-free or can be used for educational purposes.
- Search for images on the World Wide Web. Check to see if there are contact details on the site. You should email and ask for permission to use any images you will use – you must keep a record of all communication and of all permissions given. Enter the words 'copyright-free images' to find websites with images that are free from copyright.

Collecting computer graphics

- Search the World Wide Web or Microsoft Office Online, or any copyright-free websites or CD/DVD-ROMs for computer graphics. Make sure you check that the images are copyright-free or use the contact details on the site to obtain permission.
- You may have your own computer graphics from your work for other units in this course (e.g. Unit 3) or other projects that you may completed.

Collecting clipart

- Use clipart images from within an application program (e.g. Microsoft PowerPoint, Microsoft FrontPage) or search for clipart from the Microsoft Office Online website for a wider range.

Collecting animations

- Search for animations on the Microsoft Office Online website.
- You may have your own animations from your work for other units in this course (e.g. Unit 20) or other projects that you may completed.
- Ask your school/college library if they stock CD or DVD photo-libraries with animated images that are either copyright-free or can be used for educational purposes.
- Search for animations on the World Wide Web. Check to see if there are contact details on the website, you should email and ask for permission to use any animations you will use – you must keep a record of all communication and of all permissions given. Enter the keywords 'animations' or 'animated gifs' to find websites with animations that are free from copyright, or try some of the sites listed below which provide copyright free animated images.

Image resources

The following websites offer free photos for educational use:

http://www.bigfoto.com/
http://www.freedigitalphotos.net/

Some of the websites below provide copyright-free images (at the time of publication):

http://www.freeimages.co.uk/
http://www.allfree-clipart.com/clipart/index.shtml
http://www.bellsnwhistles.com

The following websites provide animations:

http://www.allfree-clipart.com/clipart/index.shtml
http://www.bellsnwhistles.com

Some schools or colleges have access to the Scran website which contains copyright-free images – ask your teacher/tutor if your school/college has access to the following website:

http://www.scran.ac.uk/

Another method of searching for images on the Web is:

1. Enter the following URL (website address) into the address bar of your browser (e.g. Internet Explorer): http://www.google.co.uk.
2. Click the link for **Images**. In the **Search** box enter a category or subject for the images you want to find. Pages displaying images that meet your search criteria will display. Click on a link.
3. The page that displays will often display the website address on which the image is displayed, click on this link and see if contact details for the image owner are given. You should email the contact to obtain permission – explain why you want to use the image (e.g. presentation for a school/college assignment).
4. Click on an image to display it in full size.
5. To download an image, right-click on the image, select **Save picture as** from the shortcut menu and save the image into your user area.

Searching for images and sounds on Microsoft Office Online

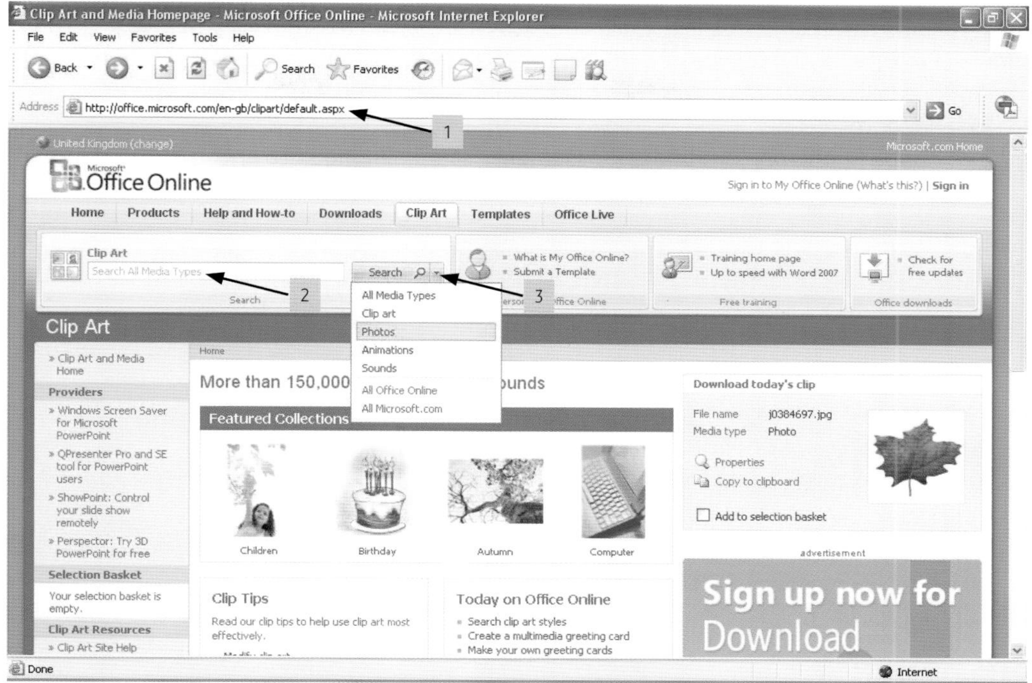

Figure 3.1: *Searching for images using the Microsoft Office Online website.*

1. Enter the following URL (website address) into the address bar of your browser: **http://office.microsoft.com/en-gb/clipart** and click **Go**.
2. In the box to the left of the **Search** button, enter a subject for the file you want to find.
3. Click the drop-down arrow to the right of the **Search** button and select the type of file you need (e.g. clipart, photos, animations or sounds).
4. Click the **Search** button to display files that meet your search criteria.
5. Examples of files will display. Click in the tick box below any thumbnail you want to download.
6. When you have selected all the files you want to download, click on **Download x item(s)** on the left of the screen below **Selection Basket** (x is the number of files you have selected – refer to Figure 3.2).

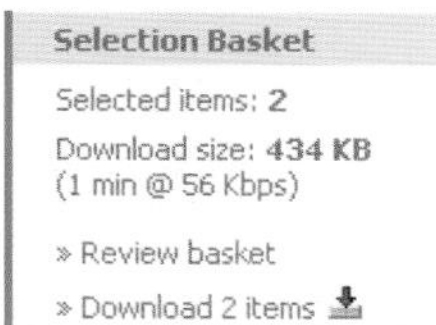

Figure 3.2: *Downloading files from the Microsoft Office Online website.*

7. Click the **Download Now** button and follow the on-screen instructions to save the files. The files will download into a folder called **Microsoft Clip Organizer**. You can leave these in this folder or copy them into your working area.

Preparing images

Whether you have been given the images, have taken them yourself, have scanned them in or obtained them from Microsoft Office Online, once you have transferred them to your computer, you should check the image quality and the image size. If you need to change the size and/or resolution, you will need to open the image in an appropriate program in order to change the file size and/or resolution. Some examples of programs in which you can manipulate images are Adobe Photoshop or Photoshop Elements, Jasc PaintShop Pro and CorelDraw.

Activity 16: Source images and animations, update record of files...

In this activity you will:

- collect and save appropriate images
- update your record of files.

➔ Refer to your design documentation produced in Chapter 2 (the description of the purpose and audience; your plan, your house style sheet and your storyboard).

➔ Find out if your teacher or tutor is able to provide you with any images that you could use in your multimedia presentation or if he/she is able to recommend any suitable sources (e.g. websites, CD/DVD-ROM photo-libraries).

➔ Source suitable images (i.e. photographs, clipart, animations and graphics) for your multimedia presentation. As a minimum you must gather suitable images – if you also use animation(s), you will achieve a higher grade.

➔ Save all image files in a suitable file format into your project folder.

➔ You MUST keep a record of all your sources. Update your **AO3_Record OfFilesCollected** form. Save this document for use later.

5. Obtain sound and video clips

Sound and video clips are available from within some application programs (e.g. Microsoft PowerPoint). As your multimedia product for the given project scenario will be an interactive presentation, you can use the sound and video files from within PowerPoint so you do not have to collect these beforehand. If you have a microphone attached to your computer, you can also record a narration directly into PowerPoint when you create your presentation.

- You can search the World Wide Web or search the Microsoft Office Online website for alternative sound and video clips. (Refer to the previous section for how to search Microsoft Office Online.)
- Use the contact details on the website if you need to obtain permission to use a clip.
- You may have your own sound and/or video clips from your work for other units in this course (e.g. Units 22 and 23) or other projects that you may have completed.

6. Back up all source files

Once you have collected and saved all the multimedia elements you will need for your multimedia product (as explained in Sections 1 to 5 above), you should create a back-up copy of your folder – you would not want to lose any files or risk any files being overwritten or corrupted! You should copy the folder(s) containing all your collected files to removable media (e.g. a memory stick or CD-ROM). As sound and video files can be quite large, you may not be able to back these up on floppy disks.

To prevent any files from being overwritten accidentally, you should also set the file or folder properties to read-only. Right-click on the folder (a menu displays) → Select **Properties** → Place a tick in the box for **Read-only** → **Apply** → **OK**.

Activity 17: Source sound and video files, update record of files...

In this activity you will:

- identify appropriate sound and video files
- update your record of files.

➔ Refer to your plans and storyboard (that you produced in Chapter 2).

➔ As a minimum you must use one sound file – to achieve a higher grade, you should also collect suitable video file(s).

➔ Ask your teacher/tutor if he/she is able to provide you with any sound and or video files that you could use in your multimedia presentation or if he/she is able to recommend any suitable sources for these items.

➔ Collect or *identify** suitable sound and/or video file(s) for your product. It is sufficient to use a minimum of one sound and one video file in your product. **If you are going to use sound and/or video files from within a program (e.g. Microsoft PowerPoint), you will not need to collect these beforehand or save them into a folder; you will simply be looking for and deciding which sound and/or video files you will use.*

➔ Save your files in a suitable file format into your folder (if appropriate).

➔ You MUST keep a record of all your sources. Update and save your **AO3_RecordOfFilesCollected** form.

Portfolio builder

By reading and understanding the guidelines in this chapter, and working through the activities, you have learned how to source text, photographs, images, animations, sound and video clips for your multimedia product. For your own portfolio, you will need to use these skills to source the multimedia elements needed to create your own product. You will also need to keep a record of the files you collect. You may use or adapt the **AO3_RecordOfFilesCollected** form provided with this book.

You should read your planning documents to remind yourself what type of product you have planned to create, what its purpose is and who the intended audience is, then go ahead and find appropriate source files. You must keep a record of all files collected. Your record should show from where and when each file was obtained, whether copyright permission has been sought and what you intend to use the file for. You should save all files into a folder.

Good luck!

Assessment Objective 4

Create the Multimedia Product

Overview

In this chapter you will create the multimedia product that you designed in Chapter 2 (Assessment Objective 2). You will use the files you collected in Chapter 3 (Assessment Objective 3). To ensure that your multimedia product meets its aims and is suitable for your target audience, you will find it helpful to take note of your findings when you reviewed three existing multimedia products in Chapter 1 (Assessment Objective 1). The multimedia product you will create in this chapter will be based on the project scenario given in the Introduction.

You should know from the work you did in Chapter 1 that there are a number of different types of multimedia products (e.g. websites, computer games, presentations and advertisements). In this chapter, you will create an interactive multimedia presentation because this best suits the aims, purpose and target audience in the project scenario. For other projects, you could create another type of multimedia product.

Key term

Interactive multimedia presentation

A presentation that is navigable by the user. The presentation will have a navigation structure allowing the viewer to choose the topics he/she wants to view by clicking a hyperlink. The presentation requires active interaction from the user. Multimedia elements like sound, video and animation are used to make the presentation more interesting and to make the information clearer.

An interactive presentation can be given to a prospective customer at, for example, a seminar, a travel/holiday/trade show or an exhibition. It can also be used for hands-on training.

Referring to the project scenario

The project scenario states that the interactive presentation that you will produce will be given on a CD-ROM to visitors attending a holiday roadshow. The intention is that users can navigate the presentation and choose to view information about adventure holidays that interest them. As the users may not be experienced at using IT, the interactive presentation should be very clearly laid out and easy to use, with lots of engaging features to keep the interest of the viewer.

How this assessment objective will be assessed...

You will need to create an interactive multimedia product based on the design documentation you have already created. This assessment objective will be graded by how effectively you create different ways of navigating your product using hyperlinks. The range of multimedia elements you use and whether or not all elements work as intended will also determine your grade.

- You will need to create a multimedia product which includes different ways for a user to navigate your product. These different ways are referred to as alternative pathways. The user should be able to choose their own route through the product.
- Your multimedia product should include a home page/slide which shows the different parts of the product. This page/slide should allow users to go to different parts of your product and also to go back.
- You should include a range of multimedia elements. As a minimum, you must include text, images and sound. To achieve a **Merit** grade, you should also include animation; for a **Distinction** grade, you should also include at least one video clip.
- To allow the user to navigate your product, you must use hyperlinks. For example, links to different slides within a presentation, links that allow the user to return quickly to the home page/slide from wherever they are in the presentation, external links to websites and/or email addresses.
- When producing the product, you should incorporate as much user interaction as possible; you should include features which encourage users to click on links to go to different parts of the product or to view sound and audio clips.
- You should use appropriate multimedia effects in your product (e.g. animations, transitions, hidden slides, action buttons to access the hidden slides).

Evidence for this assessment objective

To allow the moderator to view and navigate your interactive product and see the multimedia elements used, you or your teacher/tutor could make your product electronically, for example, on a CD-ROM, memory stick or laptop.

You will also need to include annotated printouts of each screen which should clearly show the elements used on each slide.

You should test the multimedia features to make sure they work as you intend. On the printouts, you will need to add notes to explain how the multimedia features work and to state if they work as intended.

Skills to use...

In creating your presentation, you will need to:

- set up a **Slide Master** and **Title Master**
- select slide design **templates** and colour schemes
- format **house style**
- select appropriate slide layouts, insert **text**, **images** and **animations**
- create a **navigation** bar and navigation buttons
- create internal and external **hyperlinks** using text and images
- insert at least one **sound** file
- insert at least one **video** file (**Distinction** only)
- set custom **animation** effects
- produce and annotate **printouts** of each screen
- **prepare** the multimedia product for viewing.

How to achieve...

Pass requirements

P1 You create a multimedia product which makes some use of alternative pathways through the product.

P2 Your multimedia product includes hyperlinks and multimedia effects.

P3 Your multimedia product includes text, images and sound.

P4 Some elements may not work as intended.

Merit requirements

M1 You create a multimedia product which makes good use of alternative pathways through the product.

M2 Your multimedia product makes good use of hyperlinks, user interaction and multimedia effects.

M3 Your multimedia product includes text, images, sound and animation.

M4 Most elements should work as intended.

Distinction requirements

D1 You create a multimedia product which makes effective use of alternative pathways through the product.

D2 Your multimedia product makes effective use of hyperlinks, user interaction and multimedia effects.

D3 Your multimedia product includes text, images, sound, animation and video.

D4 All elements must work as intended.

Preparing to create the multimedia presentation using the design documents and prepared files

Before you begin, remember that you are working to a given project scenario, that you have already defined your aims and target audience, that you have already created your house style guidelines and produced a plan and storyboard. You have also gathered your source files. So don't be tempted at this stage to produce a 'funky', 'jazzy' presentation with lots of interesting features – you must stick to the original plan!

There are a variety of different types of software that could be used to create your product. In this chapter we will use presentation graphics software, specifically Microsoft Office PowerPoint 2003 from the Microsoft Office 2003 suite. This software is ideal for bringing together multimedia elements to create a suitable product. Sound and video files cannot be created in Microsoft PowerPoint but these files can be easily inserted from within the program.

1. Create a presentation, set up a Slide Master and Title slides, select design templates and colour schemes, apply house style

1 Start PowerPoint 2003 and switch to the Slide Master view: **View** → **Master** → **Slide Master**.
2 Display thumbnails of the slide design templates available: **Format** → **Slide Design...** .
3 Scroll down to see the available templates (refer to Figure 4.1). (Note: the designs available will vary on different computers.) To select a template, click on it once – make sure you choose one that is appropriate for your project.

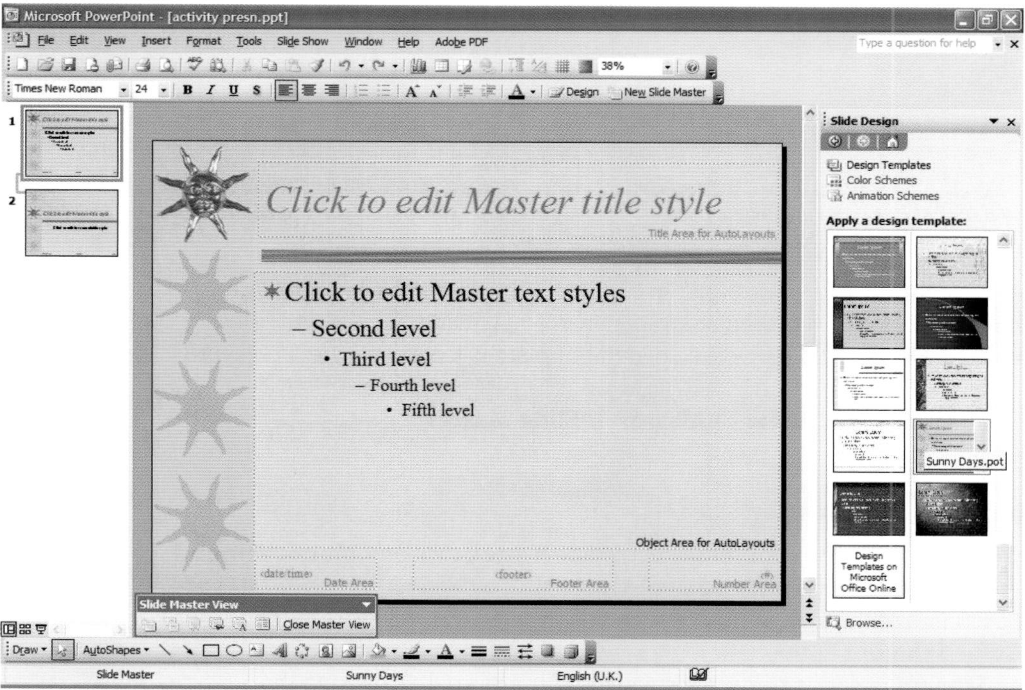

Figure 4.1: *Selecting a slide design template in Microsoft PowerPoint.*

4 Alternatively, if you have access to the Internet and are able to download files from the Internet on your computer, click on **Design Templates on Microsoft Office Online**. This will take you to the Microsoft Office Online website. Click on a category to display the templates available.

TIP

For the adventure holidays presentation, the Nature or Sports categories would be appropriate (Figure 4.2). The templates available in the Sports category are shown in Figure 4.3.

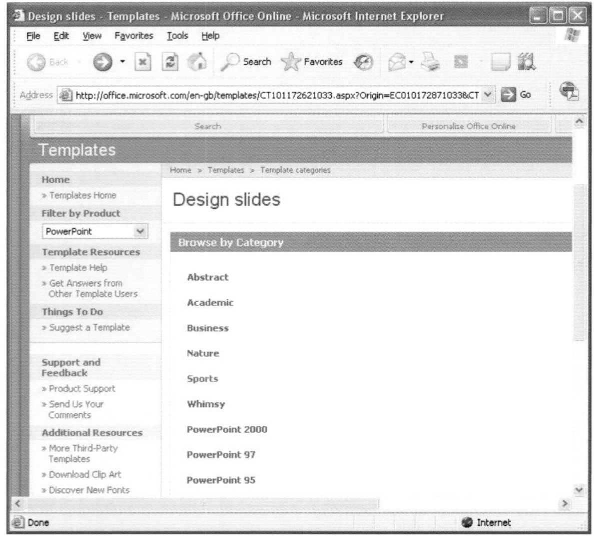

Figure 4.2: Selecting a slide design template on Microsoft Office Online.

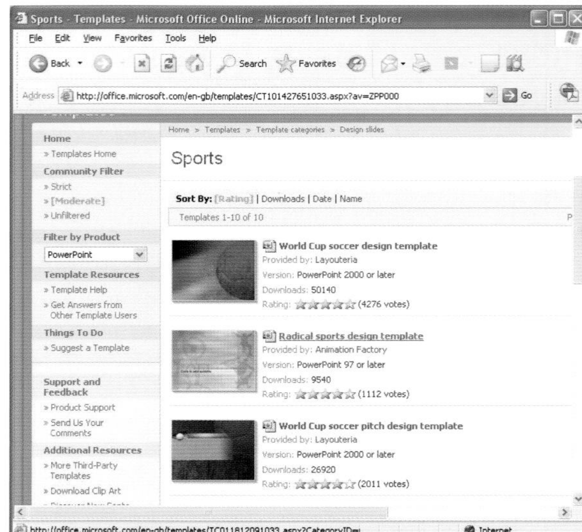

Figure 4.3: Selecting a Sports template on Microsoft Office Online.

5 Click on the name of the template you want. In Figure 4.3 the **Radical sports design template** has been selected. This template will open in a new window.
6 Click the **Download Now** button. The downloaded template will open in a new presentation.
7 Switch to the Slide Master view: **View** → **Master** → **Slide Master**.
8 Save your presentation.

Changing the colour scheme

1 To change the colour scheme on your template or Slide Master, click on **Color Schemes** in the right pane of the screen (refer to Figure 4.1).
2 Click on the thumbnails of the sample colour schemes to select alternative text colours, or click on **Edit Color Schemes** at the bottom of the pane to edit the preset colours.
3 The **Edit Color Scheme** dialogue box will display (refer to Figure 4.4). Click on the **Custom** tab and select the item (e.g. Background, Text and Lines, etc.) whose colour you want to change, then click the **Change Color** button in this window. Another window will display in which you can select the new colour you require.
4 Repeat this process for every item whose colour you want to change.

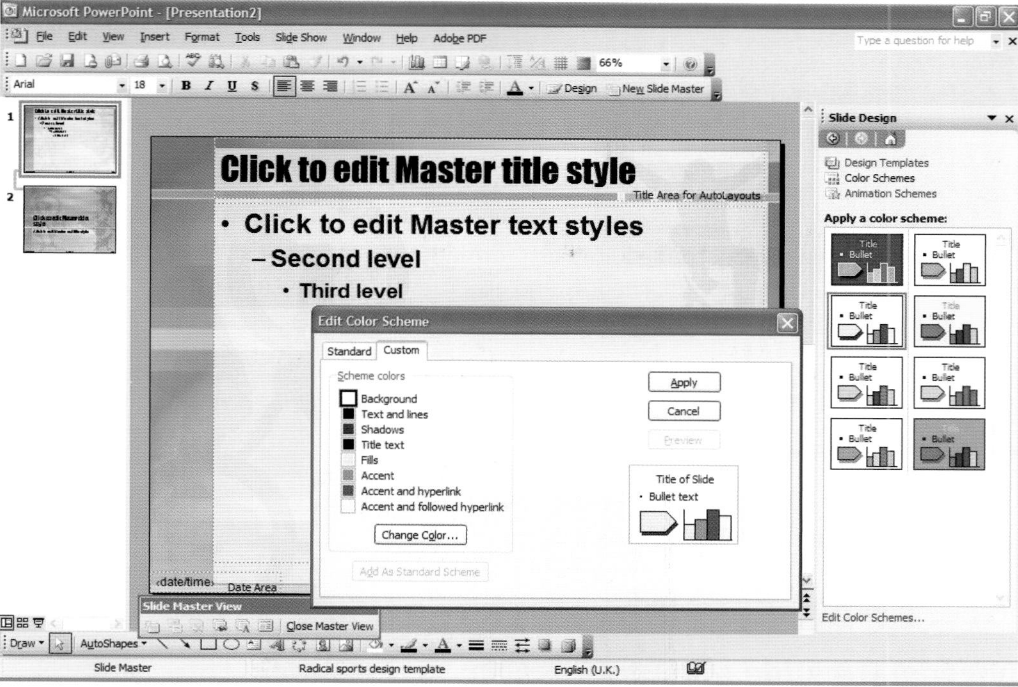

Figure 4.4: *Changing a template colour scheme.*

Activity 18: Set up master template...

In this activity you will:

- create the template for the project scenario given in the Introduction to this book
- choose a suitable design template and set the colour scheme.

➔ Refer to the design documentation you created in Chapter 2.

➔ Remember when creating your multimedia product, you must ensure you meet the purpose and audience you identified in your planning documents. To help you make sure your presentation keeps to your original plan: read the plan you produced in Activity 12; refer to the house style guidelines you produced in Activity 13; and the navigation plan and storyboard you created in Activity 14.

➔ Create a new presentation and switch to the **Slide Master** view.

➔ Set the design template according to your house style guidelines.

➔ Set the colour scheme according to your house style guidelines.

➔ Save your presentation using a suitable filename.

Applying the house style to your template

1 When setting the text style for your titles, subtitle and bullets you should do so on the **Slide Master** and the **Title Master** to ensure that all the slides have a consistent layout. Do not apply formatting to individual slides. Set the text styles following the guidelines in your house style sheet.

2 To format the text on the **Slide Master** and **Title Master** (titles, subtitles and bullets): Click anywhere within the text (the text becomes highlighted) → On the Formatting toolbar, click the drop-down arrow to set the required text formatting (e.g. font type, font size, font colour) → Click the buttons for bold, shadow and alignment as needed (refer to Figure 4.5).

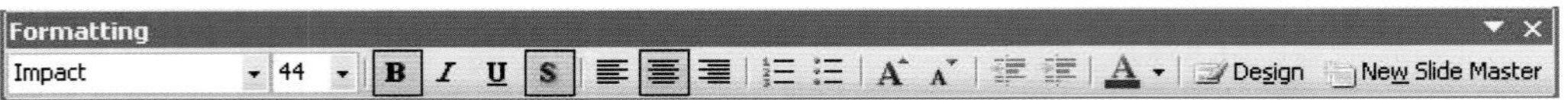

Figure 4.5: *Microsoft PowerPoint's formatting toolbar.*

3 To change the bullet character style: **Format** → **Bullets and Numbering...** to open the **Bullets and Numbering** dialogue box → Select a bullet character style or click on **Customize...** to see more options → Select an option → Click **OK**.

2. Select appropriate slide layouts, insert text, images and animations

Selecting a slide layout

1 Once you have set up your **Slide Master** and **Title Master** layout, you should switch to **Normal** view by clicking the Close Master View button on the **Slide Master View** toolbar. You can switch back the **Slide Master** view at any time if you wish to add items or make changes. (**View** → **Master** → **Slide Master**.)

2 To insert new slides, click the  button on the **Formatting** toolbar. A **Slide Layout** pane will display on the right of the screen. Use the scroll bar or arrow to scroll down to see the different types of layout available.

3 To choose a particular slide layout or to change the layout of an existing slide, click on the thumbnail of the style you want in the **Slide Layout** task pane (refer to Figure 4.6).

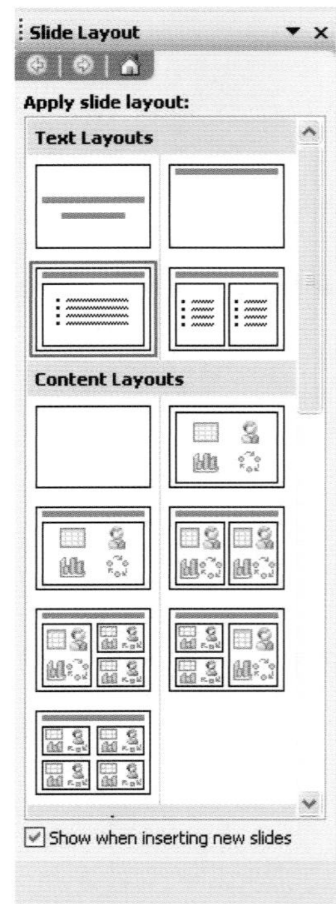

Figure 4.6: *Selecting a slide layout.*

TIP

In Microsoft PowerPoint, the first slide that displays in Normal view is a Title Slide layout. If this is not the layout you need for your first slide, remember to change the slide layout.

To enter a title and bulleted text on a slide, choose the Title and Text layout.

Entering text and inserting text

To enter titles, subtitles or text on a slide, simply click in the required text frame and type the text. The formatting you set on the **Slide Master** or **Title Master** will automatically be applied.

You have already collected your text in Chapter 4 and you should have saved it as a text file (.txt format) or as a Microsoft Word file (.doc format). All you need to do now is to copy and paste this prepared text as needed into your presentation. You will need to prepare your slides first.

1 Create the number of slides you need and select the appropriate slide layout for each slide. Save the presentation now!
2 If your text is saved in .txt format, open it in Microsoft Word: in your working folder, right-click on the text file (a menu displays) → Select **Open With** → **Microsoft Word** (refer to Figure 4.7). If Microsoft Word does not display in the sub-menu, click on **Choose Program...** and select **Microsoft Word** from the list displayed on the dialogue box.

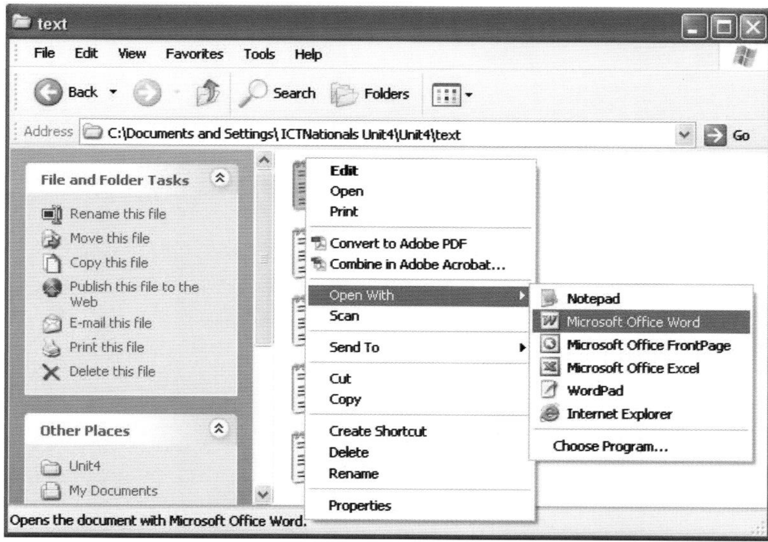

Figure 4.7: *Opening a text file in Microsoft Word.*

3 Copy the section of text your require → Switch to Microsoft PowerPoint → Select the slide on which you want to paste a section of text → Click in the text frame in which you want to paste the text → **Paste**.

When displaying text on slides, keep it simple.

Bear in mind the frequently used 6 × 7 rule for presentations: no more than 6 lines per slide, no more than 7 words per line.

Promoting and demoting text

When you paste text into the main text frame of a **Title and Text** layout slide, all text will display as first level bullets. To display text as sub-bullets: Highlight the text → Click the **Increase Indent** button on the Formatting toolbar.

Inserting images, animations and clipart

You have already collected and saved your images, animations and perhaps clipart in Chapter 3. These items are inserted in Microsoft PowerPoint as follows:

1. To insert an image that you have saved: **Insert** → **Picture** → **From File...** → Go to the folder containing the image files you collected → Click on the file → Click **Insert**.
2. To resize an image without distorting the shape: click and drag a corner handle.
3. To move an image: click in the image and drag.
4. An animation will not appear animated in normal slide view. To see it moving, click the **Slide Show from current slide** button on the bottom left of the screen.
5. To insert clipart from within PowerPoint: **Insert** → **Picture** → **Clip Art...** (the Clip Art task pane is displayed) → Enter a search word in the search box → Click **Go** → Click on a thumbnail to select it.

Activity 19: Insert text and images on to slides...

In this activity you will insert the text and images you collected in Chapter 3 into your multimedia presentation.

- Continue working on the presentation you saved in Activity 18.
- Refer to the storyboard you created in Chapter 2 to check the layout and content you had planned for the slides in the presentation.
- In normal slide view, insert the required number of slides and select the correct slide layout for each slide. Create title slides as needed for your presentation.
- Type appropriate slide titles and subtitles on the slides, then copy and paste the text you collected in Chapter 3 on to the correct slides or type the required text. Promote and demote the text as appropriate.
- Insert and position the images you have collected on to the correct slides.
- Check that all text and images are displayed correctly on all slides.
- The next thing you will do is to create a navigation bar on the master and title slides. It is important that this is created correctly, so check every slide in your presentation and make sure that the titles and content are correct on all slides.
- Save your updated presentation.

Referring to the project scenario

The project scenario is about adventure holidays in Europe. One of the aims of any interactive multimedia product is to encourage the target audience to use the interactive elements to move to different parts of the presentation. To allow them to do so, it is a good idea to create a navigation bar on the **Slide Master** and **Title Master**. But first, you must prepare appropriate slides in the presentation so that when you create the navigation bar, you can link the navigation buttons to the appropriate slides.

You should have a home page or index page as the first slide in the presentation. Then it would be appropriate to have a **Title Slide** layout for each country that you intend to feature in the presentation. After each title slide you could insert a few slides containing information about the activities in that country.

3. Create a navigation bar and navigation buttons

The navigation for the presentation should be created on the **Slide Master** and **Title Master** so that they display on every slide in the presentation. Switch to Slide Master view: **View** → **Master** → **Slide Master**. You can use some of the default action buttons and create some custom buttons on which you can insert your own text – this text could be the title you entered on the title slides.

1 **Slide Show** → **Action Buttons** → Select a button style. If you plan to enter text on the button, choose the top left option for **Action Button: Custom** (refer to Figure 4.8), otherwise select a button with an appropriate picture (e.g. the Home button would be appropriate for the link to the home page).

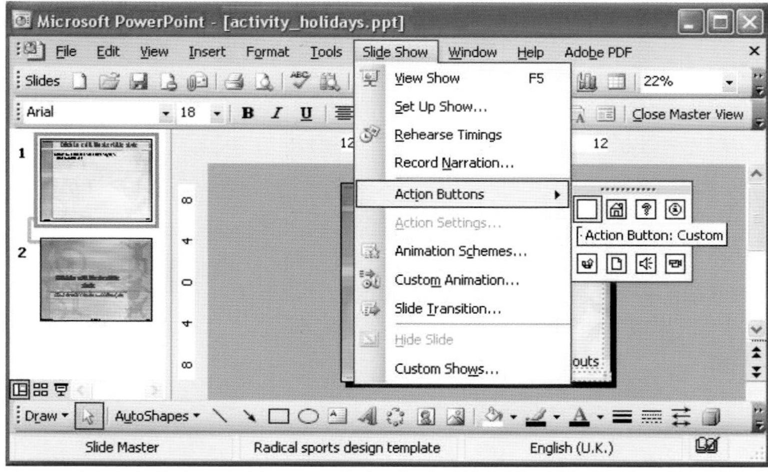

Figure 4.8: *Creating a navigation button.*

2 Draw the button in a suitable size and position it on the slide. The **Action Settings** dialogue box will display. Under the **Mouse Click** tab, click the button for **Hyperlink to:**, then click the drop-down arrow below this and scroll down the list until you see the option for **Slide...** (refer to Figure 4.9).

Figure 4.9: *Linking an action button to a slide.*

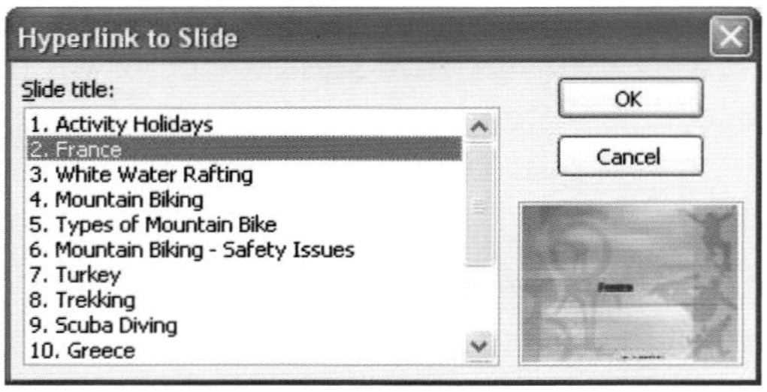

Figure 4.10: *Selecting a slide to link to.*

3 The **Hyperlink to Slide** dialogue box displays (Figure 4.10). The slide numbers and titles you entered on your slides are shown. Click to select the slide that the action button will link to, click **OK** and **OK** again. You have created the link. You should test the hyperlink before proceeding.

4 To test the link: Click the **Slide Show from current slide** button → Click the action button to test the link → Press **Esc** to close the slide show.

5 To add text to the button: Right-click the button → Select **Add Text** from the shortcut menu → a cursor will display on the button → Select an appropriate text size and style from the Formatting toolbar → type your text.

6 To resize a button, drag a corner handle. To move a button, click and drag it.

7 Repeat steps 1 to 6 to create more buttons.

TIP

Troubleshooting hyperlinks on action buttons

In Normal view: Right-click the button → Click Remove Hyperlink or Edit Hyperlink... on the shortcut menu.

TIP

Grouping action buttons

Once you have created and tested all your buttons, you could group them to prevent accidental moving. Select the first button → Hold down the Ctrl key and select the remaining buttons → Right-click to show the shortcut menu → Click Grouping → Group.

Copying action buttons

You can copy and paste individual buttons from the Slide Master to the Title Master, or better still, group them first, then copy the entire group. Click to select the button or group → Edit → Copy, select the Title Slide, Edit → Paste.

Referring to the project scenario

The example below shows hyperlink action buttons for each country featured in the presentation as well as a home button that will allow users to return to the home page and an information button that is linked to a Microsoft Word document containing booking information. The buttons were created on the **Slide Master**, then grouped and copied and pasted to the same position on the **Title Master**.

Figure 4.11: *Navigation buttons on the Slide Master and copied to the Title Master.*

Activity 20: Create navigation buttons...

In this activity you will create hyperlink action buttons for your presentation.

- Refer to your navigation plan and storyboard created in Chapter 2.
- On your **Slide Master**, create navigation buttons with appropriate text and/or images. Do not create the same buttons as in Figure 4.11!
- Position these buttons according to your design documentation.
- Test the buttons to ensure all hyperlinks work.
- Group and copy the buttons from the **Slide Master** on to your **Title Master**.
- Test the hyperlinks again.
- Save your updated presentation.

4. Create internal and external hyperlinks on individual slides using text and images

Key terms

Internal hyperlink

A link from one place in a multimedia product to another place in the same product. For example, in a presentation – a link from one slide to another; on a website – a link from one web page to another; on an interactive CD/DVD-ROM – a link from one screen to another.

External hyperlink

A hyperlink to an object outside the presentation, for example to a website (link to a URL), email address (email link), another presentation or another document (e.g. a Microsoft Word document, a spreadsheet file, etc.).

Creating internal and external hyperlinks using text or images

1 Highlight the text to be linked or click on an image to select it.
2 Click on the **Insert Hyperlink** button on the Standard toolbar. The **Insert Hyperlink** dialogue box is displayed.
3 To create a link to another slide in the presentation: Click **Place in This Document** (another window is displayed) → Click the slide number to be linked to (Figure 4.12).

> **TIP**
> If you are linking text or images on your Slide Master and/or Title Master, remember to switch back to Slide Master view.

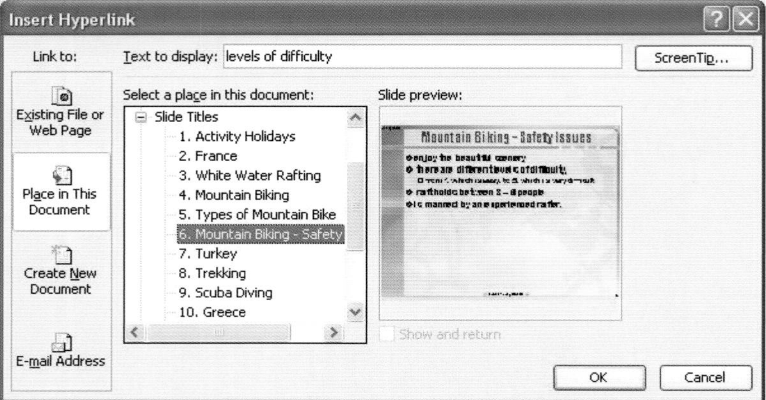

Figure 4.12: *Creating an internal hyperlink.*

4 To create a **ScreenTip** (short note) to be displayed when the user moves the cursor over a hyperlink, click the **ScreenTip...** button and then type the text you want → OK.
5 To create a link to an email address, click on **E-mail Address** (another window is displayed) → Type the email address you want to link to in the **E-mail address** box (Microsoft PowerPoint automatically inserts **mailto:** in front of the address – refer to Figure 4.13) → OK.

Figure 4.13: *Creating an email hyperlink.*

6 To create an external link to a web page, click on **Existing File or Web Page** (another window is displayed) → Type the website address in the **Address:** text box (Microsoft PowerPoint automatically inserts **http://** in front of the website address – refer to Figure 4.14) → OK.

Figure 4.14: *Creating an external hyperlink to a URL.*

Hiding slides

Slides can be hidden from view during an on-screen presentation to hide sensitive or confidential information. They could also be used to hold supplementary information that might support the main presentation. The hidden slide(s) can be accessed when needed or can be used to extend a presentation when required. They can be displayed during a presentation by clicking a hyperlink which you create on a slide to a hidden slide.

Slides can be hidden in the **Slides** pane in **Normal** view or in **Slide Sorter** view.

To hide a slide: Right-click the slide you want to hide → a shortcut menu is displayed → Select **Hide Slide**. The slide number of a hidden slide appears greyed out with a diagonal line through its slide number, e.g. 9 .

TIP

Test all your links before moving on! Click the Slide Show from current slide button and test all linked text and images.

TIP

Troubleshooting hyperlinks

In Normal view, right-click on the link → Edit Hyperlink... → Amend the link as necessary.

To remove a link: right-click on the link → Remove Hyperlink.

Activity 21: Create hyperlinks...

In this activity you will insert internal hyperlinks and external hyperlinks in your presentation.

- Refer to your storyboard.
- In your presentation, create the internal and external hyperlinks using the text and images that you identified to be linked in your original plans.
- Test every link to make sure it works as intended.
- Save the updated presentation.

5. Insert sound files

There are several options for inserting sound into your presentation: you may insert sound files available from within Microsoft PowerPoint, your own sound own files that you may have created or edited, or sound files that you have sourced previously. You can also record your own narration directly into a presentation. Sound files with the following file extensions can be inserted into Microsoft PowerPoint: .aiff, .au, .mid, .midi, .mp3, .wav and .wma.

1. In Normal view, display the slide on which you want to insert the sound effect: **Insert** → **Movies and Sounds**.
2. To insert your own sound clip: Click on **Sound from File...** → Locate the sound file from your folder → Double-click the file.
3. To insert a clip provided in Microsoft PowerPoint: Click on **Sound from Clip Organizer...** (the Clip Art task pane is displayed).
4. To find clips in a particular category: Enter the search criteria in the **Search for:** box → click **Go** → Scroll to find the clip that you want → Click on a clip to add it to the slide (refer to Figure 4.15).

TIP

The project scenario presentation is about activity holidays, so try using search words that relate to activities that would be offered. Some examples of search words that you could use are 'sport', 'swimming', 'scuba diving', 'rafting', 'skiing', 'canoeing' or 'sailing'.

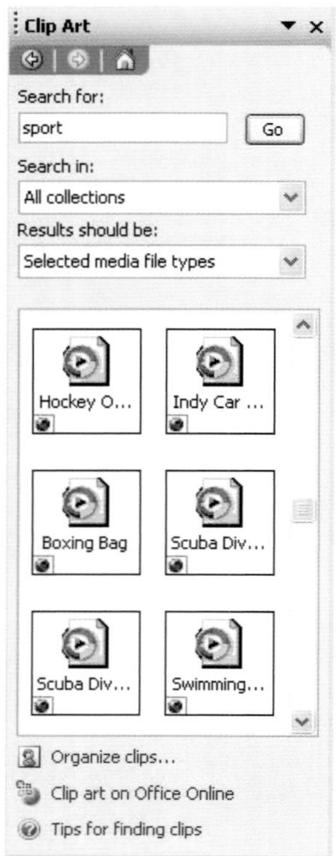

Figure 4.15: *Inserting a sound clip.*

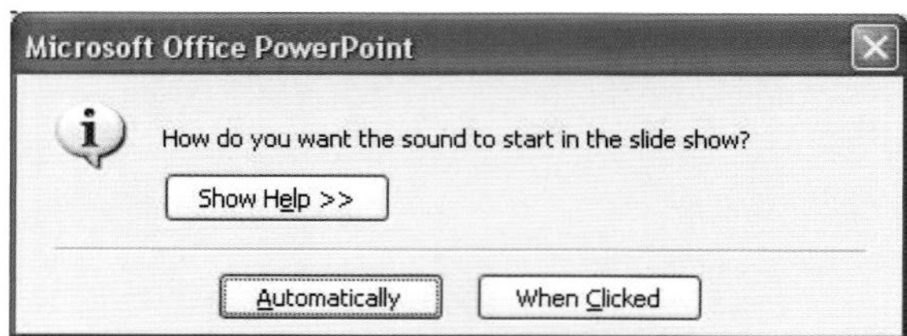

Figure 4.16: *Choosing how the sound will be played.*

5 A message will display (Figure 4.16). If you want the sound to play automatically when the user goes to the slide, select **Automatically**. To play the music or sound only when you click the sound icon, select **When Clicked**.

TIP

You need speakers and a sound card on your computer to play sounds. You may also be required to use headphones. Ask your teacher or tutor if you have these or check the sound settings in the Windows Control Panel.

Changing the sound settings

1 To change the sound settings: Right-click the sound icon on the slide (a shortcut menu is displayed) → Click **Custom Animation...** to open the Custom Animation task pane → Click the arrow to the right of the sound item you want to edit, a drop-down list is shown → Select **Effect Options...** to display the **Play Sound** dialogue box (refer to figure 4.17).

2 Choose the options you want from the **Effect** tab (refer to Figure 4.18) → Click the **Timing** tab → Choose from the options → Click the **Sound Settings** tab → Choose from the options → Click **OK**.

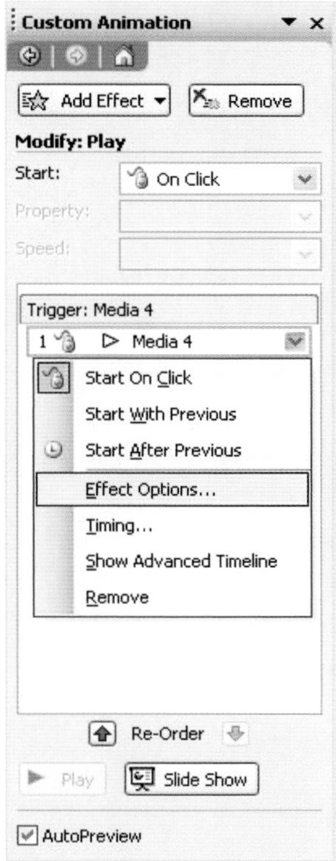

Figure 4.17: Changing sound settings.

Figure 4.18: Choosing sound options.

To add narration

1 Make sure a microphone is connected to your computer.

2 Click **Slide Show** → Select **Record Narration...** (the **Record Narration** dialogue box opens) → Click the **Change Quality...** button (the **Sound Selection** dialogue box opens) → Click the arrow to the right of the **Attributes** drop-down box → Select **48,000 kHz, 16 Bit, Mono** → Click **OK**.

3 Click the **Set Microphone Level...** button (the **Microphone Check** dialogue box opens) → Read the text displayed in this dialogue box into your microphone → Click **OK** → **OK**.

4 In slide show view, speak your narration into the microphone. The narration is automatically saved.

5 You will be prompted to save the slide timings → click **Save** or **Don't Save** as required.

Testing sound files

Click the **Slide Show from current slide** button. If you have set the option for **Automatically**, the sound will play automatically when the slide is displayed. If you have set the option for **When Clicked**, the sound will play when the sound icon is clicked.

Note: if you have recorded a narration, it will override any inserted sound file set to play automatically.

Activity 22: Insert sound file(s)...

In this activity you will insert at least one sound file in your presentation.

- Refer to your storyboard.
- In your presentation, insert an appropriate sound file on a suitable slide and in an appropriate position. Make sure the sound relates to the theme of your presentation.
- Set the sound options as appropriate to your presentation.
- Test the sound file to make sure it works as intended.
- You may add more sound files if you wish, but remember not to overdo it. Inappropriate or continuous sound can be annoying or distracting to the user.
- Save the updated presentation.

6. Insert video files (distinction only)

You may insert video files available from within Microsoft PowerPoint or your own files. Video files with the following file extensions can be inserted into Microsoft PowerPoint: .asf, .avi, .mpg, .mpeg and .wmv.

1. In Normal view, display the slide on which you want to insert the video clip → **Insert** → **Movies and Sounds**.
2. To insert your own video clip: Click on **Movie from File...** → Locate the video file from your folder → double-click the file.
3. To insert a clip provided in Microsoft PowerPoint: Click on **Movie from Clip Organizer...** (the Clip Art task pane is displayed).
4. To find clips in a particular category: Enter the search criteria in the **Search for:** box → Click **Go** → Scroll to find the clip that you want → Click on a clip to add it to the slide.

Choosing the video settings and adding sound to a video clip

1. To change how a clip is displayed: Right-click the video icon on the slide (a shortcut menu is displayed) → Click **Custom Animation...** to open the Custom Animation task pane → Click the arrow to the right of the **Add Effect** button → Choose an effect, then from the submenu, choose an option (refer to Figure 4.20).
2. In the Custom Animation task pane, click the arrow to the right of the video clip you want to edit, a drop-down list is shown → Select **Effect Options...** to display the dialogue box.
3. Choose the options you want from the **Effect** and the **Timing** tabs (refer to the example in Figure 4.20).
4. To add sound: Select the **Effect** tab → Click arrow to the right of **Sound** list box → Click an option. To add your own sound file: Click **Other sound...** → Locate your sound file → OK.

Referring to the project scenario

The project is about adventure holidays, so the clip is that of an airplane (see Figure 4.19). The **Entrance** and **Fly In** effects have been selected (see Figure 4.20).

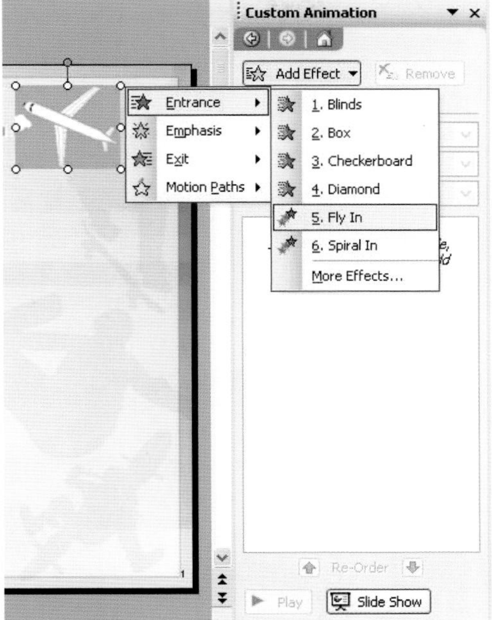

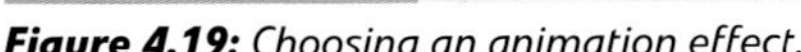

Figure 4.19: *Choosing an animation effect.*

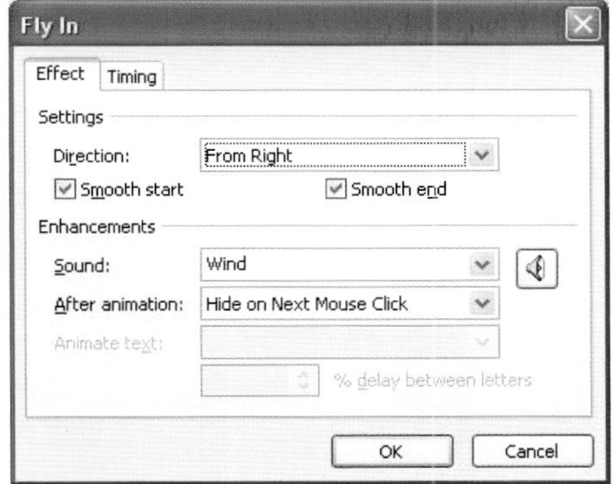

Figure 4.20: *Choosing animation options.*

Testing video files

Click the **Slide Show from current slide** button . The video will play automatically.

Activity 23: Insert video clip(s)...

In this activity you will insert at least one video clip in your presentation.

- Refer to your storyboard.
- In your presentation, insert an appropriate video clip. Make sure you insert this clip on a suitable slide and in an appropriate position.
- Set a custom animation effect and add an appropriate sound to the video clip if you wish.
- Test the video clip to make sure it works as intended.
- You may add more video clips if you wish.
- Save the updated presentation.

7. Set custom animation effects

Setting an animation scheme

1 Animations can be set in **Normal View** or in **Slide Sorter View**, but it is easier to do so in **Slide Sorter View** because you can see all the slides in your presentation at the same time.

2 Click the **Slide Sorter View** icon at the bottom left of the screen.

3 Select the slides on which you want to apply the animation. To select more than one slide: Hold down the Ctrl key and click to select the required slides. To select all the slides: **Edit** → **Select All**.

4 **Slide Show** → **Animation Schemes...** displays the Slide Design task pane showing the animation schemes available → Select an animation from the list (remember to scroll down to see all the options – refer to Figure 4.21).

5 An animation icon displays under the selected slides.

Figure 4.21: *Setting animation.*

Key term

Transition

The effect that displays when a new slide appears on screen.

Setting transitions

1 In **Slide Sorter View**, select the slides on which you want to set a transition.

2 **Slide Show** → **Slide Transition...** (displays the Slide Transition task pane) → Select an **Apply to selected slides:** option (remember to scroll down to see all the options) → Select the **Modify transition** and **Advance slide** options (refer to Figure 4.22).

Figure 4.22: *Setting slide transitions.*

Activity 24: Set animations and transitions...

In this activity you will apply custom effects to your presentation.

- In your presentation, add custom animation effects and/or slide transitions to the slides as you think appropriate. Don't overdo animation effects or transitions as too many can spoil the professional appearance of your product.
- Save the updated presentation.

8. Produce and annotate printouts of each screen

Key term

Annotate

To write notes or comments on a printout that explain what the printout shows.

Producing printouts of each screen

You will need to produce a printout of each screen of your multimedia product then annotate the printouts to show how the multimedia elements work. There are different methods for printing and annotating. The important thing to remember is that whatever style of printout you choose to produce, the printouts **must** display all elements on every slide **clearly**.

Methods of printing and annotating

Some different methods you could try to print and annotate your slides are:

- Print the presentation as individual slides or as handouts, then annotate them by hand.
- Take a screen print of each screen, paste the screen print into a Microsoft Word document and annotate it in using text boxes or by hand on a printout.

The first method is likely to be quicker whilst the last method of using text boxes is likely to look more professional.

You don't get any extra marks for the annotation method, so don't spend too much time on this. Ask your teacher or tutor what method of printing and annotating he/she prefers – he/she might not want you to print every slide individually!

Printing the presentation

- To print all slides as individual slides: **File** → **Print** → Select the button for **All** → Select **Slides** from the **Print what:** drop-down list → **OK**.
- To print only some slides as individual slides (e.g. you may want to print only the slides containing multimedia elements as individual slides and the rest as handouts): **File** → **Print** → Select the button for **Slides:** → In the **Slides:** box, type the number of each slide to be printed (separate each number by a comma) → Select **Slides** from the **Print what:** drop-down list → **OK** (refer to Figure 4.23).

- To print handouts: **File** → **Print** → select the button for **All** or select the button for **Slides:** → If you have selected **Slides:**, then in the **Slides:** text box, type the number of each slide to be printed (separate each number by a comma) → Select **Handouts** from the **Print what:** drop-down list → Click the arrow to the right of **Slides per page:** drop-down list and select a number (refer to Figure 4.24) → Click the **Preview** button and check that all the multimedia elements are clearly visible.

TIP

Do not print any more than six slides per page on a handout print because it will be difficult to see clearly the elements on the slides if the slides are too small.

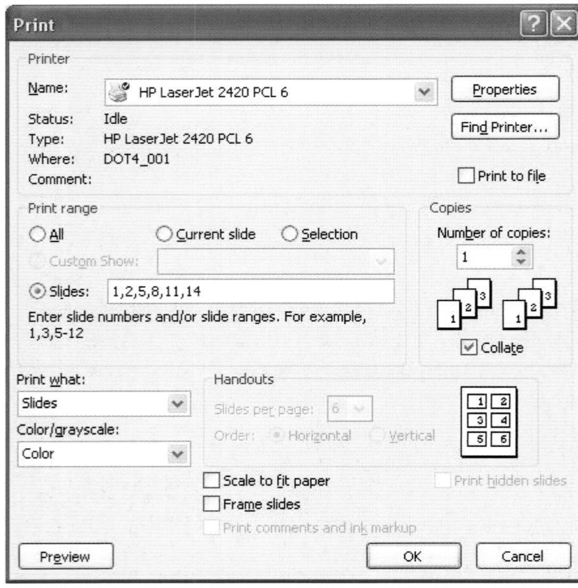

Figure 4.23: *Printing individual slides.*

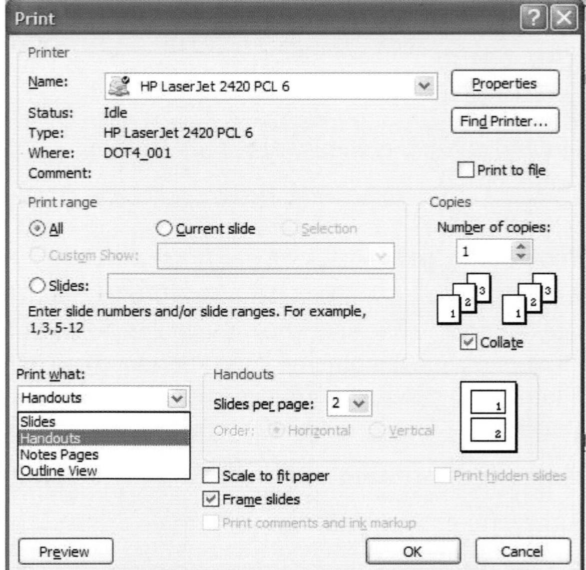

Figure 4.24: *Printing handouts (two per page).*

Annotating the printouts

Once you have printed your slides, you must remember to annotate them to explain how the multimedia elements work. Here are some example annotations:

Video clip inserted here. The plane image flies in from the right and continues to fly in while the slide is displayed – it has a wind sound effect.

Each country name on this title slide is linked to the introductory slide for a country. These action buttons are also linked to the title slide for a country – that country's title slide displays when the link is clicked.

Email link which displays a blank email message when the link is clicked.

Sound clip inserted – the clip plays automatically when the slide is displayed playing a sound of a fanfare.

Producing screen prints (optional)

Remember that taking a screen print of each screen is NOT essential. If you have printed your presentation and annotated the printouts, skip this section and the next section titled **Adding text boxes on the screen prints**.

1 Display the screen you wish to screen print – make sure the slide is displayed clearly and that any multimedia elements on the slide (e.g. a sound file icon or a video clip) are clearly displayed.
2 Press **Alt** + **PrtSc** (i.e. press the **Alt** and the **Print Screen** keys on your keyboard at the same time).
3 Open a new Microsoft Word document.
4 **Edit** → **Paste**.

TIP

To show all elements on the slide clearly, display the individual slide in Print Preview before taking a screen print.

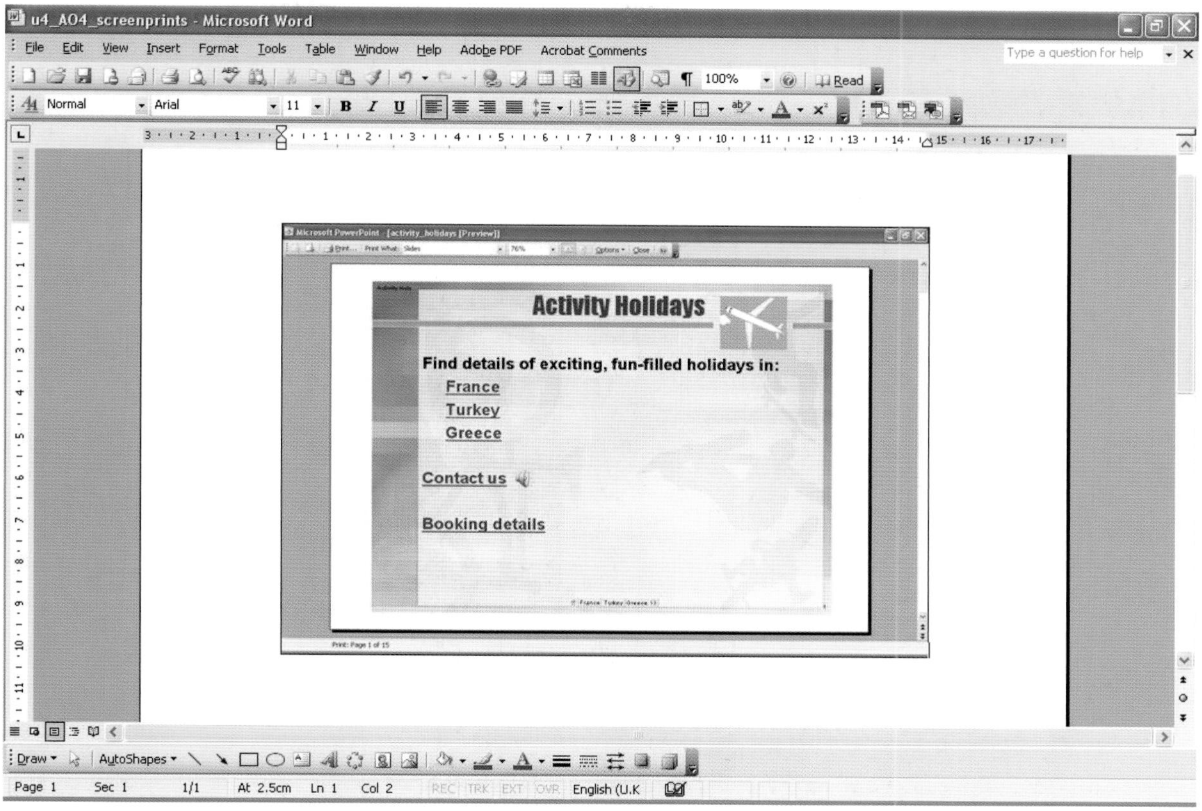

Figure 4.25: *A screen print pasted into a Microsoft Word document.*

5 Type your name in the header or footer of the screen print document.
6 Save the screen print using a suitable filename (e.g. unit4_ screenprints).

TIP

After you have pasted your first screen print, press Enter a few times so that you can paste your next prints below. If a screen print is selected (i.e. it has black handles around it) when you paste the next screen print, you will overwrite the screen print that was selected!

If you are planning to annotate the printouts using text boxes, you could set your page orientation to landscape to make room for the text boxes and paste each screen on a separate page (refer to the example in Figure 4.26).

To create a new page, insert a page break: press Ctrl + Enter.

7 You need to show printouts of each screen, so repeat steps 1 to 4 until you have produced screen prints of each screen.
8 To print the screen print document, click the Print button.

Adding text boxes on the screen prints (optional)

1 Make sure the Drawing toolbar is displayed in your Microsoft Word document containing the screen prints. This is usually docked at the bottom of the page. If it is not: **View** → **Toolbars** → **Drawing**.

2 From the Drawing toolbar, select the Text Box tool and draw a frame in your document next to your screen print. Type the text in the box to explain how the displayed feature works.

3 Use the Arrow tool on the Drawing toolbar to draw an arrow from the text box pointing to the displayed feature.

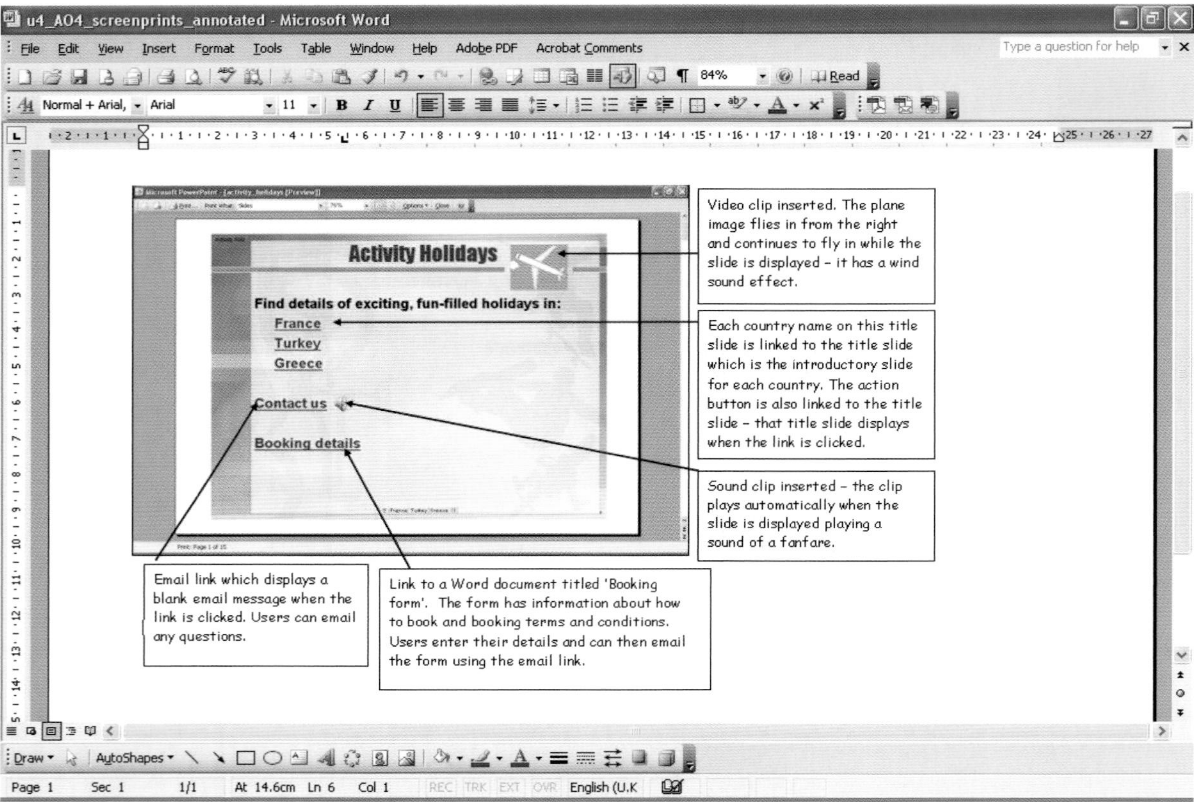

***Figure 4.26:** An annotated screen print.*

Activity 25: Produce and annotate printouts of each screen...

In this activity you will produce printouts of your presentation and annotate the printouts.

- Ask your teacher or tutor what method of printing your presentation he/she prefers.
- Print the presentation using the method suggested by your teacher/tutor.
- Annotate the printouts to show the multimedia elements and how these work.
- File all your printouts carefully.

Referring to the project scenario

The project scenario tells you that 'This presentation will be given on a CD-ROM to visitors attending a holiday roadshow.'

You have created a presentation using Microsoft Office PowerPoint 2003 but you cannot assume that everyone has this software installed on their computers. You therefore need to make your presentation suitable for viewing on all computers.

9. Prepare the multimedia product for viewing

To prepare the presentation for viewing on all computers, you will 'package' the presentation using the **Package for CD** option in Microsoft PowerPoint. Don't worry if you do not have CD-ROM or CD burning software, this is not needed.

Make sure you save the final version of your presentation. It is good practice to create a back-up copy as well!

1 Open the presentation in Microsoft PowerPoint.
2 **File** → **Package for CD...** (displays the **Package for CD** dialogue box – refer to Figure 4.27).

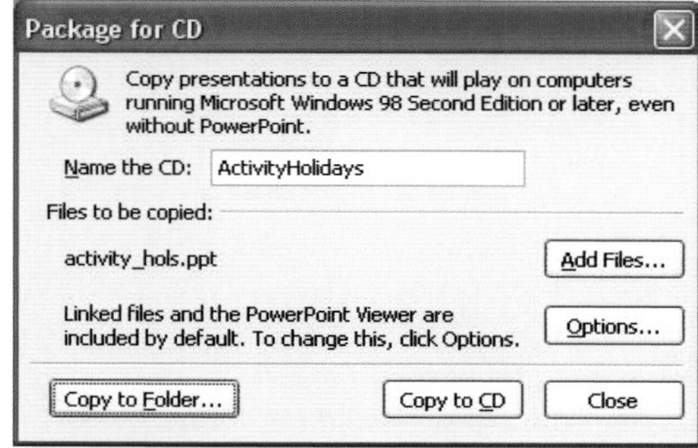

Figure 4.27: *Preparing a presentation for viewing.*

3 Type a suitable name in the **Name the CD:** box. This name will be displayed on a folder which will be automatically created and in which all the presentation files will be saved.
4 Click the **Copy to Folder...** button to display the **Copy to Folder** dialogue box (Figure 4.28).

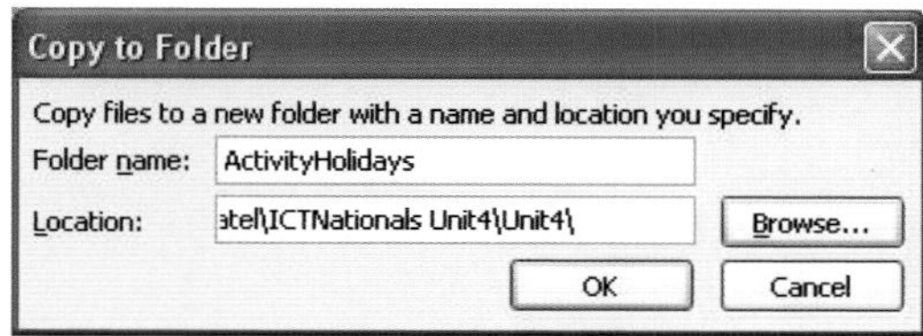

Figure 4.28: *Locating a folder for a packaged presentation.*

5 Click the **Browse...** button to display the **Choose Location** dialogue box → Locate the folder in your user area where you want to save the final multimedia presentation (all the files in your presentation and all other files needed to run the presentation will be packaged into the folder you choose) → Click the **Select** button.
6 The **Copy to Folder...** dialogue box displays again → click **OK** → click **Close** to close the **Package for CD** dialogue box.

Activity 26: Prepare your presentation for viewing...

In this activity you will package your presentation.

 Use the **Package for CD** option to prepare your presentation ready for viewing by your intended audience.

Portfolio builder

In this chapter you have learned how to use Microsoft PowerPoint to create an interactive multimedia presentation. You now need to create your own interactive multimedia product for your portfolio. As stated in this chapter, there are a number of different types of interactive multimedia products. You now need to use the practical skills you gained in this chapter to create your own product. This is the creative, fun part of this unit!

Your interactive multimedia product for your portfolio must be based on the design documentation (the plan and storyboard) that you should already have created for your portfolio. You must NOT start creating your multimedia product for your portfolio until you have created the plan and storyboard – as tempting as that might be! You must also not 'go off on a tangent' and produce a product that you have not planned!

Your multimedia product must include:

- alternative pathways (the user should be able to select their own route through the product)
- a range of multimedia elements
- hyperlinks (e.g. to websites, back to start)
- buttons/links for user interaction
- multimedia effects (e.g. transitions, animations).

You should already have sourced, organised and checked the elements to be included and decided on the house style and navigation, so creating the planned product now should be straightforward.

When you have finished creating the interactive multimedia product, you must save it in a suitable file format. You should check the completed product carefully to make sure that it is appropriate for the target audience and that it meets its identified aims.

Good luck!

Assessment Objective 5

Seek Feedback and Suggest Improvements

Overview

In this chapter you will learn how to get feedback about the interactive multimedia product you have created from a test user or from your peers (e.g. classmates). To obtain this feedback you will learn how to use questionnaires. You will also learn to evaluate your product yourself.

You will learn how to suggest possible improvement(s) to the product based on the feedback you obtained from others and based on your own evaluation.

Feedback and evaluation forms

To help you seek feedback and suggest improvements, example forms titled **AO5_FeedbackQuestionnaireTestUser** versions 1, 2, 3 and 4 and **AO5_Self-EvaluationForm** versions 1 and 2 can be downloaded from the Student Resources page on the Payne-Gallway website: **www.payne-gallway.co.uk**. You can also use the **AO1_SuggestedImprovements** form, provided for Assessment Objective 1, to record any improvements that you can think of. The forms for Unit 4 are contained in the **Unit4StudentResources** folder, in the subfolder **Unit4Forms**. The review forms are provided in Microsoft Word format. You can print the forms and handwrite your comments or type details in the Word file.

How this assessment objective will be assessed...

You will need to seek feedback from a test user or from peers, then suggest improvement(s) to your product. This assessment objective will be assessed by the range of feedback you seek from others and whether or not you carry out self-evaluation of your product. Grading will also depend on how many possible improvements you suggest and whether or not these are valid. You will also be assessed on the amount of detail you provide on how the valid improvements could be achieved.

Skills to use...

You will need to:

- use a questionnaire and/or checklist to **seek feedback** about the created multimedia product from a test user and/or from your own peers (e.g. classmates)
- **interview** a test user or peers in order to get feedback
- **evaluate** the multimedia product yourself (required by **Merit** and **Distinction** candidates only)
- suggest a possible **improvement** for your product. To achieve a **Merit** grade, you will need to suggest valid improvements. To achieve a **Distinction** grade, you should suggest valid improvements as well as give details on how the improvements could be achieved; you will not be required to carry out these improvements.

How to achieve...

Pass requirements

P1 You seek feedback from a test user or from peers.

P2 You suggest a possible improvement that could be made to the product.

Merit requirements

M1 You seek feedback from a test user or peers and through self-evaluation of your product.

M2 You suggest valid improvements that could be made to the product.

Distinction requirements

D1 You seek a range of feedback from a test user or peers and through detailed self-evaluation of your product.

D2 You suggest valid improvements that could be made to the product, providing details on how these could be achieved.

Seeking feedback from others

In order to get feedback from others, you need to think about the following:

Who will be your test user?

Can you ask your peers (e.g. classmates) to give you feedback?

What method(s) will you use to get this feedback?

Key term

Test user

In the context of testing your multimedia product, a test user is a person who reviews a product to make sure it works properly and does not have any errors or problems.

The test user makes sure that every link works correctly, that the overall layout of the product is clear, that the product is easy to navigate and provides relevant information and the right amount of information.

Reviewing multimedia products

You reviewed three existing multimedia products in Chapter 1. For your reviews, you identified the aims, the intended audience and the good and not so good features. You commented if the aims were met and suggested possible improvements.

Now that you have created your own multimedia product, you need to ask others to review your product.

Obtaining feedback

You need to ask others to test your product and give you feedback about whether *they* think your product does what you intended it to do.

If you simply ask someone this question, they may simply answer 'yes' or 'no', which may not necessarily help you identify any areas that you could improve in your product. Therefore, you need to ask for the test user's/peers' opinions on your product. Before going ahead and asking for feedback, you need to decide how best to seek this feedback.

Your aim is to try to get as much information from your test user/peers as possible. To help you do so, you could ask your test user/peers to complete a questionnaire. You should use a well-designed questionnaire that encourages the test user/peers to add comments, instead of a checklist with tick boxes or yes/no answers.

Seeking feedback is not as difficult as you may think – you have already been a test user yourself when you reviewed other multimedia products in Chapter 1. Think about the points you considered then and how you identified the good and not so good features. If you used a questionnaire to review the other products, you already have a basis for creating your own questionnaire.

Using a questionnaire to seek feedback

You are not required to design your own questionnaire, it is acceptable for your teacher or tutor to provide you with a questionnaire, or you could use or adapt the examples provided with this book.

Your questionnaire should give each test user/peers the opportunity to comment on **all** aspects of your interactive multimedia presentation.

If you use your own questionnaire, here are some examples of the factors you should encourage your test user/peers to consider:

Does the product meet its aims?

Is it clear who the target audience is? Is it suitable for the target audience?

Can the viewer use the show easily or is it too complicated?

Is the navigation clear? Do all links work?

Are there alternative pathways through the product?

Is there a range of multimedia elements? Are these appropriate?

Have multimedia effects been used appropriately?

Is there enough user interaction?

Is the amount of information in the whole product just right, too little or too much?

Is the layout of information on the pages/slides good? Or is there too much crowding, or too much empty space?

Is the product interesting and engaging? Or is it dull or boring?

Approaches to seeking feedback

There are many different ways of designing and using a questionnaire but you need to keep it simple for your test user/peers.

Seeking feedback about the aims (purpose) and audience

There are two approaches to getting feedback from your test user/peers about the aims and audience.

You could give them brief information about the aim and intended audience when you first give them the questionnaire. The questionnaire should then include questions as to whether the aims are met and whether the product is suitable for the audience. The example questionnaire **AO5_FeedbackQuestionnaireTestUser_v1** uses this method.

Alternatively, in order to assess whether or not the aims and target audience are clear to users, you should not state what the aims and who the intended audience are. Your questionnaire should then give test user/peers the opportunity to identify the aims and audience. The first two pages of the example questionnaire **AO5_FeedbackQuestionnaireTestUser_v2** use this second method.

Now tell your test user/peers what your aims are and who your intended audience is – you should start this on a new page so they only see it once they completed the first part of the questionnaire. Ask for their feedback about whether you achieved what you planned (refer to the final page of **AO5_FeedbackQuestionnaireTestUser_v2**).

You can use the provided questionnaires as they are or edit them to suit your product.

Activity 27: Seek feedback from test user/peers using questionnaires...

In this activity you will ask at least one test user (e.g. your teacher/tutor or your classmates) to give you feedback about your product.

- Look at the example **AO5_FeedbackQuestionnaireTestUser** forms provided with this book and decide which one you are going to use or adapt. Save this form into your user area.
- Make your presentation available to your test user/peers.
- Either ask your test user/peers to complete the feedback questionnaire or interview them asking the questions on the form, then enter their responses on the form yourself.
- Review the comments and any suggestions made by your test user/peers. You should bear these in mind when making your own suggestions.

Self-evaluation

Key term

Self-evaluation

Self-evaluation, as the term implies, is to assess or appraise something that *you* created by *yourself*.

Evaluating your own product

To achieve a **Merit** or **Distinction** grade, you will need to appraise your interactive multimedia product in addition to seeking feedback from a test user or from your classmates.

When you carry out a self-evaluation of your multimedia product, your aim should be to undertake an unbiased, critical appraisal with the intention of identifying its strengths and weaknesses (i.e. those areas where it could be improved).

You should try to be as objective as possible – this will help you to identify areas for improvement. You should already have sought feedback from a test user or from your peers using a questionnaire. You should now use this questionnaire to evaluate your own presentation as a whole.

You do not need to create your own self-evaluation form, your teacher or tutor may provide you with a form/table or other document, or you could use or adapt the example forms **AO5_Self-EvaluationForm** (v1 or v2).

Suggesting possible improvements

Once *you* have completed the same questionnaire that you asked your test user and/or classmates to complete, you should carry out a more detailed appraisal of *every* page/slide in your product. By doing so, you will be able to suggest appropriate, possible improvements for each page/slide.

In Chapter 1, you learned how to review other multimedia products and how to suggest possible improvements to these. Use the same methods (and forms) to review your own multimedia product. You should review every page/slide in your presentation, make some comments about the slide and suggest as many improvements as you can think of. For this evaluation, you will not need to take a screen print of each page/slide as you will have already printed and annotated your presentation.

Providing details on how improvements could be made

To achieve a **Distinction** grade, once you have suggested valid improvements to your multimedia product, you should provide details on how these improvements could be achieved.

You could provide these details in a separate document or insert a column in your evaluation form as shown in the following example table.

Slide no.	Navigation	Information	Multimedia elements	How this slide could be improved	How the improvement could be achieved

Activity 28: Evaluate your own presentation and suggest improvements...

In this activity you will evaluate your own product and suggest improvements.

*Grading: **Merit** grade candidates should carry out self-evaluation and suggest valid improvements that could be made. To achieve a **Distinction** grade, you should carry out a **detailed** self-evaluation, suggest valid improvements and **provide details of how these could be achieved**.*

- Look at the feedback given by your test user/peers.
- Evaluate each screen of your product yourself. You may use or adapt either of the example forms, titled **AO5_SelfEvaluationForm** (v1 or v2).
- Suggest improvements that could be made to each slide. If you think there is no room for improvement, give a reason why.
- Provide a suggestion of how the improvement could be made.

...and finally

For this assessment objective, you are required to evaluate your product. You have now done this. You are **not** required to make any of the suggested improvements. Therefore, it is acceptable for you to simple identify an area for improvement (e.g. 'the sound clip was too short and should be longer'), but it is not necessary for you to change the duration of the sound clip.

Portfolio builder

By reading and understanding the guidelines in this unit and by working through the activities, you have learned how to seek feedback for your multimedia product and how to evaluate it yourself. For your own portfolio, you will need to use a questionnaire and/or checklist to seek feedback about your multimedia product from a test user and/or from your own peers (classmates). You could interview your test user or peers in order to get feedback. To achieve a higher grade, you should also evaluate the multimedia product yourself. You should then collate the feedback received and your own evaluation notes, and suggest possible improvements for your product. You are not required to carry out these improvements.

For your portfolio you may use or adapt the **AO5_FeedbackQuestionnaireTestUser** and **AO5_Self-EvaluationForm** forms provided with this book. You may also find the **AO1_SuggestedImprovements** form used for Assessment Objective 1 useful.

Good luck!

Creating Sound Using ICT

In this unit you will cover the following...

- AO1 **Review several existing audio clips**
- AO2 **Design an audio clip**
- AO3 **Create an audio clip**
- AO4 **Test the audio clip**

This unit is one of the half units which you can combine with other full or half units to gain a full qualification in this course.

Sound clips may be used in many projects, for example in a website, a multimedia product and in video clips. Therefore the sound clip you create in this unit could be used in other units.

To create the sound clip in this book, a free software program called Audacity will be used.

The audio clip you will create will be based on the project scenario given in the Introduction to this book. Source sound clips have been provided for you so that you can practise the skills in Audacity. Once you have acquired the skills, you can use your own files to create your own clip.

Assessment Objective 1

Review Several Existing Audio Clips

Overview

In this chapter, you will need to review at least two different, existing audio clips. You will use the knowledge and skills gained during your reviews when planning, designing and creating your own audio clip.

You will be taught to look critically at existing audio clips. You do not need to find the audio clips for reviewing yourself: your teacher/centre may provide you with at least two different types of audio clips to review.

You will learn how to identify the aim of the clip and comment on how the aim is met. You will learn how to identify the good and not so good features of each audio clip and how to suggest possible improvements that could be made.

By looking critically at existing audio clips, you will learn to recognise what makes a good clip so that you may get some design hints for your own product, and you will learn to see the weaker features of a clip so that you avoid making similar mistakes when you create your own.

Review forms

To help you record your reviews, example review forms can be downloaded from the Student Resources page on the Payne-Gallway website: **www.payne-gallway.co.uk**. The forms for Unit 22 are contained in the **Unit22StudentResources** folder, in the subfolder **Unit22Forms**. The review forms are provided in Microsoft Word format. You can print the forms and handwrite your comments or enter details in the Word file.

How this assessment objective will be assessed...

The grade you are awarded for this assessment objective will depend on the amount of detail you include in your review of each audio clip.

As a minimum, you must list the good and not so good features of at least two different types of audio clip. However, you may review more than two audio clips if you wish.

For a **Merit** grade, your explanation of these features should be detailed and you should suggest possible improvements that could be made to each audio clip. You must also identify the aim of each audio clip.

For a **Distinction** grade, you must identify the aim of each audio clip and your explanation of the good and not so good features must be thorough. You should also suggest a range of valid improvements that could help each audio clip to meet its aims.

Key terms

You will come across the words 'thorough' and 'detailed' frequently in this qualification. 'Detailed' is usually a descriptor used for **Merit** or **Distinction** grading and 'thorough' is usually a descriptor used for **Distinction** grading. In this qualification, a 'thorough' explanation should include more detail than a 'detailed' explanation.

Detailed

A detailed explanation or detailed plan is one that is developed with care and in minute detail.

Thorough

A thorough explanation is one that is methodical and comprehensively complete. It is extremely careful and accurate and includes all the necessary information.

Skills to use...

You will need to:

- **review** two different types of audio clip – these clips may be provided by your teacher/tutor or you could find these yourself
- identify the good and not so good **features** in each clip
- identify the **aim** of each audio clip
- comment on **how** the **aims** of each audio clip are **met** and, if the aims are not met, comment on **why** they were **not met**
- suggest **possible improvements** for the audio clips reviewed.

How to achieve...

Pass requirements

P1 You will list the good and not so good features of at least two different types of audio clip.

Merit requirements

M1 You will identify the aim of each of the audio clips.

M2 You will give a detailed explanation of the good and not so good features of at least two different types of audio clip.

M3 You will suggest possible improvements for the audio clips reviewed.

Distinction requirements

D1 You will identify the aim and the audience of each of the audio clips.

D2 You will give a thorough explanation of the good and not so good features of at least two different types of audio clip.

D3 You will suggest a range of valid improvements for each of the clips reviewed to help the audio clip meet its aims.

1. Choose an audio clip

Types of audio clip

You should review two different clips of any of the following types:

Radio advertisement

Sources: radio

television channel broadcasting radio stations

radio stations which can be accessed using the Internet

Soundtrack from a film trailer

Sources: DVD-ROM

video cassette

television

the Web

Music clip

Sources: radio

television

CD or DVD-ROM

audio cassette

video cassette

the Web

Downloads from the Internet

Sources: music clips

advertisements

film soundtracks

Sources of audio clips

If you or your teacher/tutor do not have audio clips readily available to review, here are some suggestions for finding some:

Radio advertisements

Most radio stations have commercial or public service advertisements. BBC radio stations do not advertise commercial products, but they do have advertisements promoting their own television and radio programmes.

You could search for the frequencies of different radio stations on the Web. For example, the following website provides an A to Z list of radio stations in the UK and their frequencies.

http://en.wikipedia.org/wiki/Category:Radio_stations_in_the_United_Kingdom

Some other radio stations that broadcast commercial advertisements that you could review are:

Virgin radio	*105.8 MHz FM in London and the South East* *1215 kHz AM across the UK (In some areas, this may be 1197 KHz, 1233 kHz, 1242 kHz, 1260 kHz)*
TalkSPORT radio	*1089 kHz or 1053 kHz AM*

Soundtracks from film trailers

Here are some website addresses (URLs) where you could listen to soundtracks from film trailers:

http://www.apple.com/trailers/

http://www.moviecentre.net/upcomingmovies/

http://www.worstpreviews.com/

http://www.trailerdownload.net/movies

Downloads from the Internet

Search for product recalls from consumer agencies or manufacturers. (Some websites provide recorded audio clips for product recalls while others have these in text format.)

Hardware required

To review the audio clips, you will need to listen to each clip. If you are reviewing a radio advert, clip(s) on a CD/DVD, or a music clip, you are likely to need headphones so that you can listen to the clip clearly and not disturb others. If you are reviewing clips on a computer, the computer must have a sound card and either speakers or headphones. If you are listening to sounds through the speakers make sure you can hear the sounds clearly and that you do not disturb others.

Activity 1: Record details of audio clips to be reviewed...

In this activity you will start to document specific details about each audio clip that you will be reviewing.

- Ask your teacher/tutor if he/she has already identified appropriate audio clips for you to review or has a list of audio clips from which you can choose two clips.
- Choose two different types of audio clip.
- You need to start recording details of the two clips that you will review.

Note: You may review more than two clips if you wish.

- You may use or adapt the provided form titled **AO1_ReviewAudioClip**. Use a separate form for each audio clip you choose to review.
- In the Activity 1 section of each form, enter details of the audio clip in the following boxes:
  - **Type of audio clip:**
  - **Brief detail of audio clip:** (e.g. where you got the clip from)
- Save each form separately – you will update these later.

2. Identify the aim of the audio clip

Key term

Aim

The aim of an audio clip is its purpose – why the clip has been produced.

Some clips will be produced by people for fun (e.g. a music clip produced by an amateur band). However, you should be reviewing professional audio clips produced for a specific purpose.

Identifying the aim of the audio clip

Audio clips are produced for a particular purpose. A clip may have just one aim or more than one aim. When you identify the aim(s), think about whether the clip has been produced to:

- provide information (e.g. product recalls by consumer agencies or manufacturers)
- change behaviour (e.g. drink driving campaigns, benefit fraud, anti-smoking)
- attract attention (e.g. a film soundtrack)
- persuade the target audience to purchase a product (e.g. goods on sale)
- persuade the target audience to join something (e.g. keep fit classes)
- entertain (e.g. a music clip)
- teach specific skills (e.g. teaching foreign language skills).

Identifying the target audience

Any type of audio clip is created for a reason and is aimed at a specific group of people (i.e. a target audience). Refer to pages 8 and 9 in Chapter 1, Unit 4, Assessment Objective 1, for explanations of audience and target audience.

Some audio clips are aimed at a wider audience (e.g. a radio advertisement promoting discount holidays), whereas a radio advertisement promoting tickets for a country music concert would be aimed at a narrower audience.

When you describe the aim of an audio clip, one of the things you should identify is who the intended audience is. When identifying the audience, you should think about whether or not the clip is aimed at:

- a particular age group
- a particular gender (male/female)
- at people of a particular education level and/or background
- a particular family size and/or income level
- at people living in a specific location.

Activity 2: Identify the aim(s) of the audio clip...

In this activity you will begin your review of both your audio clips.

Grading: **Merit** *and* **Distinction** *grade candidates must identify the aim of the audio clip.*

➔ Listen attentively to each audio clip in turn and think about its aims as you listen. Consider the following:

- Who is the target audience?
- What is the aim of this audio clip?

➔ Continue using the **AO1_ReviewAudioClip** forms saved in Activity 1. Complete the following in the Activity 2 section on each form:

- **Target audience:**
- **Aim of audio clip:**

➔ Save your updated forms.

3. Identify the good and not so good features of an audio clip

Learning from existing reviews

Before you begin recording your own reviews, you may find it helpful to read existing reviews (e.g. reviews of music and film soundtracks). These are usually written by professional reviewers. You will find such reviews in newspapers, journals, music magazines and on the Internet.

Do not be concerned about the level of the language used in these reviews and the amount of detail – you are not expected to produce such professional reviews! In this book, you will be guided on how to record your own reviews using forms. However, by reading or listening to existing reviews, you will be prompted to think about particular points when you carry out your reviews. Reading or listening to existing reviews is not essential.

The following websites give reviews of film soundtracks:

http://www.filmtracks.com/
http://entertainment.timesonline.co.uk/ follow the links for 'Music'

How to review the different features of an audio clip

Audio clips will usually have a number of different features that you need to consider. It will be easier for you to consider the features in stages rather than produce a lengthy commentary on the whole clip.

When reviewing each audio clip, you should first identify what features have been used, then discuss whether the feature is effective or not (i.e. good or not so good). Use the questions under **Factors to consider** in the four tables on the following pages as prompts when you review your audio clips.

Identifying the speed of loading and range of components

The following table lists some factors to consider when reviewing the speed it takes for a clip to load and the range of components used in the audio clip. Note that the speed of loading will not be a factor to consider for all types of audio clips (e.g. radio advertisements are controlled by the broadcaster) – it is a factor to comment on for clips downloaded from the Internet or clips on a CD/DVD-ROM.

Feature	Factors to consider about speed of loading and range of components
Loading the clip	• Does the sound clip load quickly or is it slow to load? • Is the file size appropriate for a single clip?
Compatibility	• Is the file format compatible with most media players?
Use of different components	• Does the clip include different components (e.g. music, speech, other sounds)? • How effective are each of the components used?

Explaining the good and not so good features of the speed of loading and components in an audio clip

Here are some examples of comments about the speed of loading and range of components in an audio clip.

Example of a positive comment:

The soundtrack loaded very quickly and because the file size was not too big, I was able to copy the clip on to my memory stick. There was a very good mix of music, singing and sound effects which all worked very well to produce an impressive soundtrack.

Example of a comment about a feature that is not so good:

The soundtrack took a long time to load. It was a bit boring because the man spoke too formally and there were no other sounds except his voice.

Activity 3: Identify and comment on the speed of loading the clips and the use of components...

In this activity you will play each of your audio clips taking note of how quickly the clip loads and determining the range of components included in the clip.

Grading: **Pass** *grade candidates must list the good and not so good features; commenting on the features is not essential. For a* **Merit** *grade, your explanations should be detailed. For a* **Distinction** *grade, your explanations should be thorough.*

- Continue using the **AO1_ReviewAudioClip** forms saved in Activity 2.
- In the Activity 3 section of the form for each audio clip, comment on the good and/or not so good aspects of how quickly the clip loads (if this is not applicable to your audio clip enter 'n/a' in this box).
    - If the clip is slow to load, look at the file type and file size and comment on this.
    - Listen to the entire clip and comment on the components that have been included (e.g. music, speech, lyrics, sounds, etc.).
- Save your updated forms.

Key terms

Crescendo

A sound that gets gradually louder.

Diminuendo

A sound that gets gradually softer.

Lyrics

The words in a song or tune.

Identifying aspects of the volume, sound quality and clarity

The table below lists some factors to consider when reviewing the volume, sound quality and clarity of audio clips.

You should also try to think of additional factors, regarding sound quality and clarity, to list and comment on.

Feature	Factors to consider about volume, sound quality and clarity
Clarity of voice	• Audibility – discuss how easy it is to hear the speech/lyrics. • Can the speech/lyrics be easily understood or does the speaker/singer mumble? • Articulation – how easy is it to understand what is being said/sung? • Excitement or expression – is the speaker overly loud or excitable, to the point where it is irritating or grating to the listener?
Clarity and order of message	• Is there a logical, orderly change of different messages/scenes? • Is there a clear and logical progression of ideas/message being conveyed? • Does the overall message flow well or is it disjointed?
Pitch	• Is the pitch of speech/lyrics appropriate (e.g. do the voices sound realistic or are they too shrill or too deep)? • Is the pitch of music and other sounds appropriate (e.g. not pitched too high or too low)?
Volume	• Is the volume appropriate throughout the clip? • Can the volume be easily adjusted? • Are any changes of volume between speech, music and other sounds smooth and appropriate? • Have changes in volume (crescendo and diminuendo) been used and, if so, have they been used effectively?

Explaining the good and not so good features of the sound quality in an audio clip

Here are some examples of comments about the sound quality in a radio advertisement about smoking:

Example of a positive comment

The advert was very effective as it gave clear information about the dangers of smoking to one's own health as well as the harms of passive smoking. The sounds of the smoker with lung cancer struggling to breathe and the agonising crying of his young children were disturbing and thought provoking.

Example of a comment about a feature that is not so good

The sound quality was very poor. There was an echo throughout the advert which made it difficult to hear what was being said. The clip was badly recorded and could make the listener want to change the channel.

Activity 4: Identify and comment on the volume, sound quality and clarity...

In this activity you should listen to each of your audio clips again, this time concentrating on the volume, sound quality and clarity.

Grading: **Pass** *grade candidates should list the good and not so good features.* **Merit** *grade candidates should provide detailed explanations.* **Distinction** *grade candidates should provide thorough explanations.*

- Continue using the **AO1_ReviewAudioClip** forms saved in Activity 3.
- In the Activity 4 section of each form for each audio clip, comment on the good and/or not so good features of the different aspects of volume, sound quality and clarity.
- Identify and comment on any other aspects of volume, sound quality and clarity that you can think of.
- Save your updated forms.

Key terms

Synchronise

When two or more events occur in the proper sequence in relation to each other they are synchronised. In a sound clip 'events' are the components.

Tempo

The speed or pace at which a clip is played.

Identifying aspects of the speed (tempo) of different sounds

The table below also lists some factors to consider when reviewing the speed in audio clips. You should also try to think of additional factors to list and comment on regarding the sound quality.

Feature	Factors to consider about the speed of different sounds
Overall speed of clip	• How appropriate is the speed of the clip? For example, if it is a radio advert, does it play so quickly that the listener is likely to miss the message? (Radio adverts are costly and some advertisers tend to cram too much information into a short clip.)
Tempo	• Is the speed at which different components (music, speech, other sounds) play appropriate? • Does the speed of any music relate to speech/lyrics (e.g. if it is a sad or melancholy song, is the music also slow and soft to reflect the mood)?
Synchronising	• Do the different components synchronise well?
Pace of speech	• Is the pace of speech or song appropriate (i.e. not too fast for the listener but not too slow so the listener loses interest)?
Continuity	• Is there smooth continuity between the different types of sound or are there unnecessary silences?

Activity 5: Identify and comment on the speed (tempo) of different sounds...

In this activity you should comment on the speed (tempo) of the whole clip and of different sounds in each clip.

Grading: grade candidates should list the features. **Merit** *grade candidates should provide detailed explanations* **Distinction** *grade candidates should provide thorough explanations.*

- Continue using the **AO1_ReviewAudioClip** forms saved in Activity 4.
- In the Activity 5 section of each form, comment on the good and/or not so good features of the different aspects of the speed (tempo) of the whole clip and of different sounds.
- Identify and comment on any other aspects of speed (tempo) that you can think of.
- Save your updated forms.

Key term

Sound effects

Sound effects are artificially created or enhanced sounds that are used to emphasise the content of audio or music clips.

Identifying aspects of background sounds and sound effects

The table below lists some factors to consider when reviewing background sounds and the use of sound effects in audio clips. You should also try to think of additional factors to list and comment on regarding the sound quality.

Feature	Factors to consider about background sounds and sound effects
Background sounds	• Are backgrounds sounds used? If so, are they used effectively? • Are background sounds appropriate to the theme of the sound clip? • Are background music, sound, musical instruments intrusive and/or distracting?
Background noise	• Are there any background noises or sounds (e.g. clicks, crackles, hisses, rustling) that distract the listener? • Does the sound echo? • Is there speech in the background that is inaudible and distracting?
Sound effects	• Have sound effects been used? If so, are they appropriate for the clip (gunshot, door closing, wind blowing, chime of cash register, leaves rustling, etc.)? • Have different sounds and sound effects been faded in and out appropriately? • Have different sounds been mixed and, if so, have they been mixed well? • Do sound effects and backgrounds harmonise with each other?

Activity 6: Identify and comment on background sounds and sound effects

In this activity you should comment on the background sounds and sound effects in each clip.

Grading: **Pass** *grade candidates should list the features.* **Merit** *grade candidates should provide detailed explanations.* **Distinction** *grade candidates should provide thorough explanations.*

- Continue using the **AO1_ReviewAudioClip** forms saved in Activity 5.
- In the Activity 6 section of the form for each audio clip, comment on the good and/or not so good aspects of any background sounds and sound effects.
- Identify and comment on any other aspects of background sounds and sound effects that you can think of.
- Save your updated forms.

Commenting on the audio clip as a whole

Once you have commented on individual features, you will be quite familiar with the entire audio clip. You should then make some comments on each clip as a whole. Here are some points to consider:

- How original is the sound clip? Is it innovative?
- How does the clip maintain your interest? Does it make you want to listen? Or does it make you lose your interest?
- Does the sound convey the correct mood and message?
- How appropriate is the sound for the target audience (e.g. is classical music appropriate for teenagers or is loud rock music suitable for an older audience)?
- Have jingles or tunes been used? How appropriate are these? (They can be quite effective because people sing along to them, thus remembering the advert or music clip, etc.)

If you are reviewing a radio advert, you should comment on:

- Is it clear what is being advertised?
- Do the adverts give information about where to get a product or where to book for an event, etc?

If you are reviewing a soundtrack from a movie trailer, you should comment on:

- Does the soundtrack reflect the atmosphere, mood and content? For example, in a sad scene, is the background music sombre? (Light-hearted music or laughter would not be appropriate in such a scene.)

You should also comment on whether or not:

- the content is suitable for the aim
- the content is suitable for the target audience
- the clip is of an appropriate length. If it is too long, the listener might lose interest. If it is too short, the listener may miss the message being conveyed.

Activity 7: Comment on the audio clip as a whole...

In this activity you will complete your review of each audio clip.

*Grading: **Pass** grade candidates should list the features. **Merit** grade candidates should provide detailed explanations. **Distinction** grade candidates should provide thorough explanations.*

- Continue using the **AO1_ReviewAudioClip** forms saved in Activity 6.
- In the Activity 7 section of the form for each audio clip, insert a comment below each question about the different aspects of the audio clips.
- Comment on the effectiveness and appropriateness on the audio clip as a whole.
- Add any other comments about the audio clip and what you thought about it.
- Proofread then save your completed review forms.

4. Suggest improvements to an audio clip

For a **Merit** grade, you need to suggest possible improvements to the audio clips you reviewed and, for a **Distinction** grade, you should suggest a range of valid improvements to help the audio clip meet its aims.

In order to suggest improvements, you will need to comment on how the aims are met and if they not met, comment on why they were not met.

When you review the different features of the audio clips, you could note down suggested improvements for that aspect or you could do so after you have completed your review of individual aspects and are familiar with the entire clip.

Commenting on the aim

When you have completed your review of each audio clip, you should decide if the aim/aims was/were met and how. In doing so, you must remember who the target audience is and decide if the audio clip has met the aims for that target audience.

You should refer to your review form in which you identified the aim of the audio clip and comment on how the aim is met. To do so, see how many good and not so good features you have identified.

If you have identified more good features than not so good, and have mostly positive comments about the audio clip as a whole, it is likely that the audio clip has met its aims. On the other hand, if there are more not so good features than good features, and more negative comments about the audio clip as a whole, it is possible that the aims have not been met.

Activity 8: Comment on how the aims are met and explain why any aims are not met...

In this activity you will comment on whether the aim(s) is/are met.

Grading: Pass grade candidates are not required comment on the aims.

- Read your review form for each audio clip.
- For each audio clip that you reviewed, comment on whether or not you think the aims are met. To do so, you may use the provided form titled **AO1_SuggestedImprovementsAudioClip** for each clip.
- Comment on how the aims are met. If you think an aim is not met, give reasons why you think it was not met.
- Save the forms – you will update them in the next activity.

Suggesting improvements

You should suggest improvements that are appropriate for the type of audio clip you reviewed and appropriate for the intended target audience. You may use the provided form to do so.

When suggesting improvements, you will need to refer to the features in your review form that you identified as being not so good. When suggesting improvements, you will find it helpful to:

- copy and paste (or write) the features that you identified as being not so good on your review form into your suggested improvements form – then suggest how each feature could be improved
- list any features that were not originally included in the audio clip that would help to improve the audio clip.

Here is an example of a suggested improvement for a feature in a radio advertisement that was identified in a review as being 'not so good'. The not so good comment about the speed (tempo) was:

The information was spoken so quickly that it was difficult to understand and to take in all the information.

An example of a suggested improvement is:

The speaker should speak more slowly so that listeners can hear all the information.

Activity 9: Suggest possible improvements...

In this activity you will suggest improvements that could help to improve each audio clip.

Grading: grade candidates are not required to suggest improvements. **Merit** *grade candidates should suggest improvements.* **Distinction** *grade candidates should suggest a range of valid improvements that could help the audio clip meet its aims.*

- Continue using the form **AO1_SuggestedImprovementsAudioClip** saved in Activity 8.
- Copy the features that you identified as being 'not so good' in your review form, then suggest how that feature could be improved.
- List any features that were not originally included in the audio clip that would help to improve the audio clip.
- Proofread then save your completed review forms.

Portfolio builder

By reading and understanding the guidelines in this chapter, and working through the activities, you have learned how to review audio clips and how to record your review notes. You should now be ready to start working on your portfolio. For your own portfolio, you will need to review at least two different types of existing audio clips from any of the following types: radio advertisement, soundtrack from a film trailer, music clip, downloads from the Internet.

You do not need to source the audio clips yourself. Your teacher/tutor or someone else in your centre may provide you with appropriate clips. You should review two different types of clips (e.g. one radio advert and one soundtrack from a film trailer). You should not review two of the same type of clip (e.g. two radio adverts).

You may use the review forms provided with this book to record your reviews for your portfolio.

Before you begin, you should read the 'How this assessment objective will be assessed…' and 'How to achieve…' sections of this chapter. Discuss with your teacher or tutor what grade he/she would advise you to aim for.

For each clip you review, you should:

- identify and record the good and not so good features – to do so, you should refer to the 'Factors to consider' tables in this chapter and discuss the different features separately, then refer to the section about reviewing the clip as a whole
- identify and record the aim – you should comment on how the aim is met and if the aim is not met, comment on why
- suggest possible improvements for the audio clips reviewed.

Good luck!

CHAPTER 7

Assessment Objective 2

Design an Audio Clip

Overview

For Assessment Objective 1, you reviewed existing audio clips, so you should understand how important it is for an audio clip to meet its aims and to be suitable for its target audience. By reviewing existing clips, you learned how to recognise what makes a good clip and also recognise how to identify the weaker features of audio clips. You will now draw on your experience to plan your own audio clip.

Before you create your own audio clip, you must spend some time planning it and producing documentation to show this planning process. Planning is very important and will help to ensure that when you create your audio clip, it meets its aims and is appropriate for the target audience. Planning the clip requires more than just making notes in a plan and creating a storyboard. For this unit, you need to use source files to create your clip, so the first thing you need to do before drawing up a plan is either to decide where you will get the components to be included and to source all the files you need, or, if files are provided for you, to select which ones are the most appropriate for your clip.

In this chapter you will learn how to source and organise components for your clip and produce design documents. You will learn how to define the aim and how to describe the audience. You will learn how to plan the production of your audio clip by creating a storyboard to show which components you are going to include, the sequence in which they will appear and the other features you intend to use.

Software

Although you won't actually create the clip until the next chapter, you need to know, for your planning, that you will be using a free software program, called Audacity, to create it.

Practice files

To help you practise the skills for this unit, four sound clips are provided for use with the activities in this book (a music clip, a speech clip and two sound clips). These practice files can be downloaded from the Student Resources page on the Payne-Gallway website: **www.payne-gallway.co.uk**.

The files are contained in the **Unit22StudentResources** folder, in the subfolder **U22SourceSoundClips**.

Key terms

Storyboard

A storyboard for an audio clip provides an overview of the components of the clip. The storyboard provides information about the content of the audio clip: the source clips, the sequence in which the tracks will be played, the duration and content of each track, and any effects and edits that will be applied.

The storyboard is produced beforehand to help the sound editor see how the final audio clip will be produced before beginning the creating and editing.

Creating a storyboard will help to identify any possible problems before they happen. Storyboards often include arrows and/or instructions to show the sequence of different tracks.

Track

When a clip is imported into a sound editing program (e.g. Audacity), the clip is referred to as a track.

How this assessment objective will be assessed...

- You will need to describe the aim of the audio clip. If you also describe the audience you can achieve a **Merit** grade and if your descriptions are thorough you can achieve a **Distinction** grade.
- You will also need to provide a storyboard showing the elements to be included in your audio clip. If your storyboard shows all elements of your clip, you can achieve a higher grade.
- The grading for this assessment objective will be differentiated by the amount of detail in your description of the aim and audience of the audio clip, by how clearly structured your designs are and by how clear your storyboard is.

Skills to use...

You will need to:

- select the source **components** (music, sound and speech files) you will use from files provided or find source components
- decide what the **aim** of your audio clip will be and describe the aim
- decide who your intended **audience** is and describe the audience
- select the **software** to be used
- create a **storyboard** to show the contents of the audio clip, the type of clip (mono or stereo), the sequence of how components will be played and the timeline
- show on your storyboard where in your clip you will use **silencing** and **fading**
- show on your storyboard what **effects** you will use and where they will be used.

How to achieve...

Pass requirements

P1 You will describe the aim of your audio clip.

P2 You will produce a simple storyboard covering the main elements.

P3 Your design may lack structure.

Merit requirements

M1 You describe the aim and audience of your audio clip.

M2 You produce a storyboard covering the main elements.

M3 Your design has a clear structure.

Distinction requirements

D1 You are thorough in your description of the aim and audience for your audio clip.

D2 You produce a storyboard covering all elements.

D3 Your design is well structured.

Understanding how the audio clip will be created

In Chapter 8, you will create an audio clip using existing source files, also referred to as components or elements. These components are existing sound clips – they could be music clips, speech (i.e. someone speaking, also referred to as narration) and sounds (e.g. sounds of an aeroplane, a boat, ocean or underwater).

It is important that you understand that, in this unit, it is not essential that you use a sound recorder or microphone to record sounds – you do not have to record any sounds yourself (although you can if you want to and have the facilities to do so). This unit is not about going to a recording studio to record your own music! You will actually be creating your audio clip on a computer, using suitable software and existing source files. In order to produce a plan of the audio clip to be created, it is crucial that you know what source files you will use.

1. Source files

You cannot start producing your planning documents until you have decided which source files you will use in your audio clip.

Therefore, the first step is to find out what source files are available for you to use in your audio clip. It is no good deciding that you are going to produce an audio clip about ice dancing if you don't have any source sounds, music or speech about ice skating and dancing on ice.

You are not required to create the source elements yourself. You may source these from elsewhere, so before you can begin creating the design documents and storyboard, you need to decide what components to include.

The audio clip you will create must be at least 45 seconds long, so ensure that you collect source files that will allow you to create a clip of this length after you have done all the editing.

Note about hardware

So that you can decide what sound files to use, you will need to listen to the sounds on a computer with a sound card and a media player (e.g. Microsoft Windows Media Player). You will also need either speakers or headphones and access to the volume control settings. Check with your teacher or tutor that you have the necessary hardware.

Referring to the project scenario

The audio clip you will be creating in this book will be based on the project scenario (given in the Introduction to this book) which is about adventure holidays. You should read this scenario carefully and think about what aspect of the adventure holidays you would like to create the audio clip about.

Preparing folders for the source files

It is a good idea to prepare a folder for your source files before you begin.

If you do not have many different files, you can save all your source components in one folder. If you have many different files, then it would be better to have subfolders in your main folder for the different types of files (i.e. music, sounds and speech) – remember that the audio clip you will be creating only needs to be a minimum of 45 seconds long so you won't need many different source files.

To create a folder in your user area: **File** → **New** → **Folder** → **Backspace** to delete the existing folder name → Type the new folder name you have chosen → **Enter**. Open this folder and create subfolders in the same way.

Suitable file types that can be imported into Audacity

When you are sourcing components, you must ensure that the file formats of the clips are suitable for use in Audacity.

File types that can be imported into Audacity are: .aiff, .au, .mp3, .ogg, .wav.

File formats that are common on the World Wide Web but *cannot* be imported into Audacity are: .wma, .aac.

The file extensions listed above and their characteristics are explained in Chapter 8, but for now you should make sure that the files you collect for your audio clip, and which you will refer to in your planning documents, are in a format that can be imported into Audacity.

Selecting provided source files

Find out if your teacher or tutor can provide you with music clips, sound files and speech clips or narrations.

If your teacher or tutor cannot provide you with source files, ask at your school/college library, or public library, if they stock CD or DVD sound libraries. These may contain components that are either copyright-free or can be used for educational purposes.

If you are provided with a selection of source files or CD/DVDs, you should spend some time listening to the music clips, sounds and speech clips that are available. Decide which of these files will be suitable for your project scenario and copy them to your working area.

Bear in mind that your final clip should be at least 45 seconds long, so the total playing time for the combined source components should run for a minimum of about three to five minutes. You will be cutting out unwanted parts of the clips therefore you need to have enough original clips to work with. There is no prescribed maximum clip running time but try not to make your final clip any longer than three or four minutes.

You will need at least one music clip, at least one speech clip and at least one sound.

Recording your own sounds

If you have access to a sound recorder you could record your own sounds that will be suitable for your project. If you have access to a microphone, you could record your own speech (narration). You must find out what file format your sound recorder or microphone will record sounds in, as you will need to ensure that the recording can be imported into Audacity. As this unit does not require you to record your own sounds and as there are so many different sound recorders and microphones, recording sounds is not covered in this book.

If you record your own sounds or narration, you could also use them in other units (e.g. Unit 2 Webpage Creation, Unit 4 Design and Produce Multimedia Products).

Sourcing your own files

If you need to find your own files, you can search for them on the Internet, but you *must* look on the websites for copyright information. It is important that you find out if you need permission to use the clips. It is your responsibility to ensure that any clips you download are free from copyright or that permission has been given. Refer to the section titled 'Keep a record of files and acknowledge sources' on page 46 in Chapter 3 which covers how to obtain and reference source files. Note that for this unit you are not required to produce a reference of sources, but it is good practice to keep a record for yourself of all files and permissions given for sounds that you download from the Internet.

A note about downloading files

If network security policies in your school or centre prevent students from downloading and saving certain types of files, you will need to ask your teacher or tutor to make arrangements for suitable files to be provided for you to use. Four sound files are provided with this book for you to use as practice when learning how to create an audio clip in the next chapter.

Key terms

Mono

Mono means single. A mono audio track is a single channel of sound recorded from a single point and replayed through a single speaker. If the sound is played through two speakers, the same sound will be played in both speakers.

Stereo

A stereo audio track is sound recorded and replayed using more than one channel. If the sound is played through two speakers, a different sound will be played in each speaker.

How to download sounds from the Internet

There are a number of websites that allow downloading of clips for educational use. You will need to research these. A few websites that you could search for free sounds are given below.

http://www.findsounds.com

http://www.freeaudioclips.com

http://www.a1freesoundeffects.com

To search for clips on the findsounds.com website:

1 Type a search category in the **Search for** box on the homepage.
2 Tick the option boxes below the **Search for** box to make sure you search for the types of sound you want and that they can be imported into Audacity. For example, below **File Formats**, the three check boxes for aiff, au and wave are ticked by default – this is fine as all three file formats can be imported into Audacity. Similarly, you can work with **mono** and **stereo** files in Audacity, so these boxes can both remain ticked.
3 If you have restrictions on the size of files you can download in your school or centre, click the arrow next to the **Maximum File Size** drop-down list and select an appropriate file size, otherwise, keep the default setting.
4 Once you have entered the search criteria and selected the appropriate options, click the **Search** button. A list of available sounds will display. Read the information about the sound (e.g. sound file type, duration in seconds, file size, mono/stereo). If the file type is suitable, click on the link to listen to the sound. The sound will play in Windows Media Player (by default, unless the default setting has been changed). If the sound is suitable, close the media player window and download the file. Don't worry if the duration is longer or shorter than you need it to be, you can duplicate a sound that is too short or cut a sound that is too long. In fact, you need to show that you can edit sound clips, so it is useful to have clips that are not perfect to start with.

Some links from this site are to websites that may have moved or no longer exist. If you receive an error message, simply click the **Back** button and click on another link or change your search criteria.

To download a file:

5 Right-click the URL for the file to display a shortcut menu → Select **Save Target As...** to display the **Save As** window (a window prompting you to **Open** or **Save** may display first → Click **Save** to save the file into a folder in your working area using *an appropriate filename that describes the clip* (a **Download complete** dialogue box will display → Click **Close**.
6 Repeat Steps 1, 4 and 5 to download more clips.
7 Play each clip in a media player as you download it to make sure it is suitable for your project.

The Internet Archive website **http://www.archive.org** acts as a digital library of Internet sites. It provides free access to researchers, historians, scholars and the general public:

8 Click the link for **Audio** → In the **Sub-Collections** section, click a link for a particular category (e.g. **Open Source Audio**) → Follow the links to search for suitable sound clips.
9 Alternatively: Enter your keywords in the **Search** box → Click **Go** → Follow the links to find suitable sound clips → Download the file making sure that the clip is in a file format that can be used in Audacity.

Checking source audio clips

Once you have downloaded all your source files, you should carry out some final checks on the files.

- Play and listen to every file to make absolutely sure that it is suitable for your project's aim and/or audience before moving on – this will save you having to find more suitable files later on.
- Make sure the sounds harmonise with each other – make sure that the message they put across when they are combined is suitable for your project.
- Do not be concerned if different files have different volumes, you can edit the volume when you create your audio clip.

Checking the running time of source audio clips

The next thing to take note of is the playing time of individual downloaded clips and the total time. The duration of your edited sound file must be at least 45 seconds so you must make sure that the total duration of all your clips is long enough for you to edit them to the required length.

Activity 10: Source and store source files...

In this activity you will source the components needed to produce your audio clip, and that you will refer to in your planning documents.

- Create a new folder using a suitable folder name (e.g. U22AudioClip).
- Read the project scenario given in the Introduction to this book.
- Decide which aspect of the adventure holidays you would like to create the audio clip about.
- Find out whether your teacher/tutor is able to provide you with files to use. List the files which you will use. You must have at least one music clip, one sound clip and one speech clip or narration.
- Copy the files into the folders you prepared in your user area.
- If you need to source the files yourself, find suitable components. Download the files, rename them using suitable filenames and save them into the folder in your user area.
- Play and listen to EVERY file to make absolutely sure that it is suitable for your project before moving on. If your files are not appropriate for your aim and/or audience, you will have problems later on, so it is important to be certain at this stage that your files are appropriate.

2. Describe the aim of the audio clip

You need to decide the purpose of your audio clip (i.e. what is your intention for producing the clip?).

You are already familiar with the aim of the existing audio clips that you reviewed. You will find it useful to read the section titled 'Identifying the aim of the audio clip' and your notes from Activity 2 in Chapter 6.

Your description of the aim of your audio clip should make clear *the purpose of your audio clip*. The purpose is your *expected outcome* – the *overall objective* of your audio clip. The aim you describe at this stage will then guide you when you create the storyboard later so think about your aim carefully. Your aim should be appropriate to the project scenario.

You may use any appropriate style to present the information. As this unit is a 30-hour unit (referred to as a half unit), you will not have as much time as you would in a full unit, so don't waste time on different document styles – try to keep it simple but clear. Here is an example of a description of the aim of an audio clip:

Aim of audio clip:

To produce an audio clip for a CD-ROM that will be given at a holiday roadshow. The CD-ROM will include an interactive presentation about adventure holidays for teenage girls and boys aged 12 to 17.

My aim for producing this audio clip is to create a sound file in .wav format that can be inserted into the interactive multimedia presentation. The audio clip can also be inserted on a website about adventure holidays, on the page about scuba diving. My audio clip will talk about the underwater world that scuba divers can experience. I will add soothing background music and will have some speech about scuba diving mixed in with sounds of underwater to give listeners a feel for what it would be like to be underwater.

3. Describe the audience for your audio clip

You should describe the group of people that your audio clip is aimed at (i.e. who do you want the audio clip to appeal to?).

Your target audience could be narrow or wide or could be a combination of two categories. A narrow audience would be 'experienced snorkellers with life-guarding experience'. A wide audience would be 'anyone who can swim'. A combination of two categories would be 'teenagers who can swim and have life-guarding experience'.

If your target audience is wide, you could describe the main target audience and explain who the secondary audience is. For example, the main target audience could be 'teenagers interested in adventure holidays' and your secondary audience could be 'teenagers who can swim and would like to explore the underwater world'.

Here is an example of a description of the target audience for an audio clip:

Target audience for audio clip about scuba diving:

The target audience is teenage girls and boys aged 12 to 17 who are interested in adventure holidays, particularly those who can swim and would like to try scuba diving for the first time.

4. The plan

Key dates

Your teacher or tutor will probably have given you some deadlines for the completion of your work. In your plan it is a good idea to make a note of all key dates. You could enter these as a numbered list as shown in the example below.

Key dates:

1 Source files to be collected by: [enter date here]
2 Plan to be completed by: [enter date here]
3 Storyboard to be completed by: [enter date here]
4 Begin creating audio clip on: [enter date here]
5 Finish creating audio clip on: [enter date here]
6 Produce test plan by: [enter date here]
7 Test audio clip by: [enter date here]
8 Action improvements by: [enter date here]

Initial ideas for your plan

By now, you will have decided which source files you will use and you should have a good idea of the content of these files. You should have decided what your audio clip will be about, and you should have a fairly good idea of its aim and audience. When you create your plan, it is a good idea to make notes of your initial ideas for the audio clip. Here are some example questions you might ask yourself to help you with your initial ideas:

- Will you have background music for the whole duration of the clip?
- Which clip(s) will you use for the background sound?
- Will you have speech for the whole duration or will you mix the speech with sounds and/or music?
- How many different source clips will you use to create your own audio clip?
- How many different sound effects will you use?
- Which clips will play in the foreground (i.e. which clip will be the loudest)?

Here are examples of some initial ideas you might make in your plan for your early ideas before you create the storyboard:

Sequence	Component	Filename	How it will play
1	music	background	• music starting soft and getting louder • background music track to play for the whole duration of audio clip
2	speech	intro	• first sentence, slow down tempo to match mood of music • background music soft
3	sound	underwater	• underwater sound fade in and fade out, background music soft during underwater sound • music gets louder for a few seconds when underwater sound finishes
4	speech	intro	• second sentence, increase volume when speech is describing under-water life • background music soft
5	sound	underwater	• sound of bubbling getting louder • background music soft • repeat bubbling sound
6	speech	intro	• third sentence • background music soft and bub-bling
7	music	background	• music gets louder
8	speech	intro	• final sentence • soft background music, speech stops, music fades out

Activity 11: Describe the aim and audience...

In this activity you will:

- create your plan for the audio clip that you are going to create
- describe the aim and audience
- include other details of your planning.

Grading: Pass *level candidates should describe the aim of the audio clip;* **Merit** *level candidates should describe the aim and audience;* **Distinction** *level candidates should provide a thorough description of the aim and audience.*

- Read the project scenario given in the Introduction to this book.
- Create a new document and describe the aim of the audio clip you are going to create.
- Describe the intended target audience for the audio clip.
- Make a note of the important dates that you need to work to when planning, creating and testing your audio clip.
- Write down your initial ideas for what you will include in your clip, the sequence each component will play in and the background music/sounds. You could note these details in a table as shown on page 110.
- Save your plan using a suitable filename (e.g. PlanAudioClip).

5. Storyboards for audio clips

The storyboard layout

Storyboards for audio clips are not used as often as they are for video clips. There is no single prescribed layout that should be used. The important thing about any storyboard, drawing or sketch that you produce is that it should give enough detail for someone else to create the clip.

A storyboard can be produced in several ways, for example:

- you can display a **summary storyboard** on one page which shows an overview of all components to be displayed in the clip, the order they will be displayed and where the source files are saved. Then, accompanying the summary storyboard, you could have a more **detailed storyboard** on several pages, with each page showing two or three clips with more detail of the content of each clip and details of effects, edits, duration, volume, etc.
- you can create an **overview storyboard** which shows all the different components and the sequence of all components on one page. It will show the filename, name and location of the source files folder. The details on this overview will be brief but sufficient for the creator of the clip and others to know what will go where and how clips will be edited. Refer to the example provided in pdf format in the **Unit22Forms** folder.

You should already know how many different clips you intend to use – you have noted down some initial ideas in your plan.

As your completed audio clip needs to be at least 45 seconds long, which is not long at all, creating an overview storyboard should be sufficient.

Using a template

A template of an **overview storyboard** has been provided for you in the **Unit22StudentResources** folder in the subfolder **Unit22Forms**. The template is provided in Microsoft Word format. You can use it in a number of ways, for example:

- you can print the template and add notes by hand
- you can use the template to produce your storyboard on the computer, typing your notes in the text boxes.

If you wish you can create your own storyboard or use one provided by your teacher or tutor. Use any method that you find easy and quick, but whatever method you choose, note that it is worth spending time producing a clear storyboard for your audio clip because it will help you when you start to create the clip.

What to include on the storyboard

A well-produced storyboard should clearly display which components will be included, where they will be included and the sequence of each track in your audio clip. Your storyboard should include sufficient detail for someone else to see what the final product will look like when finished. A simple rule is that if a component is going to be included in the audio clip, it must be shown on the storyboard. There should not be much difference between the content and features shown on the storyboard and the content and features of the completed audio clip.

A useful test to find out if your storyboard is clear and displays all components and features is to see if someone else would be able to use your storyboard to create the audio clip. Remember your ideas must be noted on paper, not in your head!

As a minimum, your storyboard should show the following:

- content of the audio clip
- timeline
- where you will use fading (**Distinction** only)
- where you will insert silencing (**Distinction** only)
- the volume of each clip
- whether the clip is mono or stereo
- special effects
- audio editing that will be carried out (e.g. cut, copy, paste, split, trim).

Each of these is explained below.

Content of the audio clip

The content is everything that is included in the audio clip – its components.

Components are the source files that you will use to create your audio clip. These are the music, sound and speech clips that you should have already sourced and saved into a folder. You should display the filename, the type of component (music, sound or speech) and the file type of the component on the storyboard.

Timeline

The timeline is a chronological display of all the components (source music, sound and speech clips) that will be used in your audio clip. The timeline must also show the duration in seconds of each component (i.e. how long each track will play for once you have edited it). It is also useful to show on the storyboard the length of the original source file.

Fading

'Fade in' and 'Fade out' are effects that can be applied to any type of audio track to change the volume of the track. Fade in gradually increases the sound and fade out gradually decreases the sound.

Silencing

As the word implies, 'silencing' is when a period of 'quiet' is inserted in a track. Silencing can also be used to remove unwanted sections or background noises in a track.

Volume

In an audio clip, it is quite common to play more than one sound at the same time. For example, music can be played continuously behind other sounds such as speech and sound effects. If you intend to play two sounds together, you should show on the storyboard which sound should be played louder and which one should be played quieter.

Mono or stereo?

Mono and stereo channels were explained on page 106 of this chapter. It is useful to show on the storyboard if the original source track is a mono track or a stereo track. You could also show if you want to edit the original track as it is (i.e. mono or stereo), if you wish to split a stereo track or if you want to convert a mono track before editing.

Special effects

Effects are editing techniques that change the sound of a selected part of an audio track. They are very useful and can improve the quality of an audio file if applied correctly.

Audio editing

You will need to use some audio editing techniques (e.g. cutting, copying and pasting, splitting and trimming tracks). These techniques are covered in more detail in chapter 8, but are explained briefly below so that you can decide what editing techniques you will use and can enter these details on your storyboard. When you create your storyboard, you will find it useful to play the source files several times so that you can decide where you will edit the clip and what editing technique you will apply.

- **Cut (and paste)** – Part of an audio track can be cut out altogether or pasted in another track or in a new audio track.
- **Copy and paste** – A part of a track can be copied and then pasted in another track after existing audio or in a new audio track. It can replace an existing portion of a track or be pasted in another location in the same track.
- **Trim** – When a track is trimmed, everything to the left and right of the selection is removed.
- **Split** – When a track is split, the selected part of the track is moved to its own track and the original selection is replaced with silence.

Other information to show on the storyboard

Your storyboard should also display the following:

- your name
- audio clip filename
- source files folder name
- source folder location
- other notes (e.g. what the duration of the completed audio clip should be).

Producing your storyboard

You are ready to start creating your storyboard. Before you begin, make sure you understand audio storyboards, that you have sourced and organised your components and have looked at the example of the completed storyboard which is available in the **Unit22StudentResources** folder in the subfolder **Unit22Forms**.

1. Open the template document that you are going to use.
2. Read the project scenario.
3. Read your plan. Remind yourself of the aim and audience. Read the initial ideas you noted down.
4. Remind yourself of the content of all your components – listen to all your source sound files. This will help you decide the sequence of the files, the effects to be applied and what and where you will apply the editing.
5. Decide the order that you will play the source clips in the timeline.
6. Decide what, if any, clips will be played together and what sounds, if any, you will play in the background.
7. Decide on the filename of your completed audio clip.

Activity 12: Produce a storyboard...

In this activity you will produce a storyboard to show the content of your planned audio clip.

You may use the template provided with this book titled **AO2_AudioClipStoryboard_Template** or you may create your own storyboard. The instructions below refer to the template provided with this book.

- Read the project scenario given in the Introduction to this book.
- Refer to the plan you created in Activity 11.
- Produce an overview storyboard showing the components you will use in your audio clip.
- When creating your storyboard, you will find it useful to play the source files several times to help you decide what to edit.
- Show brief details of:
  - the type of component (e.g. **music**, **sound** or **speech**)
  - the filename and file type (e.g. **intro.wav**)
  - whether the track is **mono** or **stereo**
  - the **original** track **duration** (length of time)
  - the **edited** track **duration**
  - the **background** sound (if applicable)
  - **effects** to be applied
  - **editing** to be applied
  - the **volume** that the clip will play at in relation to other clips that will play at the same time.
- Save your storyboard in your user area using a suitable filename.
- Enter the following on your storyboard template:
  - the filename you intend to give to your audio clip
  - the location and name of the folder where the files are saved.

- Enter any other relevant notes – remember that your storyboard should show enough detail for someone else to be able to create the audio clip from the information you have given.
- Save your storyboard.

An *example* of a completed storyboard in .pdf format has been provided in the **Unit22StudentResources** folder, in the subfolder **Unit22Forms**. You may wish to compare your storyboard with the example.

Portfolio builder

By reading and understanding the guidelines in this chapter, and working through the activities, you will have learned how to plan and design an audio clip. You should now be ready to prepare your source files and produce your own planning documents for your portfolio.

It is very important that you spend time planning your audio clip at this stage. You will probably be tempted to start creating it, but planning it and producing planning documentation is essential!

Before you can start working on your plans, you should discuss with your teacher or tutor what your audio clip should be about. So far in this unit you have used the given example project scenario, but now you will need your own scenario. The next stage is to discuss with your teacher or tutor whether he/she will provide you with source components or not. If your teacher/tutor can provide you with files, you need to play the source sound, music and speech clips and decide which ones to use.

If your teacher/tutor advises you to source your own components, that will be your next task. You should find suitable sound, music and speech components. Once you have collected all your source files, you should create a folder in your working area and save your components into that folder. You must check that all source components are in file formats that can be imported into Audacity. Play and listen to your source audio clips again. This is important because having appropriate components will make the process of planning, creating and testing much smoother for you.

Next, you should read the 'How this assessment objective will be assessed…' and 'How to achieve…' sections of this chapter. Discuss with your teacher/tutor what grade he/she advises you to aim for.

Now you are ready to start working on your planning documents!

In your plan, describe clearly the aim and audience of the audio clip that you intend to create. Include the key dates that you need to work to in your plan.

Create a storyboard to show an overview of your audio clip. You may use or adapt the storyboard template provided with this book. You will be using Audacity to create your clip, so make a note of this on your storyboard as it is required in the syllabus. Remember to write down all your ideas – your plans should not be in your head! Your storyboard must show:

- the content of the clip (i.e. the source components – sounds, music and speech)
- the timeline
- where you will use fading and silencing
- special effects.

When you have completed your plan and storyboard, ask your teacher/tutor to look at your plan and storyboard. Ask him/her whether they would be able to use your plan and storyboard to create the audio clip.

Good luck!

CHAPTER 8

Assessment Objective 3

Create an Audio Clip

Overview

In this chapter you will create the audio clip that you designed in Chapter 7 (Assessment Objective 2). To ensure that your audio clip meets its aims and is suitable for your target audience, you will find it helpful to read your review notes from Chapter 6 (Assessment Objective 1). The audio clip you will create in this chapter will be based on the sample project scenario given in the Introduction to this book.

For this unit you are not required to create every element for your own sound clip yourself. You can source the components (music, sound, speech) from elsewhere then import them into the appropriate software to edit them and create your own sound clip. Sourcing of components for the sound clip is covered in Chapter 7.

To create your sound clip, you will use a software program called Audacity. For this unit, you will need a sound card with speakers or headphones and access to the volume control settings.

Practical activities in this chapter

To help you practise the skills for this unit, four sound clips have been provided for use in the activities (a music clip, a speech clip and two sound clips). You will find it helpful to use these clips as you work through the activities, as the activities and screen prints in this chapter are based on these clips. Once you have understood and learned the skills for producing a sound clip in Audacity, you may use your own clips and edit these as you wish to produce your own sound clip.

The activities should be completed in the sequence provided. If you wish to practise a particular skill again, or have not completed the previous activity successfully, you may use the relevant working project file provided. This is explained at the beginning of an activity.

Source files

To use the practice files provided, you will need to download them from the Student Resources page on the Payne-Gallway website: **www.payne-gallway.co.uk**.
The files are contained in the **Unit22StudentResources** folder, in the subfolder **U22SourceSoundClips**. The worked project files are in the subfolder **U22SoundProjects**.

Referring to the project scenario

The project scenario is about adventure holidays. The audio clip created in the examples in this chapter will be about one of the activities on offer (i.e. scuba diving). However, your clip need not be about scuba diving – you may decide to create a clip relating to another aspect of the adventure holidays.

How this assessment objective will be assessed...

You need to create an audio clip based on the design documentation you have already created in Chapter 7. This assessment objective will be graded by how you make use of importing and editing components of your audio clip. You will also be graded by the range of editing techniques you use, the features you include in your audio clip, and whether or not all these elements work as intended. Your audio clip should be fit for purpose.

- As a minimum, you need to create an audio clip of at least 45 seconds in length, into which you will import components (music, sound, speech). You must use cut, copy and paste techniques and some effects.
- You must export your completed clip in a suitable file format.
- Higher level candidates should split and/or trim clips and use silencing and fading.
- To achieve the higher grades, your audio clip must be appropriate and for a **Distinction** grade it must also meet its identified aims.

Evidence for this assessment objective

To allow the moderator to listen to your audio clip, you or your teacher/tutor could make available your audio clip electronically (e.g. on a CD-ROM, memory stick or laptop). This would be much simpler than attempting to provide printed evidence. You will need to show evidence of editing (e.g. using cut, copy and paste, splitting and trimming). To do so you will learn how to save the clips using different filenames to show the various stages of compiling and editing.

However, if you wish to supply printouts, Audacity does have the option to print the wave-forms for your audio tracks, so you could include printouts of the various stages of editing and combining your sound clips. The waveform is a visual representation of the audio track on the screen. Alternatively you could produce screen prints.

Your final clip will be exported in a suitable file format (e.g. .mp3 or .wav format). Ideally, this final clip should be available electronically for the moderator to listen to.

Skills to use...

You will need to:

- **import** audio files
- use the **editing** tools
- create and **save** a new and an updated project
- use the Audacity menus, toolbars and track controls
- play all and selected tracks and selections
- **trim** and **split** clips
- **silence** selections
- **cut**, **copy**, **paste** and duplicate selections
- apply **effects**
- **fade in** and **fade out**
- **export** a completed sound clip in a suitable file format.

How to achieve...

Pass requirements

P1 You will create an audio clip which is at least 45 seconds in length.

P2 You will make some use of importing components, cutting, copying and pasting, and using effects.

P3 Some elements may not work as intended.

P4 You will export the audio clip in a suitable file format.

Merit requirements

M1 You will create an audio clip which is at least 45 seconds in length. The audio clip must be appropriate.

M2 You will make good use of importing components, cutting, copying and pasting, splitting/trimming clips and using effects.

M3 Most elements should work as intended.

M4 You will export the audio clip in a suitable file format.

Distinction requirements

D1 You will create an audio clip which is at least 45 seconds in length. The audio clip must be appropriate and must meet the identified aims.

D2 You make good use of importing components, cutting, copying and pasting, splitting/trimming clips, silencing/fading and using effects.

D3 All elements should work as intended.

D4 You will export the audio clip in a suitable file format.

Notes for tutors/centres – downloading Audacity and the required plug-in and setting preferences

Audacity is a free, open source program which can be downloaded from the following site: **http://audacity.sourceforge.net/** (note there is no www). Please ensure that you read the information and that you download the stable version (version 1.2.6 at the time of writing this book).

As the program is continually being developed, there is often another version for advanced users (version 1.3.3 at the time of writing this book), but this is not always stable as it may not be fully tested.

Downloading the lame_enc.dll plug in

For this unit, candidates must export their sound file in a suitable file format. In the Download section on the Audacity site, there is also an additional, free plug-in which should also be downloaded. This plug-in will allow sound files to be exported in .mp3 format.

1. Click the link for **LAME MP3 encoder** → Go to the LAME download page → Click on *any* link from the list of identical **lame-3.96.1** links (there are many different links, select any one).
2. When you have finished downloading LAME, unzip it and save the file **lame_enc.dll** anywhere on the computer (preferably in the same folder as the Audacity program files).

Now, you will need to set up Audacity to export .mp3 files as follows. This set up only needs to be done once.

1. Start Audacity. Click the **Edit** menu → **Preferences** → select the **File Formats** tab. Below **MP3 Export Setup**, click the button for **Find Library** (a dialogue box will display asking if you want to locate the lame encoder) → click **Yes**.
2. Browse to the folder containing the **lame-enc.dll** file and select it → Click **Open** → click **OK**.

Learners will now be able to export files to the .mp3 format.

Setting up the preferences

Before learners begin using Audacity, you (the teacher/tutor) should check the Preferences. This is especially important if Audacity is going to be used to record, but should also be done before editing as learners will be playing back sounds.

1. Click the **Edit** menu → **Preferences**. You will need to set options in the various tabs.
2. Click the **Audio I/O** tab (I/O is short for Input/Output). Here you will 'tell' Audacity where to record sound from and where to play it back to.
3. Below **Playback**, click the arrow to the right of the **Device** list box and select the correct option from the list. (You may need to check with a technician.)
4. If Audacity will be used to record: below **Recording**, click the arrow to the right of the **Device** list box and select the correct option from the list. Select the options for the two check boxes as needed.
5. Select the **Quality** tab. Here you will set the sound quality. Click the arrow to the right of the **Default Sample Rate** list box and select an option. A higher sample rate will produce better quality audio, but the file size will be larger. For CD quality sound, record at **44,100 Hz**.
6. Leave the other settings in Audacity at their defaults.

Tutors are also advised to check the **Sounds and Audio Device Settings** in the Control Panel.

Understanding sound

Sounds are pressure waves of air. We hear sounds because our ears are sensitive to these pressure waves.

Sound waves vary in amplitude and pitch. Amplitude is measured in decibels (dB) and pitch is measured in hertz (Hz).

Key terms

Amplitude

The amount of energy in a sound wave which determines the volume of a sound (i.e. the magnitude of a sound wave).

Pitch

The perceived frequency of a sound. It is the auditory attribute of sound according to which sounds can be ordered on a scale from low to high.

Frequency

The number of sound vibrations in a given period of time (e.g. per second). Frequency determines the pitch of a sound which may range from low to high.

Decibel (dB)

A unit of measure for the intensity of a sound wave (i.e. how loud a sound is).

Hertz (Hz)

The unit of measure for frequency in cycles per second. One hertz is one cycle per second.

Waveform

A graph that shows a sound wave over a period of time. It is a visual representation of the audio track on the screen.

(Sound) wave

A disturbance that creates sound.

Sound file types that can be imported into Audacity

The following table shows common file types that can be imported into Audacity and their characteristics.

File extension	Definition	Characteristic
.aiff	Audio Interchange File Format	The default uncompressed audio format on Apple Macintosh computers. It is supported by most computer systems, although not as common as wav format.
.au	Audio File	This is the default audio format for audio files created on Sun Microsystems or Unix-based machines.
.aup	Audacity Project Format	Audacity projects are stored in an aup file – a format that allows projects to open and save quickly. This format is not compatible with any other audio programs. When you are finished working on a project and you want to import, edit or use the audio file in another program, you will need to export the file in a suitable format.
.mp3	MPEG1 layer 3	MP3 is an acronym for MPEG audio layer 3. (MPEG: Motion (or moving) picture experts groups). A compressed audio format that is a very popular way to store music. It can compress audio with little degradation in quality.
.ogg	Ogg Vorbis	A new compressed audio format. Ogg Vorbis files are not as common as MP3 files – they are about the same size as MP3 files. They are said to have better quality and have no patent restrictions.
.wav	Windows Wave format	The default uncompressed audio format in Windows. This format is supported on almost all computer systems.

Sound file types not supported by Audacity

The following table shows common file types that cannot be imported into Audacity and their characteristics.

File extension	Definition	Characteristic
.wma	Windows media audio	A compressed audio file format developed by Microsoft. It is similar to MP3 format and is often used for playing music from the Internet.
.aac	Advanced audio coding	A digital audio compression used by Apple for iTunes and the iPod.

An introduction to Audacity

To start Audacity: Click the **Start** button → **All Programs** → **Audacity** (or, if shortcuts have been created, click the shortcut icon on the desktop or taskbar). The Audacity window will display (Figure 8.1).

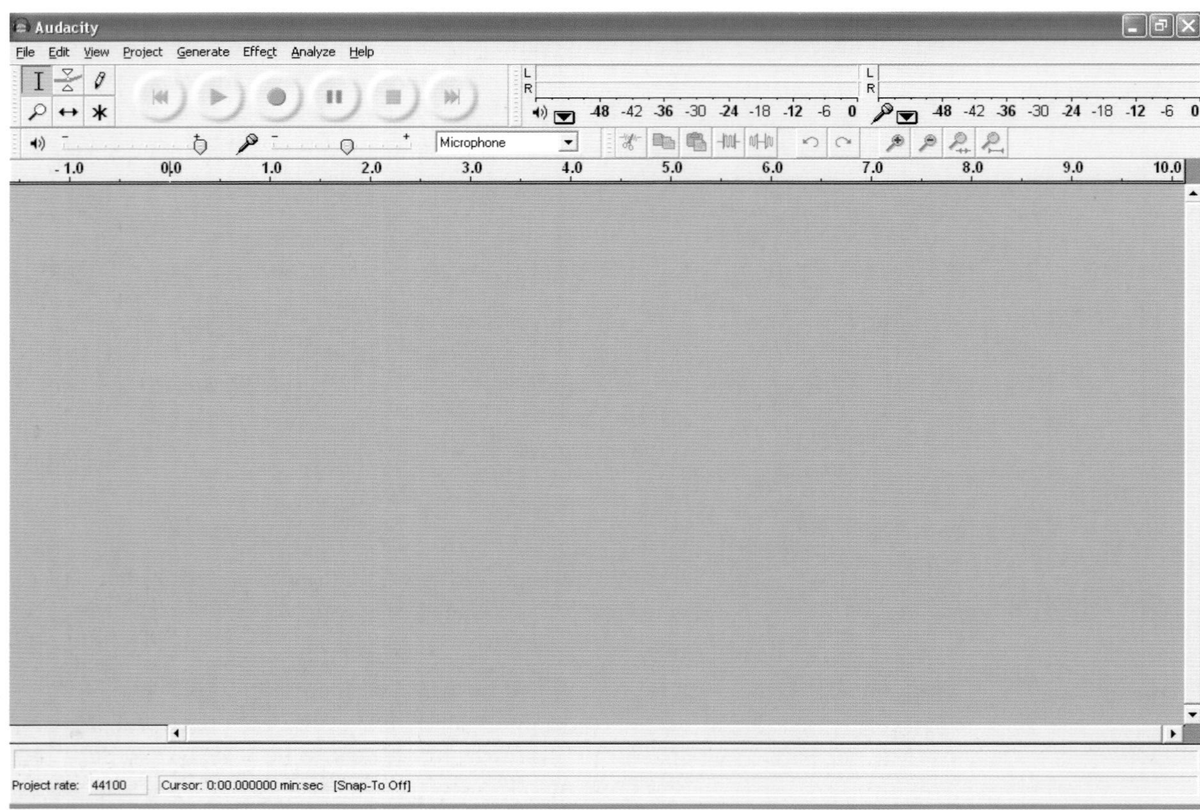

Figure 8.1: *The Audacity window.*

You should spend a little time familiarising yourself with the Audacity window.

To help you understand the basic icons and buttons in Audacity, we will open an audio file. To import an audio file: Click the **Project** menu → **Import Audio** → Navigate to the folder in your user area containing the file you want to open → Select the file → Click **Open**.

When you open an audio file in Audacity, it is displayed as a track. Each track displays the waveform of sound in that track.

Mono and stereo

An audio file recorded in mono will display one waveform, and one recorded in or converted to stereo will display two waveforms as shown in the figures on page 123. In a stereo track, the top track is the left channel and the bottom is the right channel.

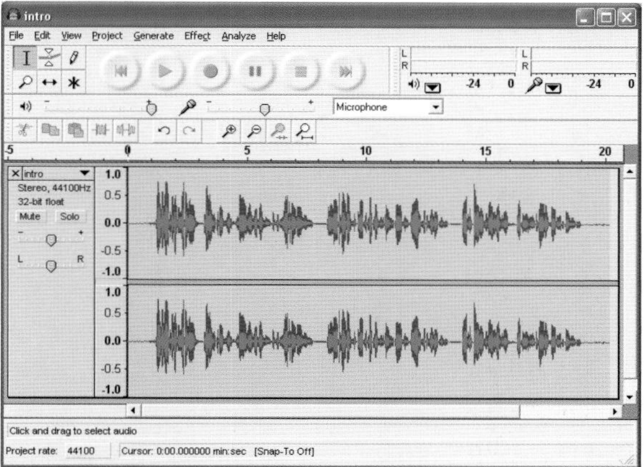

Figure 8.2: *An audio file recorded in stereo.*

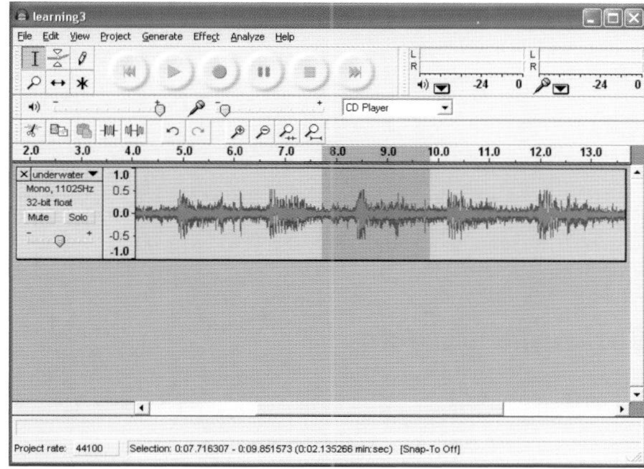

Figure 8.3: *An audio file recorded in mono. (Part of the clip is selected using the selection tool.)*

Activity 13: Import an audio file...

In this activity you will:

- open a provided speech audio clip
- become familiar with some basic icons and buttons in Audacity.

➔ Before you begin this activity, ensure that you have a copy of the folder **U22SourceSoundClips**.

➔ Start Audacity, then from the **Project** menu import the audio file **intro** into Audacity. Your screen should look similar to Figure 8.2.

➔ Keep this file open in Audacity.

Audacity toolbars

There are four toolbars in Audacity: the **Control** toolbar, the **Mixer** toolbar, the **Meter** toolbar and the **Edit** toolbar. The toolbars are shown docked in Figures 8.1, 8.2 and 8.3 – this is the default. Toolbars can also be floated by using the **View** menu, but you are advised to keep the toolbars in the default positions. When undocked, the toolbar name displays. You will not need to use all the toolbars and menus. The toolbars and tools that you will need to be familiar with are explained on the following pages.

The Control toolbar

The **Control** toolbar includes basic editing tools and audio control buttons.

The audio control buttons are the round buttons (refer to Figure 8.4). They are similar to the playback buttons on a CD player and are straightforward to use.

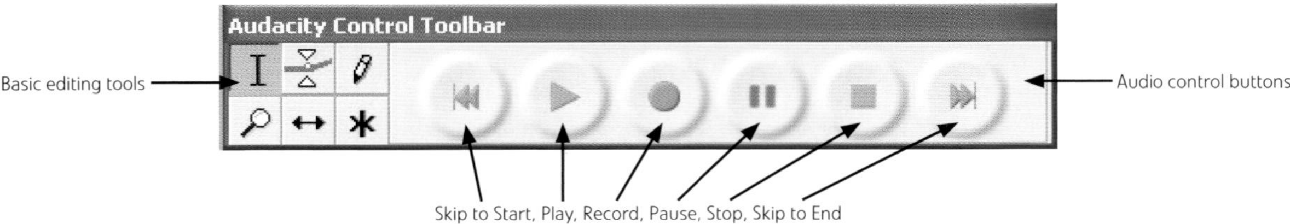

Figure 8.4: *The Control toolbar.*

Basic editing tools

Icon	Tool	What the tool is used for
I	Selection tool	Used to highlight sections of the audio clip by clicking and dragging across the audio waveform. A selected area becomes a darker grey shade on the waveform (refer to Figure 8.3). The length of the selection displays in the Status bar at the bottom of the screen. Edits and effects can be applied to a selected area. When an area is selected and you click the **Play** button, only that area is played. This is very useful when you want to try to locate or isolate a particular sound. To deselect a selection, click once anywhere in the audio track (in or outside the selection).
	Envelope tool	Used to increase and decrease volume levels at various locations in a waveform. Useful for fading music into the background and for editing recordings with two voices where one might be louder than the other. Click the tool to create handle points (white square points) around the portions of the waveform where you want to raise or lower the volume level. Blue borders will surround your audio sample. You can widen the blue border to increase the volume between those points or narrow it to decrease the volume.
	Draw tool	Used to modify individual wave samples. To use this tool you will need to zoom in until you can see individual points on the waveform. Click and drag a point on the wave to edit the points. This tool is not used frequently.
	Zoom tool	Used to zoom in and out of specific parts of your waveform. Left click once to zoom in on a selection, or right click to zoom out. To zoom in on a specific portion of a waveform, left-click and drag across the portion.

Icon	Tool	What the tool is used for
↔	Time Shift tool	Used to slide an entire track to the left or right. Useful for moving a track.
✱	Multi-tool Mode tool	Used to perform multiple editing actions with your mouse. Allows you to use all the editing tools at once.

Creating and saving a project

When you start working with files, you are working on an audio project. One of the first things you need to do when you launch Audacity is to create and save a new project. You may save the project before you have imported any files or immediately after you import a file.

When you save a project, Audacity saves the file you create in **.aup** format (Audacity project format), and also creates another folder in the same user area, using the **filename** you entered followed by **data**. In this folder, Audacity saves all the changed and recorded audio. Audacity breaks the project files into smaller sections and places these smaller sections in the data folder.

To save a project: **File** → **Save Project As** (a **Warning** dialogue box displays – refer to Figure 8.5) → Click **OK** → Navigate to the folder in your user area where you want to save the file → **Save**.

TIP

The Warning dialogue box is just a reminder that your project files cannot be opened in other programs. Do not be concerned about this; once you have completed your final audio clip, you will learn to save it as a .wav file and an .mp3 file, both of which can be opened in other programs.

To prevent this dialogue box displaying each time you save a project, you could click in the check box for **Don't show this warning again**.

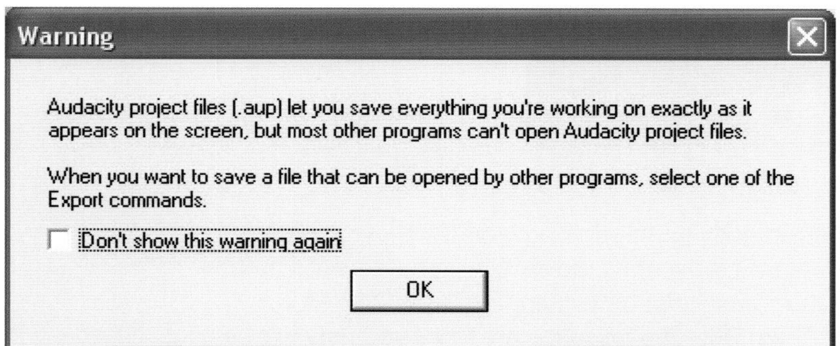

Figure 8.5: *Standard warning message that displays when saving an Audacity project.*

To open a saved project: **File** → **Open** → Navigate to the folder in your user area → Select the Audacity project file (the .aup file) to be opened (not the folder) → **Open**.

To exit Audacity: **File** → **Exit**.

Activity 14. Use the editing tools and audio control buttons...

In this activity you will:

- familiarise yourself with some basic icons and buttons in Audacity
- save a project.

➔ Ensure you have the audio file **intro** open in Audacity.

➔ Press the **Play** button to play the clip. It is a clip of somebody speaking.

➔ Use the **Selection** tool to select (highlight) any part of the audio clip and press the **Play** button again. Notice how only that part of the clip plays.

➔ Use the **Envelope** tool to create an envelope for part of the clip. Play the clip again. Notice how the sound has faded.

➔ Select the **Zoom** tool and left-click to zoom into the clip. Now right-click to zoom out again.

➔ Use the **Time Shift** tool to move the clip to the left then to the right.

➔ Save this project into a new folder called **practicework** in your user area using the filename **learning**.

➔ Close the project **learning** and exit Audacity.

➔ From **Windows Explorer** or **My Computer**, open your folder **practicework**. Notice how another folder called learning has been created. Open this folder and you will see that Audacity has created a number of **au** files in this folder.

TIP

To move to the beginning of the Timeline, press the Home key on your keyboard. To move to the end of the Timeline, press the End key.

The Edit toolbar

Figure 8.6: *The Edit toolbar.*

The **Edit** toolbar buttons perform actions quickly (as in other programs). They provide shortcuts of options that are also available via the menus. Hover your mouse over a button to see a tooltip of what it does. You will be familiar with the standard icons such as Cut, Copy, Paste, Undo, Redo, Zoom in and Zoom Out. The following are icons you may not be familiar with:

- Trim away the audio outside the selection.
- Silence the selected audio.
- Fit selection in window.
- Fit project in window.

Audacity menus and track controls

The **Track Control Panel** appears to the left of every track. The cross at the top left of the panel allows you to close a track. This will remove the track from the Audacity project, but leave the Audacity window and any other tracks, open.

To select an entire track: Click in the grey area of the control panel *below* the sliders.

To display the **Track** pop-down menu for a track: Click the down arrow or the track title on the track control panel. The options on each track menu will be slightly different depending on how the track was recorded. Refer to Figure 8.7.

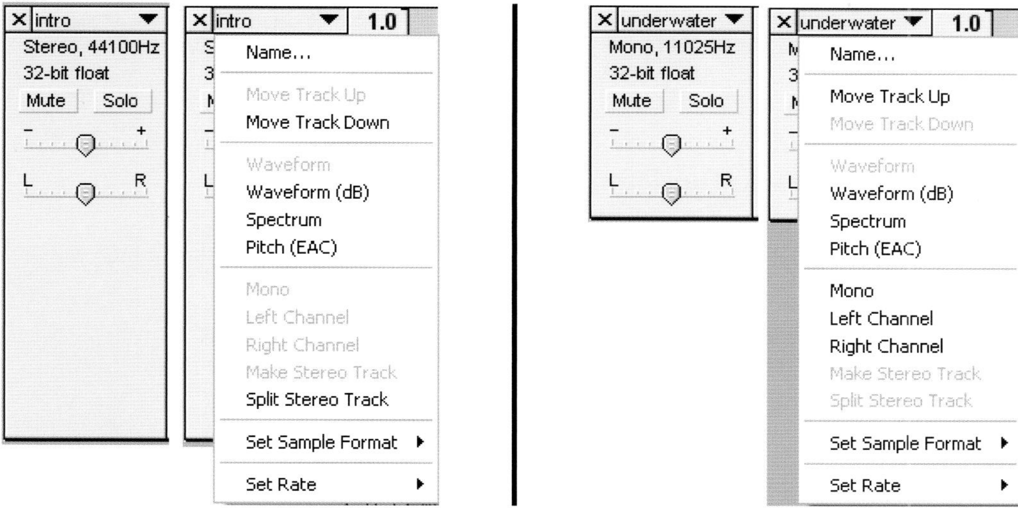

Figure 8.7: *The Track Control Panel and Track pop-down menu for two different tracks.*

The top slider in the **Track Control Panel** (below the Mute and Solo buttons) is the **gain control** – this affects the volume of the track. The bottom slider is the **pan control** – this affects the balance of the output between the left and right speakers.

To rename a track: Click the **Name...** option from the **Track** pop-down menu, and type the new name.

Playing tracks

When you have more than one track open and you press **Play**, all the tracks will be played at the same time. The **Mute** and **Solo** buttons on the **Control Panel** can be used to play individual tracks. The **Mute** button Mute stops that track from playing and the **Solo** button Solo will play only that track. The **Solo** button overrides the **Mute** button. Using **Mute** and **Solo** only affect the play back within Audacity – they will not affect editing and exporting tracks (i.e. it does not matter if the **Mute** button is pressed when you export a track).

Track volume

Between the **Track Control Panel** and the waveform is a vertical ruler. This gives a guide to the volume of the sound of the track shown by the waveform. The volume is expressed in decibels.

Audacity menus

Some of the drop-down menus in Audacity (e.g. **File**, **Edit**, **View**) are similar to other programs you will be familiar with, while others are a little different. The menu options that you need to use will be explained later when you begin editing your sound clips.

Labelling audio tracks (optional)

If you want to identify the content of different parts of your track, you can add labels to the track. Note that the labels will be added to a new, separate track, called a **Label Track**.

Use the **Selection** tool to position the cursor at the position in the track where you want to add a label → **Project** menu → **Add Label At Selection** (a **Label Track** is created *below* the open audio tracks) → Type the label. Repeat to add more labels. You can move the label track further up if you wish: Click the down arrow in the **Track Control Panel** → Select **Move Track Up**.

Changing mono and stereo tracks (optional)

If you are working with a stereo track, and *if* you want to edit the sounds in the left and right channels separately, you can split the stereo track. Similarly, if you have a stereo track, you can make it a mono track so that you can edit both channels together.

To split a stereo track: Click the arrow to the right of the **Track Title** list box → Select **Split Stereo track**.

To change a stereo track to mono: Select the arrow to the right of the **Track Title** list box → Select **Mono**.

To print a waveform

As stated on page 117 in the section titled 'Evidence for this assessment objective', it would be better to provide the moderator with your electronic files. However, if you want to print waveform(s) before and after editing, you can do this from the **Print** menu. The track name will not display on the printout, so you must ensure that you write down the track name on the printout. If you print the edited track, you should also note on the printout what edits have been made.

To print a waveform: **File** → **Print** (displays the **Print** dialogue box) → click the **Print** button. Note, Audacity does not allow you to preview a printout before printing. Alternatively you could provide 'before and after' screen prints to show the editing.

Activity 15: Open and play a speech, a sound and a music clip and save a new project...

In this activity you will:

- begin a new project
- import and play three clips.

➔ Start Audacity and import the **intro** speech clip. (Do not open the saved project **learning**.)

➔ Import the provided sound clip called **underwater**.

➔ Import the provided music clip called **background**.

- Notice how the **intro** and **underwater** clips appear to 'shrink' when you open the background clip. This is because all three clips are a different length. The background music clip is longer than the other two clips.
- Save the project using the filename **1imported** into your folder **practicework**.
- Look at the **Timeline** bar above the tracks to see the approximate time for each of the three tracks. Now using the **Selection** tool, click at the end of each track. Look at the **Status** bar at the bottom of the screen to see the precise track duration.
- Press the **Play** button. Notice how all three tracks play at the same time and that the **background** music track is longer.
- Use the **Selection** tool to adjust the height of each track. Position the mouse at the bottom edge of the track and drag upwards to resize.
- Use the **View** menu to change the view. Try **View → Zoom Normal**, **View → Fit in Window** and **View → Fit Vertically**.

You will need to be familiar with the content of each track so that you know where to apply the edits.

- Use the **Selection** tool to select different parts of each track and play the selection.
- Use the **Mute** and **Solo** buttons to isolate different tracks and play the track and selections from the track.
- Save the project keeping the name **1imported**.

Sound editing

Professional sound editors clean up dialogue tracks, add layers of special effects, place sounds at certain times, cut out unwanted sections and mix in interesting sounds. Music production engineers may cut pieces of vocals away or move them to another part in a song.

Editing is about cutting, placing, fading, moving, duplicating and adjusting the volume of audio material. Mixing is also a form of editing, often combining two or more sound files together.

Trimming and splitting clips

When a track is **trimmed**, everything to the left and right of the selection is removed.

TIP

To undo an action press Ctrl + Z or Edit → Undo.

To trim a track

1. Use the **Selection** tool to select the part of the track to be kept (the area outside the selection will be removed).
2. Play the selection to make sure that the selection is the part you want to keep.
3. **Edit→ Trim**.

Activity 16: Trim a track...

In this activity you will practise trimming a track.

Grading: ***Merit*** *and* ***Distinction*** *grade candidates should trim at least one track.* ***Pass*** *grade candidates are not required to trim tracks.*

- Open your saved project **1imported.** Alternatively, you may open the project file **1imported** from the **U22SoundProjects** folder. Fit the tracks vertically.
- Save it using the new filename **musictrim**.
- Use the **Solo** button on the **background** track to isolate this track. When you play the track, you want to identify a part of the track, lasting about 30 seconds, to keep. The rest will be trimmed.
- Play the track a few times and decide which part you will keep.
- Use the **Selection** tool to highlight the part to be kept. Trim the remaining part of the track.
- Close the **intro** and **underwater** tracks.
- Save and close the project keeping the filename **musictrim**.

Splitting tracks

When a track is **split**, the selected part of the track is moved to its own track, replacing the original selection with silence. If the split is created from the beginning of the track, the split is replaced by a blank area.

Silence in a track is represented by a straight line within the waveform (refer to Figure 8.8).

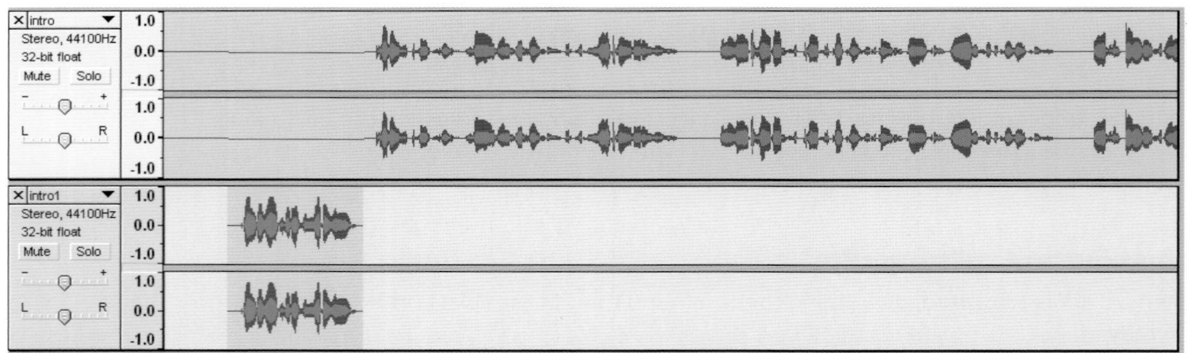

Figure 8.8: *Splitting a track – the split region has been replaced with silence.*

To split a track

1. Use the **Selection** tool to select the part of the track to be split.
2. Play the selection to ensure that your selection is correct.
3. **Edit** → **Split**. The split region is moved to a new track.

TIP

When you have split a track, it is helpful to rename the newly created track to avoid having two tracks with the same name.

Activity 17: Split and trim tracks...

In this activity you will split and trim a track.

Grading: Pass grade candidates are not required to split or trim clips.

- Open your saved project **1imported** and save it using the new filename **2splitrim**. *Alternatively, you may open the project **1imported** from the **U22SoundProjects** folder.*
- Select the first one minute of the **background** track (from the beginning of the track to the 1:00 marker). Trim this selection.
- Use the **View** menu to fit the tracks in the window and fit vertically.
- Mute the **underwater** and **background** tracks.
- Zoom in so that you can see the first four seconds of the **intro** clip clearly.
- Play the **intro** clip from the beginning a few times and watch the waveform as you do. Your aim is to identify the waves for the section of the clip where the speaker says 'Underwater lies another world…'. In particular you want to identify the waves where the speaker finishes this sentence.
- On the waveform, notice that after this line is spoken, the waveform is almost silent briefly.
- Use the **Selection** tool to highlight (select) from the beginning of the **intro** clip to immediately after the sentence 'Underwater lies another world…'. Play the selection to make sure you have selected the entire sentence and none of the end is omitted.
- Split the track so that the selection appears on a track of its own – a new track will be created at the bottom of the screen.
- Fit all the tracks vertically on the screen and fit in the window.
- Rename the new track (the split region) to be **intro1**.
- Using the **Track** pop-down menu position the tracks so they are displayed in the following sequence: **intro**, **underwater**, **intro1** and **background**.
- Save your updated project keeping the filename **2splitrim**.
- Use the **Time Shift** tool to move the beginning of the **underwater** track so that this track begins at the end of the **intro1** track.
- Move the beginning of the **intro** clip so that this track begins where the **underwater** track ends.
- Save the updated project keeping the filename **2splitrim**.
- Play the tracks.

Silencing and fading clips

Silence can be created in two ways. (Remember, silence is represented by a straight line in the waveform.)

- A portion of the track can be selected and this portion can be silenced using the **Silence** option from the **Edit** menu. Highlight a selection → **Edit** → **Silence.**
- A section of silence can be inserted at any point in the track using the **Generate** menu. Click to place the cursor in the track → **Generate** → **Silence** → the **Generate Silence** dialogue box displays → Enter a number in seconds for the period of silence you want to insert → Click the button for **Generate Silence**. Refer to Figure 8.9.

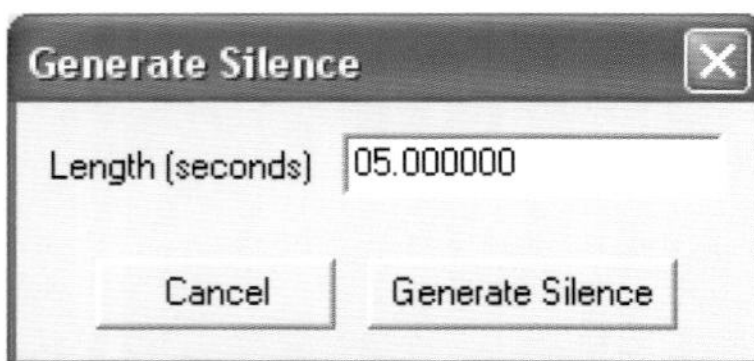

Figure 8.9: *Inserting a five second period of silence.*

Activity 18: Silence selection in track and insert silence...

In this activity you will:

- silence a selection in a track
- insert a period of silence in another part of the track.

*Grading: Pass and **Merit** grade candidates are not required to apply silencing.*

➔ Open your saved project **2splitrim** and save it using the new filename **3silenced**. *Alternatively, you may open the project **2splitrim** from the **U22SoundProjects** folder.*

➔ Select the **Solo** option for the **intro** track.

➔ Zoom in so you can see the beginning of the **intro** track more clearly. Use the scroll bars to see the required part of the track on screen.

➔ Select the beginning part of this track where there is nothing spoken, *before* the speaker starts saying 'Colours, creatures…'. This section of track will be approximately three seconds only.

➔ Silence this section of track.

➔ Play the **intro** track again – you need to find the position in the track where the speaker finishes the sentence 'Colours, creatures, sounds and sensations that have no parallel on land'. Position your cursor after the end of this sentence and insert a period of silence lasting **five** seconds.

➔ Switch off the **Solo** button for the **intro** track and play all the clips to hear the combination of the clips. (Refer to Figure 8.10.)

➔ Save the project keeping the name **3silenced**.

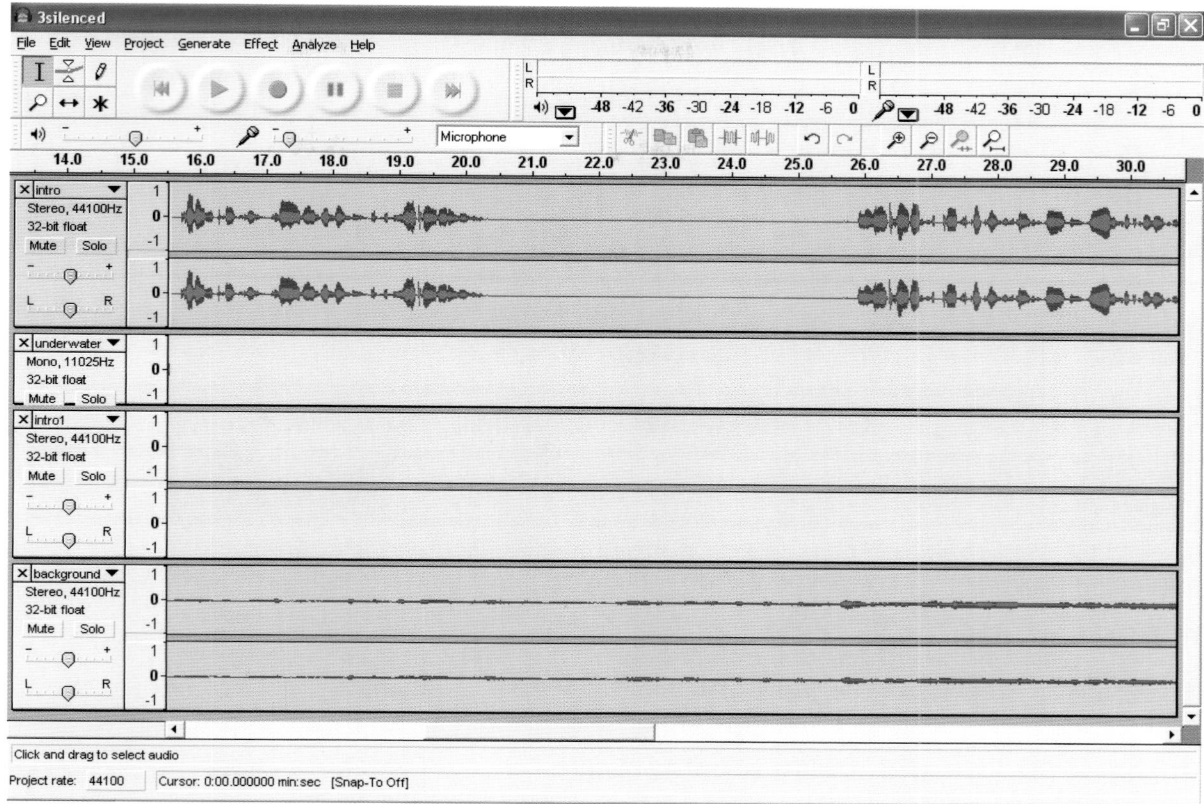

Figure 8.10: *A five second silence inserted in the* ***intro*** *track.*

Cutting, copying, pasting and duplicating

Audio selections can be cut, copied and pasted using the **Edit** menu.

To create a new audio track

Project → New Audio Track. Use the **Name** option on the **Track** pop-down menu to rename the new track.

To cut or copy and paste a selection

When a selection of audio track is cut, that selection is removed from the track and stored on the clipboard. This selection can then be pasted in another track or in a new audio track. In Audacity, only one selection can be held on the clipboard.

1. Use the **Selection** tool to highlight the section of track to be cut or copied. **Edit → Cut** or **Edit → Copy**.
2. The selection can be pasted into an existing track (**Edit → Paste**) or into a new track (**Project → New Audio Track → Edit → Paste**).

Note that if the selection is pasted in an existing track it will be pasted at the end of any existing audio (you cannot leave a gap in an audio track when pasting).

If it is pasted in a new track, it will be pasted at the beginning of the **Timeline**. If you want the pasted selection to play further along the **Timeline**, use the **Time Shift** tool to move the new audio track to the required position in the **Timeline**.

The length of track that was cut will remain highlighted (darker grey) in the **Timeline** – use this as a guide when moving the new track. Refer to figure 8.11.

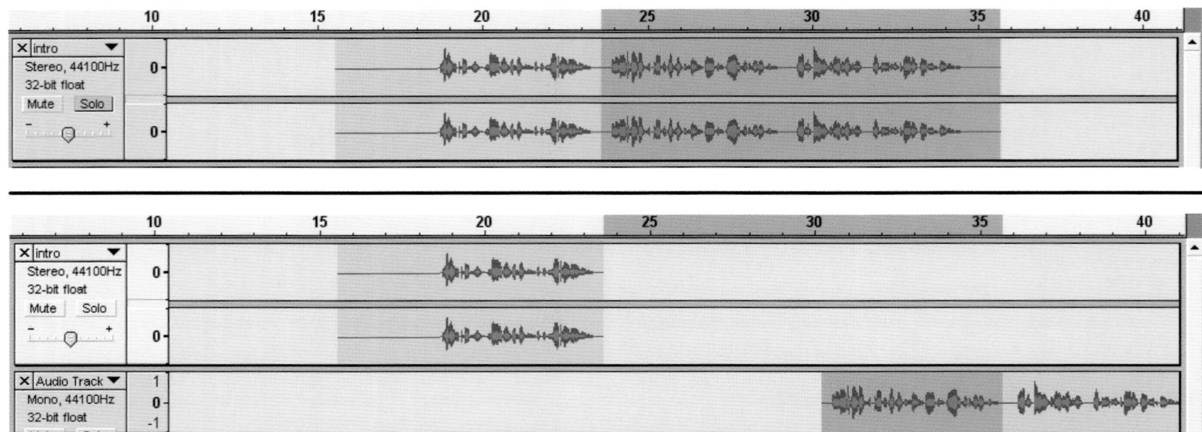

Figure 8.11: *A selection is highlighted, then cut and pasted into a new track. The length of the cut remains highlighted on the Timeline.*

To delete a selection

- Highlight the section of track to be deleted → **Edit** → **Delete**.

Activity 19: Cut and paste a selection...

In this activity you will use cut and paste techniques.

- Open your saved project **3silenced** and save it using the name **4cut**. *Alternatively, you may open the project **3silenced** from the **U22SoundProjects** folder.*
- Create a new audio track and name this **intro3**.
- Rename the track **intro** to be **intro2**.
- Change the view to fit in the window and fit vertically so that all tracks are visible on screen.
- In the **intro2** track, select the part of the track where the following is spoken: 'The marine paradise is a perfect location to learn to dive in warm tropical waters. There is an abundance of underwater life making it an unparalleled diving experience.'
- Cut this selection.
- Paste the selection on the **intro3** track.
- Use the **Selection** tool to position the cursor in the **intro3** track at 33 seconds on the **Timeline**. Use the status bar as a guide. Using the **Time Shift** tool, move the **intro3** track so that the beginning of the audio starts at 33.0 seconds on the **Timeline**.

- Use the **Selection** tool to locate the point in the **intro3** track where the speaker finishes the sentence 'The marine paradise is a perfect location to learn to dive in warm tropical waters'.
- Insert a 5 second silence at this point.
- Save the updated project keeping the name **4cut**.

To copy a selection

When a selection of audio track is copied it is copied to the clipboard without removing it from the project. This selection can then be pasted as follows:

- In another track after existing audio.
- In a new audio track.
- It can replace an existing portion of a track.
- Within an existing track.

1. Use the **Selection** tool to highlight the section of track to be copied (**Edit** → **Copy**).
2. To paste in a new track or in to an existing track: **Edit** → **Paste**.
3. To paste over an existing section of track: Highlight the section of track to be overwritten, then paste.
4. To insert the selection within a track: Place the cursor at the point where the selection is to be pasted.

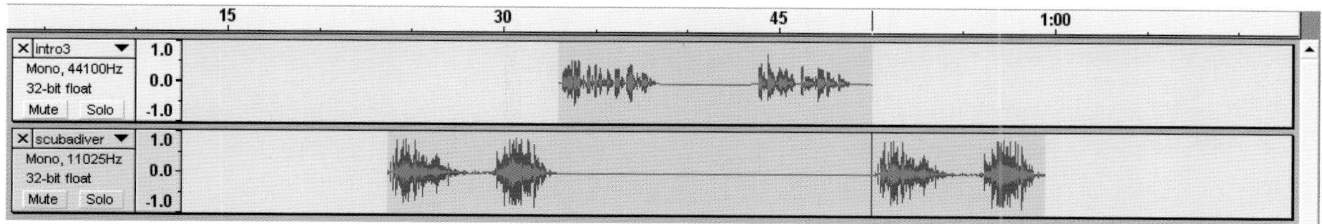

Figure 8.12: *A selection is copied, silence inserted, then pasted.*

To duplicate a selection

To create a copy of a selection in the same place in the **Timeline**, use **Duplicate**. The selection will be copied to a new track and will start and end at the same time as the original selection. The copy can, of course, be moved using the **Time Shift** tool.

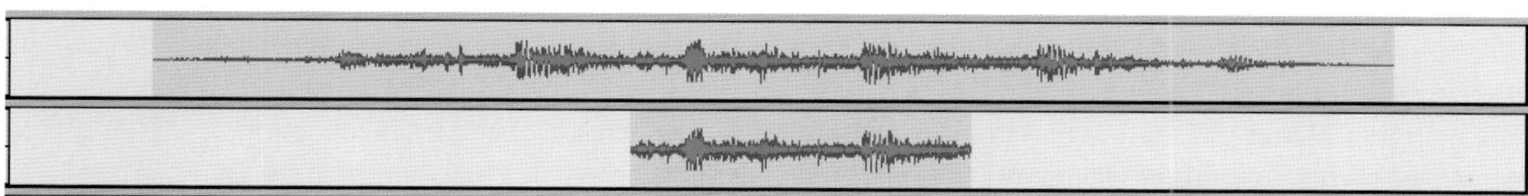

Figure 8.13: *A duplicated selection.*

Activity 20: Import a new track, copy and paste a selection...

In this activity you will:

- import another sound track
- use copy and paste techniques.

➔ Open your saved project **4cut** and save it using the new name **5copy**. *Alternatively, you may open the project **4cut** from the **U22SoundProjects** folder.*

➔ Arrange the tracks in the following order: **intro1**, **intro2**, **intro3**, **underwater**, **background**.

➔ Import the sound clip **diver**. Move this track up so it is positioned below **intro3**.

➔ Fit all the tracks on screen and fit them vertically.

➔ Use the **Time Shift** tool to move the beginning of the **diver** track so that it is positioned at the end of the waveform in **intro2** (when the speaker finishes the sentence 'Colours, creatures, sounds and sensations that have no parallel on land'.

➔ Copy the waveform in the **diver** clip.

➔ Insert a period of silence (about 15 seconds) at the end of the **diver** clip.

➔ Paste the copy after this period of silence.

➔ Save the updated project keeping the name **5copy**.

Key term

Effects

Procedures that alter the sound of the selected audio. Effects are very useful and can improve the quality of an audio file (if applied correctly).

Applying effects

Effects are applied using the **Effect** menu. All the options in this menu will be 'greyed out' unless you have a part of an audio track selected. To apply an effect, you should use the **Selection** tool to select part of a track, or, if you want to apply an effect to an entire track, select the entire track by clicking in the grey area of the **Control Panel** *below* the sliders. Next, apply the required effect, then listen to the results. Some effects have a **Preview** button in that **Effect** dialogue box – this will play about three seconds of the track, allowing you to hear what that effect will sound like before you apply it.

Audacity has over 25 effects, some of which will be covered below. You may experiment with other effects as you wish. Always listen to the audio selection before you apply the effect and listen to the selection again after applying the effect.

Use the **Undo** button or **Edit** → **Undo** to undo any effects that don't sound right.

Fading in and out

When you fade part of a track, you are gradually increasing (fading in) or decreasing (fading out) the volume of the selected part of a track. Fading can be applied to any mono or stereo track. Fading out sound behind speech (narration) tracks and fading in sound between narration, at the end of a narration or at the end of a clip, are useful techniques.

- **Fade In** gradually increases the sound based on the length of the track you have selected – the sound increases progressively.
- **Fade Out** gradually decreases the sound based on the length of the selection. Audacity decreases the volume of the selection progressively.

Note that the volume of the entire selection is not changed when you use **Fade In** or **Fade Out**. The sound is gradually reduced or gradually increased.

To fade in or out: Highlight a selection of a track → **Effect** menu → **Fade Out** or **Fade In**.

You will see a change in the waveform – the height of the blue waves will change. Refer to Figure 8.14.

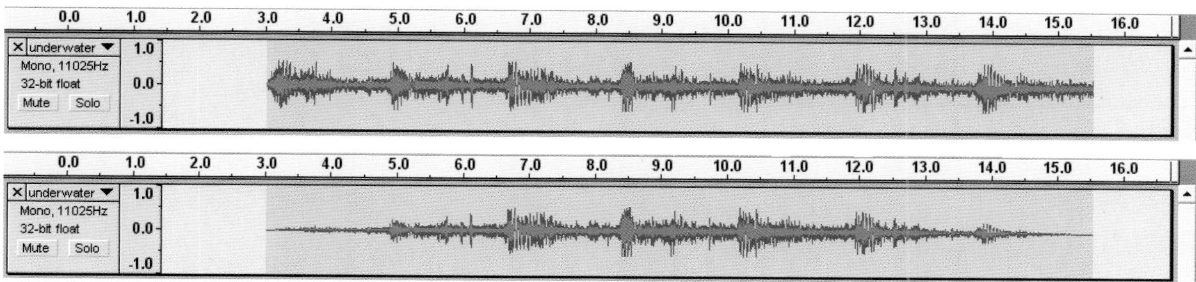

Figure 8.14: *The original track and the track with Fade In applied to the first four seconds and Fade Out applied to the last four seconds.*

Activity 21: Fading in and out...

In this activity you will apply a fade in and a fade out effect to a track.

Grading: Pass grade candidates are not required to apply fading.

- Open your saved project **5copy** and save it using the new name **6faded**. *Alternatively, you may open the project **5copy** from the **U22SoundProjects** folder.*
- Move the **underwater** track to the top so it is closer to the **Timeline** ruler. Zoom in so you can see the beginning of the track clearly.
- Use the **Solo** button to play only the **underwater** track to hear the sound before you apply fading.
- Select the first four seconds of the track and apply a fade in effect. Notice the change in the waveform.
- Select the last four seconds of the track and apply a fade out effect. Notice the change in the waveform.
- Save the updated project keeping the name **6faded**.
- Play only the **underwater** track again – notice the difference in the volume at the beginning and end of the track.

Changing tempo

Change tempo will change the length of the audio – the speed of the audio can be increased or decreased without changing the pitch. This effect can be used to 'slow down' speech that is spoken too quickly for example. Refer to Figure 8.15.

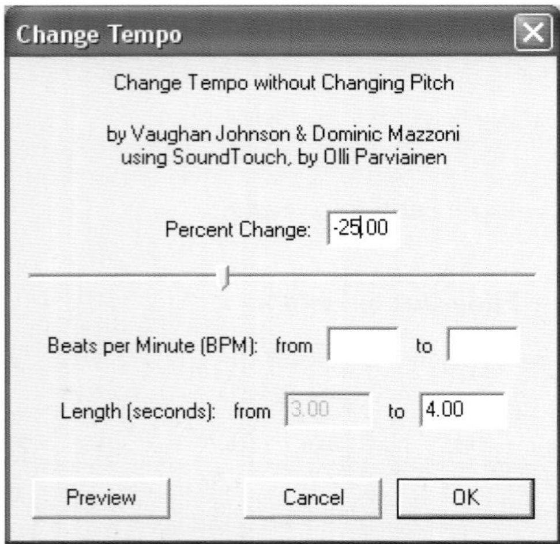

Figure 8.15: *Changing the tempo (speed) of a selection of audio clip.*

Activity 22: Changing tempo...

In this activity you will apply a 'change tempo' effect.

- Open your saved project **6faded**. *Alternatively, you may open the project **6faded** from the **U22SoundProjects** folder.*
- Save it using the new name **7effects**.
- Select the **Solo** button on the **intro2** clip so you can listen to this clip only. In the **intro2** clip, highlight the waveform where the speaker says 'Colours, creatures, sounds and sensations that have no parallel on land'. Reduce the speed (change the tempo) of this clip by a percentage change of about –25.00 (the length of this section of clip will increase).
- Play this selection.
- Optional: Zoom in and select just the word 'sensations' and reduce the speed of this a little bit more.
- You may wish to reduce the tempo to other parts of the speech clips.
- Save the project keeping the name **7effects**.

Amplifying

Amplify changes the volume of the selected audio. This effect can be used to increase or decrease the volume of the selection (but without using gradual fading). This is useful if you want to decrease the volume of background music during a narration or other sound effect and increase it during pauses or increase/decrease the volume at the end of the sound clip.

- To reduce the volume of a selection: Drag the slider so the amplification is a minus figure (below 0.00).
- To increase the volume: Drag the slider so the amplification figure is above zero.

You will need to experiment to find the correct amplification setting.

Activity 23: Amplifying...

In this activity you will apply amplification effects.

- Open your saved project **7effects**. *Alternatively, you may open the project **7effects** from the **U22SoundProjects** folder.*
- Save it using the new name **8amplify**.
- Move the **background** track to be positioned above the **underwater** track.
- In the **background** music clip, highlight the section of the waveform that will play at the same time as the **underwater** clip. Reduce the amplification of this selection (by about –3.0 to –5.0) to ***decrease*** the volume of the **background** music. Check the waveform, the waves should become smaller if you have correctly decreased the amplification. If the waves become larger, you have increased the volume!
- Play all the tracks together from the beginning and identify any other parts of the background music where it would be appropriate to change the amplification (e.g. the volume of the **background** track could be decreased during the narration in the **intro3** clip and could be increased at the very beginning).
- Change the amplification for the **background** music clip as you think appropriate.
- Listen to the other clips and change the amplification for other clips too as appropriate.
- Save the project keeping the name **8amplify**.

Bass boost

Bass Boost allows you to select the frequency and then the **Boost** in decibels (dB). You can click the **Preview** button to hear the impact your changes have made to the sound track.

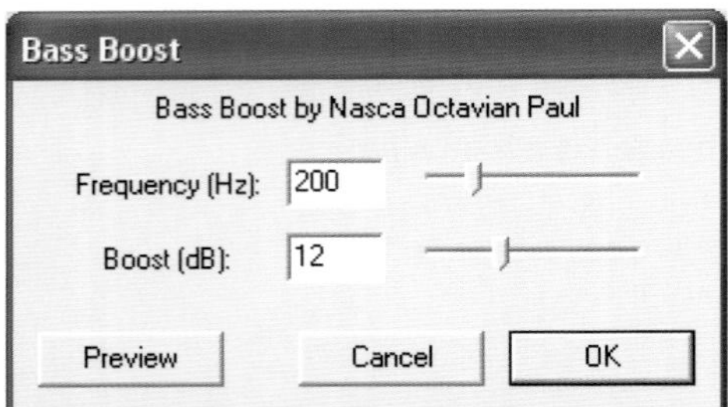

Figure 8.16: *Applying the Bass Boost effect.*

There are many different effects that can be applied, however applying too many effects does not necessarily enhance your audio – sometimes less is more. When applying effects, listen to the selection or track, apply the effect, then listen to it again. If you do not like the effect or it does not 'sound right', undo it. Here are a few more effects you may wish to try:

Change Pitch and Change Speed effects

Change Pitch changes the pitch/frequency of the audio selection without changing the tempo. **Change Speed** changes the length of the audio, increasing the speed will increase the pitch, decreasing speed will reduce the pitch.

Select the required track or a portion of track, then select **Change Pitch** or **Change Speed** from the **Effects** menu. For each, a dialogue box will display with advanced options. Drag the percentage change slider to increase or decrease the impact of the effect on your selected audio.

Noise Removal

This effect allows you to clean up noise from a selection in a track. It is effect is useful if you can hear an audible hiss, buzz or other repeated noise that you would like to remove.

To remove noise, select a piece of a track that is silent except for the noise, select the **Noise Removal** option from the **Effect** menu. From the dialogue box, select **Get Noise Profile**. Next, select the part of the track for which you want to filter out noise and click **Remove Noise**. Experiment with the slider to remove more or less noise.

Normalize

Normalize will increase the volume of all of your tracks to the maximum amount – the effect will make all tracks as loud as possible without introducing distortion. Using **Normalize** will ensure that all parts of the audio are at the same volume level. If you intend to mix tracks, it is useful to normalise all the tracks before you mix them.

Repeat

This effect is used to repeat a section of the audio a chosen number of times.

Exporting your completed sound clip in a suitable file format

As you may recall from earlier in this chapter, when you save a project, it is saved as an .**aup** file which can be only opened in Audacity. Once you have completed all your editing and are satisfied with the final result, you should save the sound clip in a file format that can be played in other programs (e.g. Windows Media Player) and can be inserted into other applications (e.g. into a Microsoft PowerPoint presentation or a web page).

- To export as a .wav file: **File** → **Export As WAV** (the **Save WAV (Microsoft) File As** dialogue box displays) → In the **File name** row, type a suitable filename → **Save**. The clip will take a few seconds to save.
- To export as an .mp3 file: **File** → **Export As MP3** (the **Save MP3 File As** dialogue box displays) → In the **File name** row, type a suitable filename → **Save**. The first time you save as an .mp3 file, a dialogue box (**Edit the ID3 tags for the MP3 file**) displays. You may enter information about your clip in this dialogue box (e.g. Title, Artist, Comments, etc.) or leave it blank. The clip will take a few seconds to save.

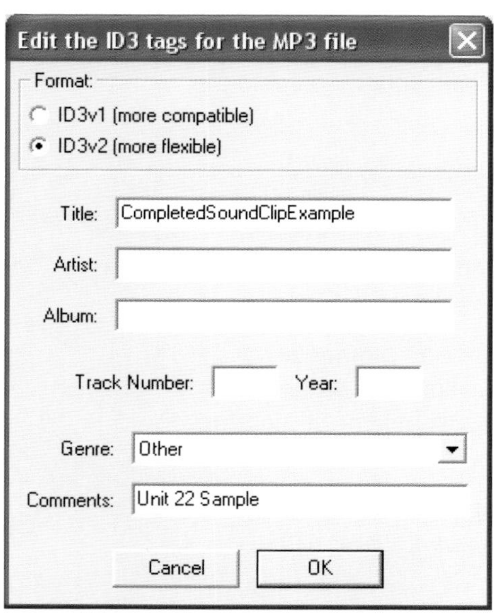

Figure 8.17: *Exporting as an MP3 file.*

WARNING!

Do not delete your latest version of the Audacity project file and folder from your working area because, in Assessment Objective 4, you will need to test your audio clip and identify areas for improvement. To do so, you will need the Audacity project file in .aup format and the folder that Audacity creates for each project.

TIP

Keep your original source components saved, do not delete these. This will help the moderator and your tutor see what you started with and what audio editing techniques you used to create the clip.

Activity 24: Export the sound clip in a suitable file format...

In this activity you will save your completed sound clip.

- Open your saved project **8amplify.** Alternatively, you may open the project **8amplify** from the **U22SoundProjects** folder and apply any effects as you wish.
- Save it as an MP3 file.
- Save the project as a WAV file.
- Exit Audacity.
- From Windows Explorer or My Computer, open each file in turn from your user area and play it in a media player, e.g. Windows Media Player.

Portfolio builder

In this chapter you have learned how to use Audacity to create an audio clip for a project scenario. You will now use the practical skills you have learned to create your own audio clip for your portfolio. This is the creative, fun part of this unit!

Your audio clip for your portfolio must be based on the design documentation (the plan and storyboard) that you should already have created for your portfolio. You must NOT start creating your audio clip for your portfolio until you have created the plan and storyboard – as tempting as that might be! You must also not 'go off on a tangent' and produce a product that you have not planned!

Your audio clip must be at least 45 seconds in length and you must import a range of components (i.e. music, sound and speech). You should already have sourced, organised and checked these components so importing them now into Audacity should be straightforward.

Before you begin creating the clip, read the 'How this assessment objective will be assessed...' and 'How to achieve...' sections of this chapter and discuss with your teacher or tutor what grade you could aim for.

Once you have imported the components you will need to edit (cut, copy and paste) and use effects. Higher level candidates should also split and trim clips, and use silencing and fading. It is very important that you have evidence of carrying out all the different types of editing and of applying the different effects. You are therefore advised to use **Save as** to save the project with different filenames in order to show the project files before and after editing.

When you have finished creating the clip, you must save it in .mp3 and/or .wav format. Check the completed clip to make sure that it is appropriate and that it meets its identified aims. You must NOT delete the saved project files as you will need these during the testing which is the next stage.

Good luck!

Assessment Objective 4

Test the Audio Clip

Overview

In this chapter you will learn how to produce a suitable test plan so that you can test your audio clip. When you were creating the clip, you were taught to carry out some testing at various stages to ensure all elements worked as intended, but now you need to identify specific areas for testing and carry out specific tests to test your completed audio clip more thoroughly. You will also learn how to suggest improvements as a result of the testing and how to action these suggestions.

Testing forms

To help you carry out and record your testing, example test tables can be downloaded from the Student Resources page on the Payne-Gallway website: **www.payne-gallway.co.uk**. The example test tables for Unit 22 are contained in the **Unit22StudentResources** folder, in the subfolder **Unit22Forms**.

How this assessment objective will be assessed...

This assessment objective will be graded by the number of tests you carry out on your audio clip. Grading will also depend on whether or not you test the main areas of your audio clip and how many of these main areas your tests cover. Another factor that will be assessed is how many of your tests are appropriate.

You will need to identify areas for improvement. If you action one of these you can achieve a **Merit** grade, and if you can action most of the areas for improvement you can achieve a **Distinction** grade.

The evidence you provide of your testing is crucial. There is no point carrying out numerous tests without clear evidence to prove you have done so. You need to be methodical in your testing and to ensure that you record details of each test as you go along. The first thing to do is to produce a good test plan.

Key term

Test plan

Also called a **test table**. It is a table showing all the elements in a product that should be tested, how they should be tested and what the expected outcome is.

Skills to use...

You will need to:

- produce a **test plan** to include specific areas for testing (given in the syllabus)
- test the content of the audio clip for **suitability**
- test the clip to check that the correct **message** is conveyed
- play the entire clip to test that it runs for at least **45 seconds**
- test that **effects** have been included and that these are suitable
- test that the final clip has been saved in a **file format** that is suitable for a media player
- identify areas for **improvement** for each of the tests listed above
- **action** one of the identified areas for improvement (**Merit** level candidates only), or action most of the identified areas for improvement (**Distinction** level candidates only).

How to achieve...

Pass requirements

P1 You will test your audio clip using a test table containing at least **three** tests.

P2 Some of your tests should be appropriate.

P3 You will identify areas for improvement.

Merit requirements

M1 You will test your audio clip using a test table containing at least **four** tests covering the main areas of your audio clip.

M2 Most of your tests should be appropriate.

M3 You will identify areas for improvement and action at least one of these.

Distinction requirements

D1 You will test your audio clip using a test table containing at least **five** tests covering the main areas of your audio clip.

D2 All your tests should be appropriate.

D3 You will identify areas for improvement and action most of these.

Key terms

Testing

The process of trying to find every possible problem, error or weakness in a product. A product is tested in order to be absolutely certain that it does what it is supposed to.

Your product is your audio clip. You will need to test your audio clip to ensure that you have actually done what you think you have done and what you had planned to do.

Criteria

The word 'criteria' is the plural of 'criterion'. A **criterion** is a standard by which something can be judged.

Testing

Before you begin the process of testing, you should understand what testing is and why testing is necessary. You may be asking yourself why you need to test your audio clip now that you have created it and have already saved it as sound file in a format suitable for most media players (i.e. in .mp3 and/or .wav format). You may also think that you have already tested your audio clip many times whilst you were creating it.

Why testing is necessary

Testing, following a methodical approach (i.e. to a defined list of test criteria, using a well-designed test plan, and recording the result of each test), will help identify any problems, errors, omissions and weaknesses. Testing your audio clip is necessary so that you can make sure that:

- there are no problems when the clip is played
- you have not made any unintentional mistakes when you created the clip
- you have not left out any components (music, sound, speech) or features during the creation
- there are no unforeseen weaknesses.

Here are some examples of issues that can be identified when testing an audio clip like the one you created:

- **Problem:** There is a long period of silence in the middle of the clip.
- **Error:** You increased the tempo instead of decreasing it.
- **Omission:** You forgot to include a speech clip.
- **Weakness:** The background music finishes before the end of the clip.

If you are going to include your audio clip in a presentation, on a website or in a video clip, it is very important that there are no such problems. Testing will help identify any such issues.

In the syllabus, you are given an example list of criteria that you could include in your test plan – you may be able to think of additional and/or alternative criteria.

Approaches to testing

There are a number of approaches that can be taken to testing and actioning any errors, problems or omissions identified.

- One approach is to:
  1. create the test plan
  2. carry out the tests
  3. select which problems/omissions to action
  4. action the solution(s).
- A second approach is to create the test plan, then carry out the tests and at the same time rectify any problems.
- Another approach is to create the test plan and at the same time test each criteria and action any solutions.

This chapter will follow the first approach. This will encourage you to work methodically and to concentrate on one thing at a time – i.e. firstly create the plan, secondly carry out the tests needed (depending on what grade you are working towards), and then, if you are working towards a **Merit** grade, you can action one identified area of improvement and, if you are working towards a **Distinction** grade, you can action most identified problems, omissions or weaknesses.

Following the second approach can become confusing – if you start to rectify areas identified for improvement whilst you are testing, you may find you correct another problem before you have had the chance to test it and record the testing.

Following the third approach is not recommended as you will be attempting to do three things at the same time. This can become very confusing as you can easily get sidetracked with the testing and correcting and forget to create a good plan, leading to a lack of evidence of the testing.

Test criteria

The test criteria are simply what needs to be tested. The syllabus identifies the following areas to be tested:

- suitable content
- whether the correct message is conveyed (communicated)
- runs for the correct length of time (at least 45 seconds)
- suitable effects
- suitable file format.

How to test an audio clip

The best way to test your audio clip is to produce a good test plan which should ideally include the above test criteria given in the syllabus and any other criteria that you may think of. You should also refer to your design documents created for Assessment Objective 2 (in Chapter 7) to see *what* you had intended to include in your clip, *who* you had intended to produce it for and what the original *aim* of your clip was.

Creating a test plan (test table)

As a minimum, your test plan should show:

- all the **elements** that need to be tested
- **how** each element will be tested
- what **should happen** when the element is tested
- what **actually happened** when the element was tested.

Merit and **Distinction** grade candidates should also show:

- what **action** was taken to solve the problem, weakness or omission.

The first three items are what you plan to test and the last two will show the results of the tests. Each of these criteria is discussed in more detail in the section 'Understanding the test criteria and how to test them' (pages 149–150).

Starting to create the test plan

For this assessment objective, you are required to produce a test plan. You could create a test checklist instead. This is very similar to creating a test plan – the differences are explained on page 147 in the section titled 'Creating a test checklist'.

When producing your test plan, it would be a good idea to use the above list of test criteria (as suggested by the syllabus) as headings in your test table. You can then add extra tests that you can think of, as well as add details of how to test the element and the expected outcome.

Two slightly different examples of the first stage of creating a test plan are shown in the following tables.

Element to be tested	How to test this element	Expected outcome	Actual outcome	Action taken
Suitability of content for aim				
Suitability of content for audience				
Message communicated				
Length of time of clip				
Suitability of effects				
Suitability of file format				

Example 1 *of the first stage of creating a test plan for your audio clip.*
(Note: the actual test plan would have more room in each cell to enter data.)

Element to be tested	How to test this element	What should happen	What actually happened	Action taken
Suitable content				
For aim				
For audience				
Correct message communicated				
message				
Audio clip runs for correct length of time				
Clip duration				
Suitability of effects				
effects				
Suitability of file format				
File format				

Example 2 *of the first stage of creating a test plan for your audio clip.*

Creating a test checklist

If you want to create a checklist instead of a test table, you can do this in a very similar way, except that the column heading for column four would be different. Instead of the heading **Actual outcome** or **What actually happened**, the heading would be something like:

Expected result produced? or **Did the test produce the expected result?**

If you used this method, then when you carry out the test, you could simply enter a ✓ if the actual result is the same as the expected result or a ✗ if it is not.

Creating a table in Microsoft Word

You can create a table using any word-processing program or even draw it by hand. The advantage of using a word processor is that the table will be neater and you can correct mistakes and add rows and columns more easily.

In Microsoft Word: Open a new blank document → Click the **Table** menu → **Insert** → **Table...** to display the **Insert Table** dialogue box → Enter the number of rows and columns required → Select the button for **AutoFit to window** → **OK**.

You can set the page orientation to **Portrait** or **Landscape**, but selecting **Landscape** will give you more width in each column, which is preferable. If you change the orientation the table width will automatically adjust because you selected **AutoFit to window** when you created the table.

The table in Example 1 (on page 147) has five columns and seven rows. If you think of additional test criteria, you can add extra rows and/or columns to your test table.

To add more rows below an existing row: Click in the row above where you want the new row to be inserted (this will be the last row if you want to add a new row at the bottom of the table) → **Table** menu → **Insert** → **Rows Below**. Rows above an existing row, and columns can be added in a similar way.

The table in Example 2 has five columns and twelve rows. The cells in some rows have been merged and shaded.

To merge cells: Highlight the cells in the row to be merged → **Table** menu → **Merge Cells**.

To shade cells: Click in the cell → **Format** menu → **Borders and Shading...** → Select the **Shading** tab → Select the required colour → Click the arrow on the **Apply to:** list box and select **Cell** → **OK**. Refer to Figure 9.1.

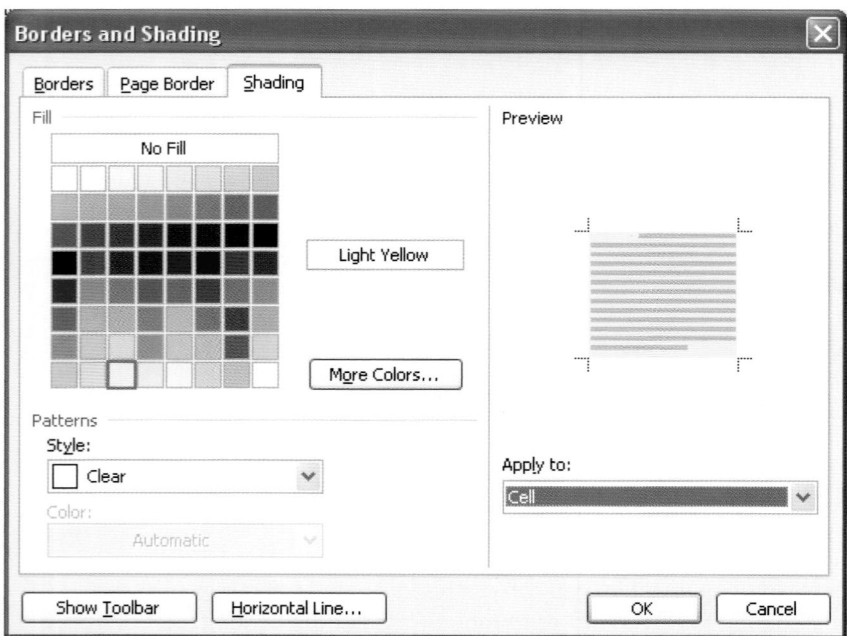

Figure 9.1: *Shading table cells in Microsoft Word.*

Activity 25: Create your test plan...

In this activity you will start to create a test plan for your audio clip.

- Refer to your planning documents.
- Identify what tests you will need to carry out. You are advised to use the test criteria given on page 147 as a basis.
- Enter the column headings in row one and the elements to be tested (i.e. the test criteria) in column one.
- Save your test plan using a suitable filename (e.g. Audio Clip Test Table) – you will update this in the next activity.

Adding other test criteria to your test plan

Look at your design documents created for Assessment Objective 2 and the 'How to achieve…' requirements for Assessment Objective 2 (Chapter 8, page 118) and Assessment Objective 3 (Chapter 9, page 144). These will remind you of what you included in your planning documentation and storyboard, and what you included in the actual clip. Looking at this documentation may give you some ideas of more tests that you could carry out. Here are some additional criteria you could add in the **Element to be tested** column of your test plan:

- software used
- editing clips: cutting, copying and pasting clips and splitting/trimming clips
- silencing and fading
- using effects
- volume (of different clips and of background sounds).

Activity 26: Identify other elements to be tested...

In this activity you will add a few more test criteria to your test plan.

- Refer to your planning documents and storyboard.
- Identify other additional elements in your storyboard that you had planned to include in your clip.
- Add extra rows to your table and details for all the other elements that should be tested.
- Save your updated test plan.

Understanding the test criteria and how to test them

1 Suitability of content?

At the beginning of this unit, you reviewed two existing audio clips. During your review you identified the aim and target audience, and commented on whether the aims were met.

When you planned your audio clip, you decided on the aim of your clip and who your target audience would be. You then went on to create your audio clip. Now, as part of your testing, you need to ensure that it meets your original stated aim and that the content is suitable for your stated target audience.

Your work during your reviews should make you realise how important it is for the aim and audience of your clip to be clear to the listener, how important it is for your aim to be met and how important it is for your clip to be suitable for your intended audience.

Testing that the content meets the stated aim

To test that the aim has been met, you should refer to your planning documents, read the stated aim, then play your audio clip to make sure that it does indeed meet your stated aim. Use the **Pause** button if you need to pause the clip in order to make notes, or the **Rewind** button if you need to review part of the clip again. You need to consider if **every** component (source music, sound and speech clips) and every edit and effect in the clip is suitable for your aim. If any aspect or component is not suitable for your aim, you need to record this fact in your test plan.

Testing that the content is suitable for the target audience

Testing that your audio clip is suitable for your target audience is very similar to testing whether it meets your stated aim. Look at your planning documents and remind yourself of your stated intended audience. Play your clip and check that all the components in the clip are suitable for your target audience. If any components are not suitable, you need to record this in your test plan. The importance of recording every aspect of your testing in the test plan is repeated here because it is so crucial. Without evidence of the stages of your testing, there is no evidence that you have tested your audio clip.

It could be possible that you have included the content according to your storyboard, but that your original planning and/or storyboard were incorrect. Testing will identify this and you should note this in your test plan. You are not required to change your plan or storyboard.

Updating the test plan

Once you have understood how to test a test criterion (in this case, test for suitable content and what the expected outcome should be), you should update your test plan. You need to enter details in the columns headed **How to test this element** and **Expected outcome**. (Note: your column headings may be slightly different.)

Refer to the example of part of a test plan below. The text in italics has now been added so that it explains how this particular criteria (i.e. suitability of content) will be tested and what should happen.

Element to be tested	How to test this element	Expected outcome	Actual outcome	Action taken
Suitability of content for aim	*Read stated aim in planning document and listen to entire clip carefully.*	*Should be about scuba diving and must include underwater sound in between speech.*		
Suitability of content for audience	*Read stated audience in planning document and listen to entire clip carefully.*	*Should be suitable for teenagers aged 12–17.*		

Activity 27: Add details of testing for suitable content...

In this activity you will add details in your test plan of how to test for suitability of content and details of the expected result.

- Read your planning document to remind yourself of your stated aim and audience.
- Add brief details in your test plan of **how** you will test for suitability of content and what the **expected result** should be.
- Save your updated test plan.

2 Correct message conveyed?

You may be wondering how an audio clip that may contain only a little speech and mostly music and/or sounds can convey a message. However a message can be put across quite effectively using sounds. For example the sound of an ocean or an aeroplane taking off can provide information to the listener without anything actually being spoken.

Your audio clip was created for a specific purpose and you now need to test whether the message given to listeners of your clip meets that purpose. Any information given should be accurate.

You also need to think about whether the message being put across in your audio clip is appropriate for your target audience.

Testing that the correct message is communicated

To test that the correct message is put across (conveyed), you should read the stated aim and target audience in your planning document again. You may think by now that you know what the aim and audience are and don't need to read it but it is surprising how sometimes what you have actually written is not what you think you have written.

Next, listen to your audio clip, keeping a clear idea of the aim and audience in your head, and decide if your audio clip delivers the message that meets your stated aim and is also appropriate for your stated target audience. This is important and also easy to test incorrectly. For example, don't get sidetracked by how impressively you have used background music or the super effects that you have applied – they are not what you are supposed to be testing!

As with testing for suitable content, it may be possible that the message being communicated in your audio clip does not match the project scenario because your plans or storyboard were incorrect. Testing will identify this and you should note this in your test plan.

Updating the test plan to add details of testing for correct message

You should update your test plan to add details of how to test for correct message and what the expected outcome is.

Activity 28: Add details of testing for correct message...

In this activity you will add details in your test plan of how to test that the correct message is communicated and of the expected result.

- Read the project scenario and your planning documents to remind yourself of your stated aim and audience.
- Add brief details in your test plan of how you will test whether the correct message is conveyed and what the expected result should be.
- Save your updated test plan.

3 Runs for correct length of time?

This is a straightforward test. Remember your audio clip should be at least 45 seconds long.

Testing the total running time

The total time can be checked easily in Windows Media Player. Open the audio clip in a media player, e.g. Windows Media Player, and press the **Play** button and check the overall timing. You can drag the play head or press forward to go to the end quickly.

In Windows Media Player, the overall time will display somewhere on the screen (where it displays will depend on the version of your player). Refer to the examples in Figure 9.2.

Figure 9.2: *Testing the total running time of an audio clip in Windows Media Player.*

Activity 29: Add details of testing total clip time...

In this activity you will add details in your test plan of how to test the total running time of the clip.

- Add brief details in your test plan of what you expect the duration of the clip to be and how you will test it.
- Save your updated test plan.

4 Suitable effects?

You applied some effects to parts or all of your source sound clips when you created it. Some of the effects available in Audacity are described in Chapter 8 (pages 136–140).

Testing effects

Listen to the entire clip VERY carefully to check that the effects you used are suitable. Sound effects are not always easy to test by just listening to the clip in a media player. To make sure that effects have been applied and to make sure that the applied effects are suitable, you really need to listen to the 'before' and 'after' clips. You need to open the final project file in Audacity and open each of the source clips. Play the first original source clip then play your final audio clip. Locate the part of your created audio clip which contains that source clip and use the **Selection** tool to highlight the part of your audio clip where the effect has been applied. Play the original source clip again and play the highlighted selection. You should be able to hear the effect more clearly and test whether or not the effect is suitable. Testing in this way will also show if you have omitted an effect you planned to include.

Activity 30: Add details of how to test for effects...

In this activity you will add details in your test plan of how to test the effects.

- Add details in your test plan of how you will test the effects and the expected result. You should state what effects should have been applied.
- Save your updated test plan.

5 Suitable file format?

Audacity allows you to save an audio clip in several different formats, some of these formats are not compatible with the most common media players. For example an Audacity project file can only be opened and played in Audacity. It is therefore important to test that the final audio clip has been exported in a file format that is suitable and can be played on the more common media players (e.g. in .wav or .mp3 format).

Testing for suitable file format

The file format can be tested by checking the file format in your working area. You will need to display the file extensions (if they are not already displayed). To display file extensions: Open the folder in your working area → **Tools** → **Folder Options...** → Select the **View** tab → Make sure there is no tick in the box for **Hide extensions for known file types** → **Apply** → **OK**.

Check that the file type is in a suitable format (you may have saved the file in more than one format). Refer to Figure 9.3.

Another way of testing the file format is to play the clip in a player other than the program in which you created the clip.

Figure 9.3: *Checking the file format.*

Activity 31: Check the file format...

In this activity you will add details in your test plan of how to test the file format.

- Add details in your test plan of how you will check the file format and the expected result.
- Save your updated test plan.

Now that you have created your own test plan, you may wish to compare it with the two example test plans **AO4_AudioTestTable** v1 and v2 provided with this book. Also provided is a test plan which contains examples of 'What should happen' when the test is carried out. This file is titled **AO4_AudioTestTablev2_WithExamples**. The example form contains sufficient detail for **Distinction** level.

- You may use the ideas in the example form to make changes to your plan.
- You should now be familiar with how to test the various elements in your audio clip. You may add other criteria to your plan if you wish (remember the minimum number of tests for **Distinction** level candidates is five). Additional criteria you could add are 'software used' and 'editing techniques'.
- Save your completed test plan. Next, you will begin the tests themselves.

Carrying out the tests

Once you have produced your test plan, and included details of how to test each element, and what should happen when each element tested, you will find the actual testing quite straightforward.

To do the testing, you will need:

- your completed audio clip in .mp3 or .wav format
- your final project file in .aup format (Audacity format)
- access to a computer with a media player, e.g. Windows Media Player, and Audacity
- your test plan.

You can handwrite or type comments in your test plan as you carry out each test. The advantage of using a computer to update your test plan is you can copy and paste during the testing. You are not required to produce any screenshots to prove that you have carried out the tests – the evidence of the testing in the test plan is sufficient.

You should now look at your test plan and decide how many, and which, tests you will carry out: at least three tests for **Pass** level; at least four for **Merit** level; and at least five tests for **Distinction** level. If you want to carry out all the tests you have identified in your plan, that's good practice and absolutely fine! **Merit** and **Distinction** level candidates are required to test the *main areas* of the audio clip.

The main areas of the audio clip are the music, speech and sounds – these are the parts of the audio clip that listeners 'hear'. Use of editing and effects are not considered to be the main areas of the clip. Note: the use of silencing and fading effects need to be used only by **Distinction** level candidates.

Recording evidence of testing

When carrying out the tests, you should complete one test at a time and make sure you make notes in the **Actual Outcome** (or equivalent) column of your test plan as you perform each test. Record the outcome immediately – it is easy to record details inaccurately or even forget them altogether if you leave it till later! If you do not have evidence of a test, you cannot prove that you have actually carried it out.

1. Carry out the first test.
2. Record the actual result in your test plan.
3. Then carry out the second test, record the result, and so on.

If the actual outcome is the same as the expected outcome, you can record it in any of the following ways:

- Write (or type) details of what happened during the test.
- Copy and paste the detail from the **Expected Outcome** column into the **Actual Outcome** column.
- Write (or type) 'As expected' in the **Actual Outcome** column.

If you have created a test checklist, you could simply enter a ✓ if the actual result is as expected.

TIP

You can copy and paste 'As expected' from one cell to another too.

If you carefully followed the instructions when creating the clip, and checked your work at each stage, you should find that the actual result is the same as the expected result. But mistakes can happen, so even if you think you were very careful as you created your clip, testing carefully is important too.

TIP

Remember to save your test plan frequently (if you are using a word processor).

If, as a result of testing an element, you find that the result is different to what is expected, or that you have forgotten to do something, enter a comment in the **Actual Outcome** column. You have identified an area for improvement.

Activity 32: Carry out the testing...

In this activity you will carry out various tests on your audio clip.

Grading: *Pass level candidates must carry out at least three tests;* **Merit** *level candidates must carry out at least four tests;* **Distinction** *level candidates must carry out at least five tests.* **Merit** *and* **Distinction** *level candidates* ***must*** *test the main areas of the clip.*

- Refer to your test plan and decide how many and which tests you will carry out on your audio clip.
- Carry out the first test and record the result in your test plan. Then carry out the second test, record the result and so on.
- Save your updated test plan.

Identifying and actioning areas for improvement

In your test plan, look at the areas where the actual outcome and the expected outcome differ. Decide what improvement you need to make (if any) and add it to your test plan for each area.

Pass level candidates are not required to action any areas identified for improvement. **Merit** level candidates must action at least one area and **Distinction** level candidates should action most areas identified for improvement. This is not as difficult you may think – you already know how to do this! The skills required to correct any errors or omissions found are the same as the skills you learned for creating the audio clip.

To action any problems or omissions, you will need:

- your final project file in .aup format (Audacity format)
- access to a computer with Audacity
- your test plan.

Action each area, one at a time, and record details of each change as you make it. Be careful not to get so involved with making changes to your audio clip that you forget to record details of the changes. Providing evidence of the changes is very important at this stage. Your evidence will be:

- the notes you make in your test plan
- your amended sound project file in .aup (Audacity) format
- the final amended, exported sound clip in .mp3 or .wav format.

Correcting areas identified for improvement

Remember, when actioning any areas identified for improvement, you should make changes in your Audacity project file, not in the .mp3 or .wav file. The advantage is that the project file has all the individual tracks as separate tracks, whereas the .mp3/.wav format file will display just one track which will be more difficult for you to edit.

1 Changing the content to make it suitable for the aim, audience and message conveyed

If, during your testing, you find that the content of your audio clip is not suitable for your audience, that it does not meet your stated aim or that it does not convey the right message, then the content will need to be changed. If the actual source music, speech and sound tracks are not appropriate, then you will need to do one or more of the following:

- Delete the inappropriate parts of the track by trimming the unwanted part(s).
- Replace the inappropriate components with more suitable tracks.
- Move tracks to another position.

If you need to trim, cut, move or delete tracks, refer to the section **Reducing timing** on page 158. To increase the timing of a component, refer to the section **Increasing timing** on page 158.

When you have finished making any changes, make sure you check the running time of the whole clip to make sure that it is still at least 45 seconds long.

2 Changing the length of time of the audio clip

If, during your tests, you find that the length of the audio clip is more than 45 seconds, it is not essential that you reduce the timing as there is no prescribed maximum time. However, if you think that your clip is far too long, you can reduce its length by cutting or trimming parts of tracks or deleting individual tracks.

Reducing timing

To reduce the timing of the audio clip, you can trim, cut or delete one or more parts of one or more tracks.

When a track is **trimmed**, everything to the left and right of the selection is removed.

To trim a track: Use the **Selection** tool to select the part of the track to be kept (the area outside the selection will be removed) → **Edit** menu → **Trim**.

To cut part of a track: Use the **Selection** tool to highlight the section of track to be cut → **Edit** → **Cut**.

To delete a track: Select the entire track by clicking in the grey area of the **Control Panel** *below* the sliders. The track **Control Panel** is at the left of every track. Press the Delete key.

Play all the tracks in the edited clip from the beginning again to ensure that the new timing is correct.

Increasing timing

If the length of the audio clip is less than 45 seconds, you will need to increase the length. To increase the total running time you could:

- import a new track
- duplicate an existing track or selection of a track.

If you think you have cut out too much of an original track, you could import the original track again and insert parts of it again.

Remember to apply suitable effects to any tracks or selections that you have added or duplicated.

Once you have made any changes, check the running time of the whole clip again. You could do so by checking the end time on the **Timeline**. Use **View** → **Fit in Window** first. Alternatively, to check the exact total running time more accurately, select the **Selection** tool and position it at the end of the longest track, then check the time of the status bar at the bottom left of the screen. Refer to Figure 9.4.

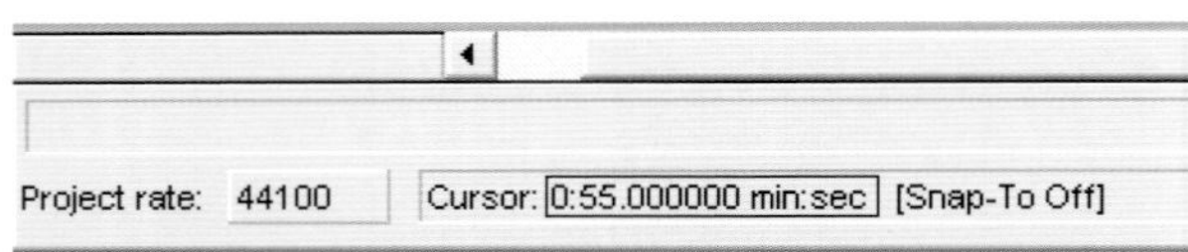

Figure 9.4: *Checking the running time on the Status Bar.*

3 Changing effects (including changing fading and volume)

If, during your tests, you find that the effects you have applied are not suitable, you can edit the clip by:

- replacing that part of the audio clip with a selection from the original clip (by copying part of the original track)
- deleting a selection of track (but make sure that the audio clip duration is not less than 45 seconds)
- applying the same or another effect again.

Editing tracks includes cutting or deleting, copying and pasting, replacing, splitting and trimming tracks (refer to Chapter 8, pages 129–130).

Changing effects

You cannot undo an effect easily in Audacity. If, during your testing, you find that an effect has been applied incorrectly, you will need to import the original track again, and edit and apply effects as needed. If you had originally used only a part of the original track, remember to cut or trim unwanted tracks. Once you have applied the effects again, use the **Time Shift** tool to move the track into the appropriate position on the **Timeline**.

After applying the effect (refer to Chapter 8, pages 136–140), listen to the selection or track again, to ensure it is suitable.

Changing volume

If you want to increase or decrease the volume of a single track or of a selection in a track, you need to apply the **Amplify** effect to that track or selection (refer to Chapter 8, page 139). You must not change the volume slider on the **Mixer** toolbar – this only changes the volume of *all* the clips you can hear through your speaker or headphones, it will not affect the volume of a particular track or selection when it is played together with the other tracks.

Changing or adding silence

If, during your tests, you find that a period of silence is too long, you can cut out part of the clip, or if it is too short, you can increase its length.

If you find that you need to add a silent period, you can insert silence (refer to Chapter 8, page 132).

4 Saving an amended project in a suitable file format

You must save the amended project file as either a .wav file or an .mp3 file (or in both formats if you wish).

During testing, if you find that you have not saved your audio clip in a suitable file format, then import the final version of the project file into Audacity once again and export it as described in Chapter 8 (page 141).

Activity 33: Identify area(s) for improvement and action the improvements...

In this activity you will make change(s) to your audio clip as a result of the testing.

Grading: ***Pass*** *level candidates are not required to make any changes;* **Merit** *level candidates must correct at least one identified problem/omission;* **Distinction** *level candidates must correct most of the problems/omissions identified as a result of the testing.*

- Refer to your test plan, identify areas that could be improved and decide how many you will correct.
- Make the changes to your audio clip as required.
- Save your amended sound project file using a different filename from the last saved version (e.g. if your final project file was 8amplify, this corrected version could be saved as audioclipfinal).
- Export your amended audio clip as an .mp3 or .wav file using a different filename to the filename you used before testing.

Portfolio builder

By reading and understanding the guidelines in this chapter, and working through the activities, you have learned how to test an audio clip and how to record your tests. For your own portfolio, you will need to create a test table or checklist and test the audio clip that you created for your portfolio.

You should read the 'How this assessment objective will be assessed...' and 'How to achieve...' sections of this chapter – the number of tests you carry out, what you test and whether or not you action any identified areas of improvement will all affect your grading.

For your portfolio, you will need to produce a test plan, then test the clip and identify any areas for improvement. Depending on the grade you are working towards, you will also need to action one or most of the areas identified for improvement. You may use or adapt the example test plans provided with this book. You must make sure you write down every aspect of your testing and correcting.

Good luck!

UNIT 23

Creating Video

In this unit you will cover the following...

- AO1 **Review several existing video clips**
- AO2 **Design a video clip**
- AO3 **Create a video clip**
- AO4 **Test the video clip**

This unit is one of the half units which you can combine with other full or half units to gain a full qualification in this course.

Video clips may be used in many projects, for example in a website or a multimedia product. Therefore the video clip you create in this unit could be used in other units.

To create the video clip in this book, a software program called Windows Movie Maker, which is available in the Microsoft Office suite, will be used.

The video clip you will create will be based on the project scenario given in the Introduction to this book.

If you have completed Unit 22 Creating Sound Using ICT, you will find Assessment Objectives 1, 2 and 4 of this unit are similar and require similar skills (there are some differences too). However, no assumption is made in this unit that any previous units have been completed – the unit is complete in its own right and does not refer to other units. Assessment Objective 3 is to create a video clip – the skills and software for creating a video clip are, of course, quite different to the skills for creating a sound clip.

Assessment Objective 1

Review Several Existing Video Clips

Overview

In this chapter, you will need to review at least two different, existing video clips. You will use the knowledge and skills gained during your reviews when planning, designing and creating your own video clip.

You do not need to find the video clips for reviewing yourself: your teacher/ tutor may provide you with at least two different types of video clips to review.

You will learn how to identify the aim of the clip and comment on how the aim is met. You will learn how to identify the good and not so good features of each video clip and how to suggest possible improvements that could help improve the features that are not effective.

By looking critically at existing video clips, you will learn to recognise what makes a good video clip so that you may get some design hints for your own product, and you will learn to see the weaker features of a video clip so that you avoid making similar mistakes when you create your own.

Review forms

To help you record your reviews, example review forms can be down-loaded from the Student Resources page on the Payne-Gallway website: **www.payne-gallway.co.uk**. The forms for Unit 23 are contained in the **Unit23StudentResources** folder, in the subfolder **Unit23Forms**. The review forms are provided in Microsoft Word format. You can print the forms and handwrite your comments, or enter details in the Word file.

How this assessment objective will be assessed...

The grade you are awarded for this assessment objective will depend on the amount of detail you include in your review of each video clip.

As a minimum, you must list the good and not so good features of at least two different types of video clip. However, you may review more than two video clips if you wish.

For a **Merit** grade, your explanation of these features should be detailed and you should suggest possible improvements that could be made to each video clip. You must also identify the aim of each video clip.

For a **Distinction** grade, you must identify the aim of each video clip and your explanation of the good and not so good features must be thorough. You should also suggest a range of valid improvements that could help each video clip to meet its aims.

Key terms

You will come across the words 'thorough' and 'detailed' frequently in this qualification. 'Detailed' is usually a descriptor used for **Merit** or **Distinction** grading and 'thorough' is usually a descriptor used for **Distinction** grading. In this qualification, a 'thorough' explanation should include more detail than a 'detailed' explanation.

Detailed

A detailed explanation or detailed plan is one that is developed with care and in minute detail.

Thorough

A thorough explanation is one that is methodical and comprehensively complete – it is extremely careful and accurate and includes all the necessary information.

Skills to use...

You will need to:

- **review** two different video clips – they may be provided by your teacher/ tutor or you could find these yourself
- identify the good and not so good **features** in each clip
- identify the **aim** of each video clip
- comment on **how** the **aims** of each video clip are **met** and if the aims are not met, comment on **why** they were **not met**
- suggest **possible improvements** for the video clips reviewed.

How to achieve...

Pass requirements

P1 You will list the good and not so good features of at least two different types of video clip.

Merit requirements

M1 You will identify the aim of each of the video clips.

M2 You will give a detailed explanation of the good and not so good features of at least two different types of video clip.

M3 You will suggest possible improvements for the video clips reviewed.

Distinction requirements

D1 You will identify the aim and the audience of each of the video clips.

D2 You will give a thorough explanation of the good and not so good features of at least two different types of video clips.

D3 You will suggest a range of valid improvements for each of the clips reviewed to help the video clip meet its aims.

1. Choose a video clip

Types of video clips

You may review two different clips of any of the following types:

Television advertisement

Sources: TV stations that can be accessed using the Internet

Movie trailer

Sources: DVD-ROM
video cassette
television
the Web

Music video or promotional video

Sources: television – particularly music channels (e.g. MTV, VH1)
CD or DVD-ROM
video cassette
the Web

Promotional videos include:
Free CD/DVD-ROM or videos advertising holidays, hotels, etc.
Videos promoting companies or professions (e.g. working for a company such as an airline or becoming a teacher)
Videos advertising property for sale

Online media clips

Sources: The Web

Sources of video clips

If you or your teacher/tutor do not have video clips readily available to review, here are some suggestions for finding some:

TV advertisements

Most television channels show commercial or public service advertisements. BBC television stations do not advertise commercial products, but they do promote their own programmes.

Movie trailers

A movie trailer is an advertisement for a film that will be exhibited in the future. A movie trailer is a preview of a forthcoming attraction – it consists of a series of selected shots from the film. The purpose of the trailer is to attract an audience to the film.

The selected scenes (referred to as excerpts) are usually abbreviated shots of the most exciting, amusing or memorable parts of the film.

Here are some website addresses (URLs) where you could watch or download movie trailers:

http://www.trailerdownload.net/movies

http://www.bbc.co.uk/films/trailers/

http://www.apple.com/trailers

http://www.moviecentre.net/upcomingmovies

http://entertainment.timesonline.co.uk

http://www.filmtracks.com

http://www.sonypictures.com/movies/index.html

http://www.movie-list.com

Hardware required

To review the video clips, you will need to watch and listen to each clip. If you are reviewing a television advert, a clip on a DVD-ROM, a music or promotional video, you will need access to the correct hardware (e.g. television, video recorder). If you are reviewing video clips on a computer, the computer must have a sound card and either speakers or headphones.

Activity 1: Record details of video clips to be reviewed...

In this activity you will start to document specific details about each video clip that you will be reviewing.

- Ask your teacher/tutor if he/she has already identified appropriate video clips for you to review or has a list of video clips from which you can choose two clips.
- Choose two different types of video clip.
- You need to start recording details of the two clips that you will review.

Note: You may review more than two clips if you wish.

- You may use or adapt the provided form titled **AO1_ReviewVideoClip**. Use a separate form for each video clip you choose to review.
- In the Activity 1 section of each form, enter details of the video clips in the following boxes:
  - **Type of video clip:**
  - **Brief detail of video clip:** (e.g. where you got the clip from)
- Save each form separately – you will update these later.

2. Identify the aim of the video clip

Key term

Aim

The aim of a video clip is its purpose – why the clip has been produced.

Identifying the aim of the video clip

A video clip may have just one aim or more than one aim. They are produced for a particular purpose. When you identify the aim(s), think about whether the clip has been produced to:

- provide information (e.g. product recalls by consumer agencies or manufacturers)
- change behaviour (e.g. drink driving campaigns, benefit fraud, anti-smoking)
- attract attention, entertain or persuade people to watch a film (e.g. a movie trailer)
- persuade viewers to buy a product or attend an event (e.g. buy clothes or attend a concert)
- persuade the target audience to join something (e.g. swimming classes)
- teach specific skills (e.g. learning to use a software program).

Identifying the target audience

Any type of video clip is created for a reason and is aimed at a specific group of people (i.e. a target audience). Refer to pages 8 and 9 in Chapter 1, Unit 4, Assessment Objective 1, for explanations of audience and target audience.

Some video clips are aimed at a wider audience (e.g. a TV advert promoting a reduction in the price of fruit), whereas a TV advert promoting tickets for an opera would be aimed at a narrower audience.

When you describe the aim of a video clip, one of the things you should identify is who the intended audience is. When identifying the audience, you should think about whether or not the clip is aimed at:

- a particular age group
- a particular gender (male/female)
- people of a particular education level and/or background
- a particular family size and/or income level
- at people living in a specific location.

Activity 2: Identify the aims of the video clip...

In this activity you will begin your review of both your video clips.

Grading: **Merit** *and* **Distinction** *grade candidates must identify the aim of the video clip.*

- Watch each video clip in turn and think about its aims as you watch. Consider the following:
  - Who is the target audience?
  - What is the aim of this video clip?
- Continue using the **AO1_ReviewVideoClip** forms saved in Activity 1. Complete the following in the Activity 2 section on each form:
  - **Target audience:**
  - **Aim of video clip:**
- Save your updated forms.

3. Identify the good and not so good features of a video clip

Learning from existing reviews

Before you begin recording your own reviews, you may find it helpful to read or watch existing reviews by professional reviewers (e.g. film review shows on television, or reviews on the Web or magazines). You will find such reviews on TV, in newspapers, journals, magazines and on the Internet.

Do not be concerned about the level of the language used in these reviews and the amount of detail – you are not expected to produce such professional reviews! In this chapter, you will be guided on how to record your own reviews using forms. By reading or watching existing reviews, you will be prompted to think about particular points when you carry out your reviews. Reading or watching existing reviews is not essential.

The following websites give film reviews:

http://www.trailerdownload.net/reviews

http://www.radiotimes.com/film

http://www.channel4.com/film

http://entertainment.timesonline.co.uk/tol/arts_and_entertainment/film/film_reviews

http://www.bbc.co.uk/films/gateways/release/review/cinema/index.shtml

http://www.movie-list.com/reviews/index.shtml

The following site has recorded reviews which you can listen to on the Internet if you have a sound card and headphones:

http://www.bbc.co.uk/fivelive/entertainment *follow the link for film reviews*

How to review the different features of a video clip

Video clips will usually have a number of different features that you need to consider. It will be easier for you to consider the features in stages rather than produce a lengthy commentary on the whole clip.

When reviewing each video clip, you should first identify what features have been used, then discuss whether the feature is effective or not (i.e. good or not so good). Use the questions under **Factors to consider** in the four tables on the following pages as prompts when you review your video clips.

Identifying the speed of loading and range of components

The following table lists some factors to consider when reviewing the speed it takes for a clip to load and the range of components used in the video clip. Note that the speed of loading will not be a factor to consider for all types of video clips (e.g. TV advertisements are controlled by the broadcaster) – it is a factor to comment on for clips downloaded from the Internet or clips on a CD/DVD-ROM.

Feature	Factors to consider about speed of loading, components and clarity
Loading the clip	• Does the video clip load quickly or is it slow to load? • Is the file size too big for a single clip?
Compatibility	• Is the file format compatible with most media players?
Use of different components	• Does the clip include different components (e.g. music, speech/song, other sounds, images and animation)? • Are all components used appropriately and effectively?
Clarity	• Can the speech be easily understood or does the speaker/singer mumble? • Articulation – can you understand what is being said? • Excitement or expression – is the speaker overly loud or excitable to the point where it is irritating or grating to the listener?

Activity 3: Identify and comment on the speed of loading the clips and the use of components...

In this activity you should play each of your video clips taking note of how quickly the clip loads and determining the range of components included in the clip.

Grading: Pass grade candidates must list the good and not so good features; commenting on the features is not essential. For a **Merit** *grade, the explanations should be detailed. For a* **Distinction** *grade, they should be thorough.*

- Continue using the **AO1_ReviewVideoClip** forms saved in Activity 2.
- In the Activity 3 section of the form for each video clip, comment on the good and/or not so good aspects of how quickly the clip loads (if this is not applicable to your video clip enter 'n/a' in this box.
- If the clip is slow to load, look at the file type and file size and comment on this.
- Watch the entire clip and comment on the components that have been included.
- Save your updated forms.

Key terms

Special effects

Special effects are simulations used in videos to accomplish scenes that cannot be achieved by live action or when it would be too expensive to create the actual scene (e.g. the sinking of a cruise ship).

Synchronisation

When two or more events occur in the correct sequence in relation to each other, they are synchronised (e.g. in a video clip the sound of a bomb exploding occurs at the same time as the bomb is seen exploding in the film).

Identifying aspects of the picture quality, special effects, synchronisation and transitions

The table below lists some factors to consider when reviewing the picture quality, special effects, synchronisation and transitions in video clips. You should also try to think of additional factors regarding these factors, to list and comment on.

Feature	Factors to consider about the picture quality, special effects, synchronisation and transitions
Picture quality	• How good is the quality of the images and the colours? Are any images or colours blurred or distorted? • Is the lighting appropriate? Does it allow you to see the images and backgrounds clearly? • Is lighting appropriate for each scene (e.g. in a scary scene, the lighting should be dark and eerie)?
Special effects	• Have special effects been used (e.g. an explosion. a fire, a car crash, a car chase)? Do they add to the drama of the video? Are they appropriate?
Synchronisation	• Do background sound effects coincide with the event in the video clip? • Does speech lag behind the movement of the mouth (or vice versa)?
Transitions	• How smooth is the changeover from one scene to another?

Activity 4: Identify and comment on the picture quality, special effects, synchronisation and transitions...

In this activity you should watch each of your video clips again, this time concentrating on the picture quality, special effects, synchronisation and transitions.

Grading: **Pass** *grade candidates should list the good and not so good features.* **Merit** *grade candidates should provide detailed explanations.* **Distinction** *grade candidates should provide thorough explanations.*

- Continue using the **AO1_ReviewVideoClip** forms saved in Activity 3.
- In the Activity 4 section of the form for each video clip, comment on the good and/or not so good features of the different aspects of each of the following: picture quality, special effects, synchronisation and transition.
- Identify and comment on any other aspects of these features that you can think of.
- Save your updated forms.

Key term

Sound effects

Artificially created or enhanced sounds that are used to emphasise the content of video clips.

Identifying aspects of the volume, sound quality, background sounds and sound effects

The table below lists some factors to consider when reviewing the volume, sound quality, background sounds and sound effects in video clips. You should also try to think of additional factors to list and comment on regarding these features.

Feature	Factors to consider about the volume, sound quality, background sounds and sound effects
Volume	• How appropriate is the volume throughout the clip? • How easily can the volume be adjusted? • How clearly audible is the volume of the speakers? Are speakers' voices drowned by background sounds or sound effects? • Are any changes of volume between speech, music and other sounds smooth and appropriate? • How effective are changes in volume?
Sound quality	• How is the sound quality of foreground and background sounds? Do they synchronise well? • How appropriate is the pitch of speech/lyrics (e.g. do the voices sound realistic or are they too shrill or too deep)? • How appropriate is the pitch of music and other sounds (e.g. is the pitch too high or too low)?
Background sounds	• Have background sounds been used? How appropriate are these? • How do sounds convey the correct mood (e.g. in a happy scene, cheerful music, or in a funeral scene, soft, sombre music)? • How appropriate are any background music, sounds, musical instruments? Are any background music, sounds or musical instruments intrusive and/or distracting? • Are there any background noises or sounds (e.g. clicks, crackles, hisses, rustling) that distract the listener?
Sound effects	• How have sound effects been used to enhance the message in the video (e.g. cars screeching, sirens and other traffics sounds during a police car chase)? • How have different sounds and sound effects been faded in and out? Has fading been used appropriately?
Speech	• How appropriate is the pace of speech (i.e. not too fast for the listener but not too slow so the listener loses interest)? • How easy is it to understand what the actors are saying (e.g. accents not too strong)?
Continuity	• Is there smooth continuity between different scenes?

Activity 5: Identify and comment on the volume, sound quality, background sounds and sound effects...

In this activity you should comment on the volume, sound quality, background sounds and sound effects in the whole clip and of different sounds in the clip.

Grading: grade candidates should list the features. **Merit** *grade candidates should provide detailed explanations.* **Distinction** *grade candidates should provide thorough explanations.*

- Continue using the **AO1_ReviewVideoClip** forms saved in Activity 4.
- In the Activity 5 section of each form, comment on the good and/or not so good features of each of the following features: volume, sound quality, background sounds and sound effects.
- Identify and comment on any other aspects of these features that you can think of.
- Save your updated forms.

Key terms

Title

The text that appears on a screen at the beginning of a movie or in between clips. A title can be displayed on its own screen or can be overlaid on an existing clip.

Credits

The text that displays at the end of a movie. In a longer movie, credits can provide information about those involved in the movie production.

Caption

The text describing an item (e.g. photo, graphic, table or illustration). Captions may be displayed during a TV advert or during a music or promotional video or media clip.

Identifying aspects of titles, credits and captions

The following table lists some factors to consider when reviewing the use of titles, credits and any other captions in video clips. You should also try to think of additional factors to list and comment on regarding these features.

Feature	Factors to consider about titles, credits and captions
Titles and credits	• How appropriate are titles? Are they brief and to the point? How appropriate to the clip are titles or introductions? • Are titles displayed at an appropriate point in the clip (e.g. in some clips the title might be displayed some time into the movie instead of near the beginning)? • Are titles displayed on the screen for an appropriate length of time (i.e. not too long and not too short)? • Have appropriate text style, formatting and text effects been used (e.g. a 'chiller' type font would be appropriate for a scary movie)? • Are credits displayed for an appropriate length of time (e.g. some movie credits roll so quickly that the viewer cannot read any information)?
Captions	• Are captions displayed clearly (e.g. not obscuring important parts of the pictures)? • Have appropriate font sizes, styles and images been used in the captions? • Is the text displayed relevant to the clip? Does it help clarify the message being given in the clip?

Activity 6: Identify and comment on titles, credits and captions...

In this activity you should comment on the use of text on the screen.

Grading: **Pass** *grade candidates should list the features.* **Merit** *grade candidates should provide detailed explanations.* **Distinction** *grade candidates should provide thorough explanations.*

- Continue using the **AO1_ReviewVideoClip** forms saved in Activity 5.
- In the Activity 6 section of the form for each video clip, comment on the good and/or not so good aspects of any titles, credits and other captions.
- Identify and comment on any other aspects of these features that you can think of.
- Save your updated forms.

Commenting on the video clip as a whole

Once you have commented on individual features, you will be quite familiar with the entire video clip. You should then make some comments on the clip as a whole. Here are some points to consider.

- How effectively does the video clip portray the message? For example: Does a movie trailer give too much away or does it entice you to watch the full film? Does a TV advert persuade you to buy the product being advertised? Does a promotional video (e.g. on health) persuade you to change your behaviour?
- How does a movie trailer entice you to watch the full film?
- How does a TV advert persuade you to buy the product being advertised?

- How does the clip succeed in persuading you to do something? For example: how does an anti-smoking trailer persuade you to change your behaviour? How does an advert promoting the rewards of a teaching career persuade you to follow that career?
- How original is the video clip?
- How captivating is the clip? How does it sustain your interest?
- How is the video clip appropriate for the target audience? For example, does a film aimed at children avoid sexual or violent scenes?

You should also comment on whether or not:

- the content is suitable for the aim
- the content is suitable for the target audience
- the clip is of an appropriate length. If it is too long, the listener might lose interest. If it is too short, the listener may miss the message being conveyed.

Explaining the good and not so good features of the video clip as a whole

Here are some examples of comments about a TV advert.

Example of a positive comment

The TV advert was very good at showing how gratifying the job of a nurse can be. It encourages people to want to train to work in the nursing profession.

Example of a negative (not so good) comment

The TV advert was not appropriate for the target audience. It was aimed at school leavers and youngsters thinking about their career path. The advert focused on the pension benefits and job security of nurses – this is not something that would be a priority for young people.

Activity 7: Comment on the video clip as a whole...

In this activity you will complete your review of the video clip.

Grading: **Pass** *grade candidates should list the features.* **Merit** *grade candidates should provide detailed explanations.* **Distinction** *grade candidates should provide thorough explanations.*

- Continue using the **AO1_ReviewVideoClip** forms saved in Activity 6.
- In the Activity 7 section of the form for each video clip, insert a comment below each question about the different aspects of the video clips.
- Comment on the effectiveness and appropriateness on each video clip as a whole.
- Add any other comments about each video clip and what you thought about it.
- Proofread then save your completed review forms.

4. Suggest improvements to a video clip

For a **Merit** grade, you need to suggest possible improvements for the video clips you reviewed and, for a **Distinction** grade, you should suggest a range of valid improvements to help the video clip meet its aims.

In order to suggest improvements, you will need to comment on how the aims are met and if the aims are not met, comment on why they were not met.

When you review the different features of the video clips, you could note down suggested improvements for that aspect or you could do so after you have completed your review of individual aspects and are familiar with the entire clip.

Commenting on the aim

When you have completed your review of each video clip, you should decide if the aim/aims was/were met and how. In doing so, you must remember who the target audience is and decide if the video clip has met the aims for that target audience.

You should refer to your review form in which you identified the aim of the video clip and comment on how the aim is met. To do so, see how many good and not so good features you have identified.

If you have identified more good features than not so good, and have mostly positive comments about the video clip as a whole, it is likely that the video clip has met its aims. On the other hand, if there are more not so good features than good features, and more negative comments about the video clip as a whole, it is possible that the aims have not been met.

Activity 8: Comment on how the aim is met and explain why any aims are not met...

In this activity you will comment on whether the aim(s) of each clip is/are met.

Grading: Pass grade candidates are not required to comment on the aims.

- Read your review form for each video clip.
- For each video clip that you reviewed, comment on whether or not you think the aims are met. To do so, you may use the provided form titled **AO1_SuggestedImprovementsVideoClip** for each clip.
- Comment on how each aim is met. If you think an aim is not met, give reasons why you think it was not met.
- Save the forms – you will update them in the next activity.

Suggesting improvements

You should suggest improvements that are appropriate for the type of video clip you reviewed and appropriate for the intended target audience. You may use the provided form to do so.

When suggesting improvements, you will need to refer the features in your review form that you identified as being not so good. When suggesting improvements, you will find it helpful to:

- copy and paste (or write) the features that you identified as being not so good in your review form into your suggested improvements form, then suggest how each feature could be improved
- list any features that were not originally included in the video clip that would help to improve the video clip.

Here are two example comments about a video clip of a movie trailer that were identified during the review as being not so good:

The file size of the video clip was very large for a 2½ minute trailer; it therefore took a long time to download from the Internet and was also slow to load on my computer.

The trailer did not portray the film as an exciting, action-packed adventure that viewers would be keen to watch. Instead it gave the impression that the movie was a little boring and predictable.

Here are examples of suggested improvements for these two not so good features:

Movie trailers on the Internet should be compressed to keep the file size as small as possible so that the clip can be downloaded and played quickly.

As the aim of the trailer was to attract the audience to the film, the extracts from the film should be from the most tense and thrilling parts of the film without giving too much away.

Activity 9: Suggest possible improvements...

In this activity you will suggest improvements that could help to improve each video clip.

Grading: **Pass** *grade candidates are not required to suggest improvements.* **Merit** *grade candidates should suggest improvements.* **Distinction** *grade candidates should suggest a range of valid improvements that could help the video clip meet its aims.*

- Continue using the form **AO1_SuggestedImprovementsVideoClip** saved in Activity 8.
- Copy the features that you identified as being 'not so good' in your review form, then suggest how that feature could be improved.
- List any features that were not originally included in the video clip that would help to improve the video clip.
- Proofread then save your completed review forms.

Portfolio builder

By reading and understanding the guidelines in this chapter, and working through the activities, you have learned how to review video clips and how to record your review notes. For your own portfolio, you will need to review at least two different types of existing video clips from any of the following types: TV advertisement, movie trailer, music video, online media clips.

You do not need to source the video clips yourself, your teacher/tutor or someone else in your centre may provide you with appropriate clips. You should review two different types of clips (e.g. one TV advert and one movie trailer). You should not review two of the same type of clip (e.g. two TV adverts).

You may use the review forms provided with this book to record your reviews for your portfolio.

Before you begin, you should read the 'How this assessment objective will be assessed…' and 'How to achieve…' sections of this chapter. Discuss with your teacher or tutor what grade he/she would advise you to aim for.

For each clip you review, you should:

- identify and record the good and not so good features – to do so, you should refer to the 'Factors to consider' tables in this chapter and discuss the different features separately, then refer to the section about reviewing the clip as a whole
- identify and record the aim – you should comment on how the aim is met and if the aim is not met, comment on why
- suggest possible improvements for the video clips reviewed.

Good luck!

CHAPTER 11

Assessment Objective 2

Design a Video Clip

Overview

For Assessment Objective 1, you reviewed existing video clips, so you should understand how important it is for a video clip to meet its aims and to be suitable for its target audience. By reviewing existing clips, you learned how to recognise what makes a good clip and also recognise how to identify the weaker features of video clips. You will now draw on your experience to plan your own video clip.

Before you create your own video clip, you must spend some time planning it and producing documentation to show this planning process. Planning is very important and will help to ensure that when you create your video clip, it meets its aims and is appropriate for the target audience. Planning the clip requires more than just making notes in a plan and creating a storyboard. For this unit, you need to use source files to create your clip, so the first thing you need to do before drawing up a plan is either to decide where you will get the components to be included and to source all the files you need, or, if files are provided for you, to select which ones are the most appropriate for your clip.

In this chapter you will learn how to source and organise components for your clip and produce design documents. You will learn how to define the aim and how to describe the audience. You will learn how to plan the production of your video clip by creating a storyboard to show which components you are going to include, the sequence in which they will appear and the other features you intend to use.

Software

Although you won't actually create the clip until the next chapter, you need to know, for your planning, that you will be using a software program called Windows Movie Maker (which is part of the Microsoft Office suite) to create it.

Key term

Storyboard

A storyboard provides a visual layout of events – it is like a large comic of a film. As the name implies, a storyboard tells a story of the film as it will be viewed. It shows the main events that will occur. Pictorial storyboards are used in the film industry. They are produced beforehand to help the film crew visualise the scenes before they film them.

Producing a storyboard will help to identify any possible problems before they happen. Storyboards often include arrows and/or instructions to show the sequence of different scenes.

How this assessment objective will be assessed...

- You will need to describe the aim of the video clip. If you also describe the audience you can achieve a **Merit** grade and if these descriptions are thorough you can achieve a **Distinction**.
- You will also need to provide a storyboard showing the elements to be included in your video clip. If your storyboard shows all elements of your clip, you can achieve a higher grade.
- The grading for this assessment objective will be differentiated by the amount of detail in your description of the aim and audience of the video clip, by how clearly structured your designs are and by how clear your storyboard is.

Skills to use...

You will need to:

- select source files from provided files or find the **components** you will need – source files are the images and/or animations, sound files and video clips that you will need to use to create your video clip
- decide what the **aim** of your video clip will be and describe the aim
- decide who your intended **audience** is and describe the audience
- select the **software** to be used
- create a **storyboard** to show a visual overview of the content of your video clip and the timeline
- show on your storyboard what text (**titles** and **credits**) you will include
- decide the **sequence** in which you will display your source files and show on your storyboard where these will be included in your video clip
- show on your storyboard where you will add **transitions** in your video clip
- show on your storyboard what special **effects** you will use and where these will be used.

How to achieve...

Pass requirements

P1 You will describe the aim of your video clip.

P2 You will produce a simple storyboard covering the main elements.

P3 Your design may lack structure.

Merit requirements

M1 You will describe the aim and audience of your video clip.

M2 You will produce a storyboard covering the main elements.

M3 Your design has a clear structure.

Distinction requirements

D1 You are thorough in your description of the aim and audience for your video clip.

D2 You will produce a storyboard covering all elements.

D3 Your design is well structured.

Understanding how the video clip will be created

In Chapter 12, you will create a video clip using existing source files, also referred to as components or elements. These components are existing video clips, images (clipart, photographs, drawings), sounds and animations.

It is important to understand that this unit is about *creating* video using existing elements. It is *not* about using a video camera to capture (shoot) and produce short films. You will create your video clip on a computer using suitable software and existing source files. In order to produce a plan of the video clip to be created, it is crucial that you know what source files you will use.

1. Source files

You cannot start producing your planning documents until you have decided which source files you will use in your video clip.

Therefore, the first step is to find out what source files are available for you to use in your video clip. It is no good deciding that you are going to produce a video clip to promote a luxury ski resort and skiing holidays in the Alps if you don't have any source videos, sounds and images of skiing in the Alps!

You are not required to create the source elements yourself. You may source these from elsewhere, so before you can begin creating the design documents and storyboard, you need to decide what components to include.

The video clip you will create must be at least 45 seconds long, so ensure that you collect source files that will allow you to create a clip of this length after you have done all the editing.

Note about hardware

So that you can decide what sound files to use, you will need to listen to the sounds on a computer with a sound card. You will also need either speakers or headphones.

Some video clips have sound that was recorded as part of the clip. Others do not. You will need to be able to watch the source videos (e.g. on Windows Media Player) as well as listen to any sounds. You will need access to the volume control settings.

Check with your teacher or tutor that you have the necessary hardware.

Referring to the project scenario

The video clip you will be creating in this book will be based on the project scenario given in the Introduction to this book and is about adventure holidays. You should read this scenario carefully and think about what aspect of the adventure holidays you would like to create the video clip about.

Source video clips about any of the activities that may be available during the adventure holidays would be suitable. Examples are video clips of skiing, scuba diving, mountain biking, water sports, diving, etc.

Preparing folders for the source files

It is a good idea to prepare a main folder for all your source files and subfolders for the different types of files (i.e. videos, sounds and images) to keep your source files organised.

To create a folder in your user area: **File** → **New** → **Folder** → **Backspace** to delete the existing folder name → Type the new folder name you have chosen → **Enter**. Open this folder and create subfolders in the same way.

Activity 10: Prepare folders for your source files...

In this activity you will create and name folders for your source files (components).

- Create a new folder using a suitable folder name (e.g. U23VideoClip).
- Inside this folder, create another three subfolders using the following folder names: **videos**, **sounds** and **images**.

Suitable file formats for video clips

When you are sourcing video clips, you must ensure that the file formats of the clips are suitable for use in Windows Movie Maker.

Some of the video file types that can be used in Windows Movie Maker are: .avi, .mpeg and .wmv.

Other video file types also suitable for use in Windows Movie Maker are: .m1v, .mp2, .mp2v, .mpe, .mpg, .mpv2 and .wm.

WARNING!

Note that .mov files that play in QuickTime player are **not** supported by Windows Movie Maker. These files are common on the World Wide Web, but you are advised **not** to download .mov files. It is possible to convert this and other file types to a file format suitable for use in Windows Movie Maker but this is beyond the syllabus requirements for this unit.

Suitable file formats for sound clips

Similarly, when sourcing sound clips, you must make sure that the file formats are suitable for use in Windows Movie Maker.

Common sound (audio) file types which can be used in Windows Movie Maker are: .wav, .wma and .mp3.

Other audio file types also suitable for use in Windows Movie Maker are: .aif, .aifc, .aiff, .asf, .au, .mp2, .mpa and .snd.

Suitable file formats for images and animations

Image file types which can be used in Windows Movie Maker are: .bmp, .dib, .emf, .gif, .jfif, .jpe, .jpeg, .jpg, .png, .tif, .tiff, and .wmf.

Animations are usually in .gif or .fla format.

All the file extensions listed on this page and their characteristics are explained in Chapter 12, but for now you should make sure that the files you collect for creating your video clip, and which you will refer to in your planning documents, are in any of these formats.

Selecting provided source files

Find out if your teacher or tutor can provide you with source video clips, sound files, images and animations.

If your teacher or tutor cannot provide you with source files, ask at your school/college library, or public library, if they stock CD or DVD photo and/or video libraries. These may contain sound and video clips, images and animations that are either copyright-free or can be used for educational purposes.

If you are provided with a selection of source files or CD/DVDs, you should spend some time looking at all the images, source video clips, animations and listening to sound files that are available. Decide which of these files will be suitable for your project scenario and copy them to your working area.

Bear in mind that your final clip should be at least 45 seconds long, so the total running time for the combined source video files should run for a minimum of about three to five minutes. You will be cutting out unwanted parts of the clips therefore you need to have enough original clips to work with. There is no prescribed maximum clip running time but try not to make your final clip any longer than three or four minutes.

You will need several source video clips, several sound clips, at least one image and/or at least one animation. Sound clips could include music, speech and sound effects (e.g. water bubbles, a narration, aeroplane taking off, etc.).

Using files from other units

If you have completed or are intending to complete other units, you may use the files you created or sourced in other units if they are suitable for the project scenario. Examples of files that could be used from other units are:

Unit 3 Digital imaging – plan and produce computer graphics: graphic images are created and edited in this unit.

Unit 20 Creating animation for the WWW using ICT: an animation is created in this unit.

Unit 22 Creating sound using ICT: a sound file is created in this unit.

Capturing your own video

If you have access to a video camera (or a digital camera that has the facility to take video clips), you could capture your own short video clips but you must ensure that any captured clips relate to your project. You must also find out what file format your video camera or digital camera captures movies in, as you will need to ensure that the file can be imported into Windows Movie Maker. As this unit does not require you to capture your own video and as there are so many different camera models, this skill is not covered in this book.

Sourcing your own files

If you need to find your own files, you can search for them on the Internet but you *must* look on the websites for copyright information. It is important that you find out if you need permission to use the clips. It is your responsibility to ensure that any clips you download are free from copyright or that permission has been given. Refer to the section titled 'Keep a record of files and acknowledge sources' on page 46 in Chapter 3 which covers how to obtain and reference source files. Note that for this unit you are not required to produce a reference of sources, but it is good practice to keep a record for yourself of all files and permission given for all files that you download from the Internet.

How to download video clips from the Internet

There are a number of websites that allow downloading of clips for educational use. You will need to research these. This section refers to two websites which provide free video clips (at the time of publication) that will be suitable for the sample project scenario.

The example video clip created in Chapter 12 is about scuba diving. The clips used were downloaded with permission from **http://www.reefvid.org** which contains free coral reef video clips for educational use.

To search for clips on this site: either click on one of the links on the page or enter a search category in the **Search** box. You can search by *Topic*, *Species* or *Location*. When you have followed the links to a clip, click on **Details** to read more about that clip to ensure it is suitable for your project (e.g. file size, description). The file types on this site are in .avi format (at the time of publication) which are suitable for use in Windows Movie Maker.

Click on **Download File**. You will be prompted to enter your email address in order to download clips.

To download a file: right-click it (a shortcut menu displays) → Select **Save Target As** (a **Save As** window may display, or a window prompting you to **Open** or **Save** may display first) → Click **Save**, and save the file into a folder in your working area using *an appropriate filename that describes the clip*. A **Download complete** dialogue box will display → Click **Close**.

Repeat to download more clips. Play each clip in a media player, e.g. Windows Media Player, as you download it to make sure it is suitable for your project.

The Internet Archive, **http://www.archive.org**, acts as a digital library of websites. It provides free access to researchers, historians, scholars and the general public.

Click the link for **Moving Images** → Click a link for a particular category (e.g. Open Source Movies) → Follow the links to search for suitable video clips. Alternatively, enter your keywords in the **Search** box → Click **Go** → Follow the links to find a suitable movie clip. Some clips can be viewed as thumbnails before downloading. Look for the option to download a file. Make sure that the clip is in a file format that can be used in Windows Movie Maker (some clips on this website are available in more than one file format).

A note about downloading files

If network security policies in your school or centre prevent students from downloading and saving certain types of files, you will need to ask your teacher or tutor to make arrangements for suitable files to be provided for you to use.

Checking source video clips

Once you have downloaded the clips, you should play each one to ensure the content and message it contains are suitable for your project and your intended target audience.

If they are not, it is important that you find other suitable clips before you move on.

Checking the running time of source video clips

The next thing to take note of is the playing time of individual downloaded clips and the total time. The duration of your edited video file must be at least 45 seconds so you must make sure that the total duration of all your clips is long enough for you to edit them to the required length.

Sourcing sound clips

You may use sound files provided by your teacher or tutor. If you have completed or are working towards 'Unit 22 Creating Sound Using ICT', you could use your own created audio clip.

Sound clips can also be found on various sites on the Internet and can be easily sourced from the Microsoft Online website. As with video clips, you must make sure that any clips you download from websites are free from copyright or that permission has been given.

Before you begin searching for sound clips, remember that the sound clips you search for must be suitable for the project scenario and the sounds must be compatible with the content of the video clips that you have already sourced. For example, it would not be appropriate to use a sound clip of a car speeding if the video clip is of a scuba diver! Play the video clips that you have collected before you search for sound files.

To search for suitable files from Microsoft: Go to **http://office.microsoft.com/en-gb/clipart** → In the box to the left of **Search**, type a subject for the type of sound you want to find → Click the arrow to the right of **Search** drop-down list box and select **Sounds**.

Available sounds that meet your chosen search criterion will display. Click on the sound icon  → Listen to the sound and if it is suitable, note down the details (caption, filename and duration) → Click the check box to select that sound (refer to Figure 11.1).

TIP

If the video clips you have downloaded are about scuba diving, suitable search criteria for sound files would be 'scuba diving', 'underwater', 'water', 'ocean', etc.

Figure 11.1: *Selecting a sound file and taking note of the caption, filename and duration.*

When you have selected all the sounds you want, click **Download x items** on the left of the screen below 'Selection Basket' (x being the number of sounds you have selected).

Click the **Download Now** button and follow the on-screen instructions to save the clips.

The sound files from the **Microsoft Online** website will be downloaded into the **My Pictures** folder into a subfolder called **Microsoft Clip Organizer**. This subfolder will open automatically once the clips have been downloaded.

TIP

The sound files in the My Pictures folder will have filenames that do not describe the sound itself. If you display the Details view, in the Downloaded Clips folder, the Caption will provide a description of the sound. Alternatively, look at the notes you made of the caption, filename and duration when downloading the files.

You will find it helpful to rename the sound files in the My Pictures subfolder so that each file has a useful, descriptive name, then copy the renamed sound files from the My Pictures folder into your working area.

Sourcing images and animations

Copyright-free images and animations can be found on a number of websites. Refer to the section titled 'Collect images (photographs, graphics, clipart, animations)' on pages 49–51 in Chapter 3, or search for **photos** or **animations** from the Microsoft Office Online website – the technique is very similar to searching for sounds except that you would select photos or animations from the drop-down list after you have entered your search criterion.

Checking source files

Once you have collated all your source files, you should carry out a final check on the files. Play and listen to every source video clip, play and listen to every audio clip, and view all images and animations, to make absolutely sure that the files are suitable for your project before moving on. Make sure the sounds harmonise with each other and that the sounds will synchronise with the video clips. Make sure that the images and animations are all appropriate to your theme. Do not be concerned if some video clips have attached sound and some do not – you can edit the audio when you create your video clip.

If your files are not appropriate for your aim and/or audience, you will need to find more suitable files later on, so it is important to be certain that your files are appropriate now.

Activity 11: Source and store source files...

In this activity you will source the components you will need to produce your video clip, and that you will refer to in your planning documents.

- Read the project scenario.
- Decide which aspect of the adventure holidays you would like to create the video clip about.
- Find out what files your teacher/tutor is able to provide for you to use. Go through the files and select the video clips, sound files, image(s) and animation(s) which you will use.
- Copy the files into the folders you prepared in your user area.
- If you need to source the files yourself, find suitable video clips, sound files, image(s) and animation(s). Download the files, rename them using suitable filenames and save them into the folders you prepared in your user area.
- Play and listen to EVERY file to make absolutely sure that it is suitable for your project before moving on. If your files are not appropriate for your aim and/or audience, you will have problems later on, so it is important to be certain at this stage that your files are appropriate.

2. Describe the aim of the video clip

You need to decide the purpose of your video clip (i.e. what is your intention for producing the clip?).

You are already familiar with the aim of some existing video clips that you reviewed. You will find it useful to read the section titled 'Identifying the aim of the video clip' and your notes from Activity 2 in Chapter 10.

Your description of the aim of your video clip should make clear *the purpose of your video clip.* The purpose is your *expected outcome* – the *overall objective* of your video clip. The aim you describe at this stage will then guide you when you create the storyboard later so think about your aim carefully. Your aim should be appropriate to the project scenario.

You may use any appropriate style to present the information. As this unit, is a 30-hour unit (referred to as a half unit), you will not have as much time as you would in a full unit, so don't waste time on different document styles – try to keep it simple but clear. Here is an example of a description of the aim of a video clip:

Aim of video clip:

To produce a video clip for a CD-ROM that will be given out at a holiday roadshow. The CD-ROM will include an interactive presentation about adventure holidays for teenage girls and boys aged 12 to 17.

The aim of producing this video clip is to show one of the activities that will be available during the adventure holidays (i.e. scuba diving). The clip aims to show a brief view of the island where the scuba diving will take place and the views of fish and anemone underwater as well as images of scuba divers in their diving clothing with their diving equipment.

This video clip about scuba diving will be included as a Windows Movie File in .wmv format on the CD-ROM. It will also be inserted on the slide about scuba diving in the interactive multimedia presentation that is to be given on a CD-ROM to visitors.

3. Describe the audience for your video clip

You should describe the group of people that your video clip is aimed at (i.e. who do you want the video clip to appeal to?).

Your target audience could be narrow or wide or could be a combination of two categories. A narrow audience would be 'boys aged 14 to 16 with ten A-grades at GCSE'. A wide audience would be 'all Londoners'. A combination of two categories would be 'teenagers in the West Midlands area'.

If your target audience is wide, you could describe the main target audience and explain who the secondary audience is. For example, the main target audience could be 'teenagers interested in adventure holidays' and your secondary audience could be 'teenagers who can swim and would like to explore the underwater world'.

Here is an example of a description of the target audience for a video clip:

Target audience for video clip about scuba diving:

The target audience is teenage girls and boys aged 12 to 17 who are interested in adventure holidays, particularly those who can swim and would like to try scuba diving for the first time.

4. The plan

Key dates

Your teacher or tutor will probably have given you some deadlines for the completion of your work. In your plan it is a good idea to make a note of all key dates. You could enter these as a numbered list as shown in the example below.

Key dates:

1 Source files to be collected by: [enter date here]
2 Plan to be completed by: [enter date here]
3 Storyboard to be completed by: [enter date here]
4 Begin creating video clip on: [enter date here]
5 Finish creating video clip on: [enter date here]
6 Produce test plan by: [enter date here]
7 Test video clip by: [enter date here]
8 Action improvements by: [enter date here]

Initial ideas

By now, you will have decided which source files you will use and you should have a good idea of the content of these files (particularly the source video clips). You should have decided what your video clip will be about, and you should have a fairly good idea of its aim and audience. When you create your plan, it is a good idea to make notes of your initial ideas for the video clip. Here are some examples questions you might ask yourself to help you with your initial ideas:

- Will you include a title? If so, what will the title be? Will you display it on a plain back-ground or will you overlay it on an existing video clip?
- How many different scenes will you include in your clip?
- Where will you include the image(s) and/or animation(s)? (As a minimum, you need to include one image and/or one animation.)
- What background sounds will you use for each of the different source video clips?
- Will you have a screen showing credits at the end of the clip?

Here is an example of some initial ideas you might make in your plan for your early ideas before you create the storyboard:

Scene 1	*Photo of scuba diver*	*Title: 'Scuba Diving'*
Scene 2	*Animation of scuba diving*	*Narration*
Scene 3	*Video clip of aerial view*	*Sound of aeroplane*
Scene 4	*Video clip of boat to site*	*Sound of boat*
Scene 5	*Video clip of fish underwater*	*Sound of underwater*
Scene 6	*Video clip of diver and shark*	*Sound of scuba diver 1*
Scene 7	*Video clip of divers in cave*	*Sound of scuba diver 2*
Scene 8	*Video clip of anemone*	*Sound of underwater bubbles*
Scene 9	*Plain blue background*	*Credit: 'The End'*

Activity 12: Describe the aim and audience...

In this activity you will:

- create your plan for the video clip that you are going to create
- describe the aim and audience
- include other details of your planning.

*Grading: Pass level candidates should describe the aim of the video clip; **Merit** level candidates should describe the aim and audience; **Distinction** level candidates should provide a thorough description of the aim and audience.*

- Read the project scenario given in the Introduction to this book.
- Create a new document and describe the aim of the video clip you are going to create.
- Describe the intended target audience for the video clip.
- Make a note of the important dates that you need to work to when planning, creating and testing your video clip.
- Write down your initial ideas for what you will include in your clip and where you will include the image(s), animation(s), video clips and sounds. Think about how many different scenes you will have in your clip.
- Save your plan using a suitable filename (e.g. PlanVideoClip).

5. Understanding storyboards

The storyboard layout

A storyboard can be produced in several ways, for example:

- you can display a **summary storyboard** on one page which shows an overview of all components to be displayed in the clip, the order they will be displayed and where the source files are saved. Then, accompanying the summary storyboard, you could have a more **detailed storyboard** on several pages, with each page showing two or three scenes with more detail of the content of each scene and details of transitions, effects, titles and credits.
- you can create an **overview storyboard** which shows all the different scenes and the sequence of all components. It will show the filename, name and location of the source file folders. The details on this overview will be brief but sufficient for the creator of the clip and others to know what will go where. It will show the type (video or image, etc.) and name of the component, duration of clips, text for titles and credits. It will also show where transitions and effects will be used and the name of the transition or effect. Refer to the example provided in .pdf format in the **Unit23Forms** folder.

You should already know how many different scenes you intend to have – you have noted down some initial ideas in your plan. The number of different scenes will be the same as the number of different boxes on your overview storyboard.

As your completed video clip needs to be at least 45 seconds long, which is not long at all, creating an overview storyboard should be sufficient. However, if you wish to provide more detail by using a summary storyboard and a detailed storyboard that is fine.

Using a template

A template of an **overview storyboard** has been provided for you. This can be downloaded from the Student Resources page on the Payne-Gallway website: **www.payne-gallway.co.uk**. The template is contained in the **Unit23StudentResources** folder within the subfolder **Unit23Forms**. It is provided in Microsoft Word format; you can use it in a number of ways, for example:

- you can print the template and add sketches and notes by hand – it does not matter if your drawings are rough (stick drawings are fine!). You should not spend too much time producing an artistic storyboard, but make sure your handwriting is legible.
- you can use the template to produce your storyboard on the computer – type your notes in the text boxes, and if you have good graphics skills you could take a screen print of the clips and insert the images into the thumbnails on the storyboard (but this is quite an advanced skill); otherwise print the storyboard and draw sketches of the clip content to give a visual idea of the clip.

If you wish you can create your own storyboard or use one provided by your teacher or tutor. Use any method that you find easy and quick, but whatever method you choose, note that it is worth spending time producing a clear storyboard for your video clip because it will help you when you start to create the clip.

What to include on the storyboard

A well-produced storyboard should display clearly which components will be included, where they will be included and the sequence of each scene in your video clip. Your storyboard should include sufficient detail for someone else to see what the final product will look like when finished. A simple rule is that if a component is going to be included in the video clip, it must be shown on the storyboard. There should not be much difference between the content and features shown on the storyboard and the content and features of the completed video clip.

TIP

A useful test to find out if your storyboard is clear and displays all components and features is to see if someone else would be able to use your storyboard to create the video clip. Remember your ideas must be noted on paper, not in your head!

As a minimum, your storyboard should show the following:

- content of the video clip
- timeline
- text (titles and credits) (**Distinction** only)
- components: image(s), animation(s), sounds, video clips
- transitions
- special effects (higher levels only).

Each of these is explained below.

Content of the video clip

The content is everything that is included in the video clip.

Content includes the components which are your source files, as well the title, credit, transitions and effects.

Timeline

The timeline is a chronological display of all the components: source video clips, sounds, image(s) and animation(s). The timeline must also show the duration in seconds of each component (i.e. how long each image, animation, sound and video clip will display on the screen).

Text (titles and credits)

A **title** is text that appears on a screen at the beginning of a movie or in between clips. The title plays for a specified amount of time. A title can be displayed on a background or can be overlaid on an existing video clip.

A **credit** is text that displays at the end of a clip. In a longer movie, credits show names of people involved in the movie production. In shorter productions, such as your video clip or in cartoons, a credit can simply be 'The End' or 'Produced by xx [producer's name/your name].

Components

Components are the source files that you will use to create your video clip. They include the source video clips, sound files, image(s) and animation(s). Earlier in this chapter you sourced or selected and organised your components. Remember you will need more than one source video clip and more than one source sound, but a minimum of one image and/or one animation will be enough. On the storyboard, you should display the filename and the file type of each component.

Transitions

A transition is a visual change between two separate scenes. Often it provides a smooth change between clips in a movie (rather than the abrupt change of one clip ending and another starting).

Special effects

Special effects refer to video effects. A video effect is a special filter that can be added to an image, animation or video clip (e.g. blur, ease in or ease out, fade in or fade out). A video effect changes how the picture or clip displays on the screen.

Some transitions and special effects are described in more detail later in this chapter.

Other information to show on the storyboard

Your storyboard should also display the following:

- your name
- final video clip filename
- file type
- source files folder name
- folder location
- subfolder name for source images and animations
- subfolder name for source video clips
- subfolder name for source sound files
- other notes (e.g the total running time)
- detail of clips to be cut or edited.

You could enter this information in a table with the headings shown below so it is clear, for example:

Video clip name	Original duration	New duration	Section to be cut or edited

Transitions and effects available in Windows Movie Maker

On your storyboard, you need to show where and what transitions and effects you will use. As you have not yet learned how to use Windows Movie Maker, you probably won't know what transitions and effects are available! The figures below show the transitions and effects available in Windows Movie Maker.

Bars
Bow Tie, Horizontal
Bow Tie, Vertical
Checkerboard, Across
Circle
Circles
Diagonal, Box Out
Diagonal, Cross Out
Diagonal, Down Right
Diamond
Dissolve
Eye
Fade
Fan, In
Fan, Out
Fan, Up
Filled V, Down
Filled V, Left
Filled V, Right
Filled V, Up
Flip
Heart
Inset, Down Left
Inset, Down Right
Inset, Up Left
Inset, Up Right
Iris
Keyhole
Page Curl, Up Left
Page Curl, Up Right
Pixelate
Rectangle
Reveal, Down
Reveal, Right
Roll
Shatter, In
Shatter, Right
Shatter, Up Left
Shatter, Up Right
Shrink, In
Slide
Slide, Up Center
Spin
Split, Horizontal
Split, Vertical
Star, 5 Points
Stars, 5 Points
Sweep, In
Sweep, Out
Sweep, Up
Wheel, 4 Spokes
Whirlwind
Wipe, Narrow Down
Wipe, Narrow Right
Wipe, Normal Down
Wipe, Normal Right
Wipe, Wide Down
Wipe, Wide Right
Zig Zag, Horizontal
Zig Zag, Vertical

Figure 11.2: *Transitions available in Windows Movie Maker.*

Blur
Brightness, Decrease
Brightness, Increase
Ease In
Ease Out
Fade In, From Black
Fade In, From White
Fade Out, To Black
Fade Out, To White
Film Age, Old
Film Age, Older
Film Age, Oldest
Film Grain
Grayscale
Hue, Cycles Entire Color Spectrum
Mirror, Horizontal
Mirror, Vertical
Pixelate
Posterize
Rotate 90
Rotate 180
Rotate 270
Sepia Tone
Slow Down, Half
Smudge Stick
Speed Up, Double
Threshold
Watercolor

Figure 11.3: *Effects available in Windows Movie Maker.*

Name:	**Candy Date**
Final video clip filename:	ScubaDivingClip
File type:	.wmv
Source files folder name:	Unit23_product
Folder location:	C:\MyDocuments\CandyDate
Subfolder name for source images and animations:	images
Subfolder name for source video clips:	video_downloads
Subfolder name for source sound files:	sounds
Other notes:	Total running time 1 minute

Video clip name	**Original duration**	**New duration**	**Section to be cut or edited**
Beach	**40 secs**	**3 secs**	**Split clip. Delete first 27 secs of clip. Delete last 5 secs from the end. Trim the remaining clip to be 3 secs. Make sure all sections with people swimming are cut out.**
Aerialview	**17 secs**	**10 secs**	**Cut out 5 secs at end of clip where wing is flapping. Cut approximately 8 secs from the beginning where part of plane is blocking island view. Trim rest of the clip to keep 10 secs.**

Example of other details on storyboard

Producing your storyboard

You are ready to start creating your storyboard. Before you begin, make sure that you understand video storyboards, have sourced and organised your components and have looked at the example of the completed storyboard which is available in the **Unit23StudentResources** folder in the subfolder **Unit23Forms**. Note, your storyboard will have sketched drawings instead of screen shots as shown in the example.

1. Open the template document that you are going to use.
2. Read the project scenario.
3. Read your plan. Remind yourself of the aim and audience. Read the initial ideas you noted down.
4. Remind yourself of the content of all your components – look at all the images and animations, listen to all the sound clips, watch all the source video clips.
5. Decide the order that you will display your source video clips, image(s) and animation(s).
6. Decide which sounds will play with each clip or image.
7. Decide what the filename of your completed video clip will be.

Activity 13: Produce a storyboard...

In this activity you will produce a storyboard to show the content of your planned video clip.

You may use or adapt the template provided with this book titled **AO2_VideoStoryboard_Template** or you may create your own storyboard. The instructions below refer to the template provided with this book.

- Read the project scenario given in the Introduction to this book.
- Refer to the plan you created in Activity 11.
- Produce an overview storyboard showing the number of scenes in your video clip.
- Below each thumbnail enter brief details of the:
  - type of component, the filename and file type (e.g. component: **video, aerialview.avi**)
  - length of time (**clip duration**) that the clip or image will display on screen
  - name of the **sound** file and the file type that will play when the clip displays on screen (e.g. sound: **IntroFoz.wav**). If a sound clip will play for longer than the duration of one video clip, it is helpful to show that the same sound clip will be continued
  - **duration** that the sound will play
  - type of **effect** that you intend to use. If you are not planning to apply an effect, either enter 'none' or delete the effect row.
- Between each thumbnail, if you intend to display a transition, enter the type of transition you intend to display (e.g. page curl up, bars, etc.). If you are not going to display a transition, enter 'none' (or delete the transition arrow and text box).
- Save your storyboard in your user area using a suitable filename.

- Enter your name in the template header.
- Enter the following on page 2:
  - The filename you intend to give to your video clip.
  - The name of the folder where the files are saved.
  - The name of the subfolders in which your source files are saved.
- Enter any other relevant notes (e.g. whether or not you are going to add narration to your sound clip).
- In the table on page 2 of your storyboard, enter details of clips that are too long and need to be cut.
- Enter details of clips that need to be edited.
- Remember that your storyboard should show enough detail for someone else to be able to create the video clip from the information you have given.
- Save your storyboard.
- An *example* of a completed storyboard in .pdf format has been provided in the **Unit23StudentResources** folder, in the subfolder **Unit23Forms**. You may wish to compare your storyboard to the example.

Portfolio builder

By reading and understanding the guidelines in this chapter, and working through the activities, you will have learned how to plan and design a video clip. You should now be ready to prepare your source files and produce your own planning documents for your portfolio.

It is very important that you spend time planning your video clip at this stage. You will probably be tempted to start creating it, but planning it and producing planning documentation is essential!

Before you can start working on your plans, you should discuss with your teacher or tutor what the topic of your planned video clip will be. So far in this unit you have used the given example project scenario, but now you will need your own scenario. The next stage is to discuss with your teacher or tutor whether he/she will provide you with source components or not. If your teacher/tutor can provide you with files, you need to play the source video and sound clips and look through the images and animations and decide which ones to use use.

If your teacher/tutor advises you to source your own components, that will be your next task. You should find suitable video and audio clips and suitable images and/or animations. Once you have collected all your source files, you should create folders in your working area and organise your files into folders. You must check that all source components are in file formats that can be imported into Windows Movie Maker. Play and listen to your video and audio clips and check the images and animations again. This is important because having appropriate components will make the process of planning, creating and testing much smoother for you.

Next, you should read the 'How this assessment objective will be assessed…' and 'How to achieve…' sections of this chapter. Discuss with your teacher/tutor what grade he/she advises you to aim for.

Now you are ready to start working on your planning documents!

In your plan, describe clearly the aim and audience of the video clip that you intend to create. Include the key dates that you need to work to in your plan.

Create a storyboard to show a visual overview of your video clip. You may use or adapt the storyboard template provided with this book. You will be using Windows Movie Maker to create your clip, so make a note of this on your storyboard as it is required in the syllabus. Remember to write down all your ideas – your plans should not be in your head! Your storyboard must show:

- the content of the clip including the different source components (i.e. sounds, videos, images and animations)
- the timeline
- text (titles and credits)
- transitions
- special effects.

When you have completed your plan and storyboard, ask your teacher/tutor to look at your plan and storyboard. Ask him/her whether they would be able to use your plan and storyboard to create the video clip.

Good luck!

Assessment Objective 3

Create a Video Clip

Overview

In this chapter you will create the video clip that you designed in Chapter 11 (Assessment Objective 2). To ensure that your video clip meets its aims and is suitable for your target audience, you will find it helpful to read your review notes from Chapter 10 (Assessment Objective 1). The video clip you will create in this chapter will be based on the sample project scenario given in the Introduction to this book.

For this unit you are not required to create every element for your own video clip yourself. You can source the components (images, animations, video, sound) from elsewhere then import the components into the software and edit them to create your own video clip. Sourcing of components for the video clip is covered in Chapter 11.

To create your video clip, also referred to as a movie clip, you will use a software program called Microsoft Windows Movie Maker. This program is easy to use and is included with Microsoft Windows XP. This program's features (e.g. menus, icons) and techniques (e.g. drag and drop, right-click) are very similar to other Microsoft Windows programs that you will be familiar with.

How this assessment objective will be assessed...

You need to create a video clip based on the design documentation you have already created in Chapter 11. This assessment objective will be assessed by how you make use of importing and editing components into your video clip. You will also be graded by the range of editing techniques you use, the features you include in your video clip, and whether or not all these elements work as intended. Your video clip should be fit for purpose.

- As a minimum, you need to create a video clip of at least 45 seconds in length, into which you will import components (image/animation, video, sound), edit clips, add transitions, add a soundtrack and export the clip in a suitable file format.
- To achieve the higher grades, your video clip must be appropriate and you should also add effects and titles.
- For a **Distinction** grade, you will need to add narration as well as split and/or trim clips, and the clip must also meet its identified aims.

Skills to use...

You will need to:

- create a project folder and subfolders within Windows Movie Maker for your source files (videos, images, sounds) and **import** these components
- check video and sound clip **properties**
- add **video** clips, **images** and **animations** to a movie project
- **edit** clips (including splitting, trimming and combining clips)
- add **transitions** and **effects**
- add **sound** clips and **narration** to a movie project
- add **titles** and **credits**
- **save** the final movie clip (export) in a suitable file format.

How to achieve...

Pass requirements

P1 You will create a video clip which is at least 45 seconds in length.

P2 You will make some use of importing components, editing clips, transitions and a soundtrack.

P3 Some elements may not work as intended.

P4 You will export the video clip in a suitable file format.

Merit requirements

M1 You will create a video clip which is at least 45 seconds in length. The video clip must be appropriate.

M2 You will make good use of importing components, editing clips, transitions and effects, titles and a soundtrack.

M3 Most elements will work as intended.

M4 You will export the video clip in a suitable file format.

Distinction requirements

D1 You will create a video clip which is at least 45 seconds in length. The video clip must be appropriate and must meet the identified aims.

D2 You will make good use of importing components, editing clips, splitting/trimming clips, transitions and effects, titles and a soundtrack/narration.

D3 All elements must work as intended.

D4 You will export the video clip in a suitable file format.

Notes for Tutors/Centres – Windows Movie Maker version

This chapter is written for version 2 of Windows Movie Maker (the latest version available at the time of writing this book). Please check the version that learners will be using. In Windows Movie Maker, click the Help menu → About Windows Movie Maker. The version number is displayed on a window – version2 begins with 2, e.g. Windows ® Movie Maker Version 2.1.4026.0 (refer to Figure 12.1).

Figure 12.1: *Checking the version of Windows Movie Maker.*

If required, the latest version of Windows Movie Maker can be downloaded from the Microsoft website or from within Windows Movie Maker: Click the Help menu → Windows Movie Maker on the Web → Follow the on-screen instructions.

Sound card and speakers/headphones

All candidates will need to add a soundtrack to their created video clip, so they will need a sound card and speakers or headphones. Candidates should have access to the volume control settings.

Distinction level candidates will need to add narration, so they will need a microphone.

Teacher and tutors are also advised to check the **Sounds and Audio Device Settings** in the Control Panel.

Files used in this chapter

For the activities and screen prints in this chapter the following video clips were downloaded from the ReefVid site (**http://www.reefvid.org**). These were renamed as shown below. All video file types are .avi format. Refer to Chapter 11 for guidelines on how to download and save source video clips from this site.

Topic	Clip title	Renamed as
Anemones	Red and black anemonefish	Anemone
Divers	Diver surveying whilst shark passes behind	Diver+Shark
Field activities	Boat journey to dive site	ToDiveSite
Reef fish	School of surgeonfishes	SurgeonFish
Islands	Beach on Lifou	Beach
Islands	Aerial views of St John and St Thomas	Aerialview
Caves	Caves in reef	Diversincave

The following sound clips were downloaded from the Microsoft Office Online website (**http://office.microsoft.com/en-us/clipart/default.aspx**).

Caption	Filename	Renamed as
Underwater sound	j0074970.wav	underwater
Ocean waves	j0388289.wav	oceanwaves
Scuba diver 1	j0074968.wav	scubadiver1
Scuba diver 2	j0074969.wav	scubadiver2

The following image and animation were also downloaded from the Microsoft Office Online website and renamed as shown.

Search category	Filename	Renamed as
Scuba diver	j0255531.jpg	scubadiver
Scuba diving	j0309766.gif	underwater

Other components (video clips, images and sound) of scuba divers and diving which you may use as practice are provided in the **Unit23StudentResources** folder in the subfolder **PracticeFiles**.

Practice activities and files

The activities in this chapter must be completed in sequence.

By now, you should have sourced all your files. To learn the skills for creating a video clip, you may:

- download the files listed on page 198 and work through the activities in this chapter
- use your own files, or
- use the practice files provided.

Referring to the project scenario

The project scenario is about activity holidays. The video clip created in the examples in this chapter will be about one of the activities on offer (i.e. scuba diving). However, your clip need not be about scuba diving – you may decide to create a clip relating to another aspect of the activity holidays.

Evidence for this assessment objective

To allow the moderator to view your video clip, you and/or your teacher/tutor could make available your product electronically (e.g. on a CD-ROM, memory stick or laptop). This would be much simpler than attempting to provide printed evidence (Windows Movie Maker does not have an option to print).

You will need to show evidence of the edits (e.g. of splitting, trimming and using effects). To do so you need you will learn how to save the clips using different filenames to show the various stages of compiling and editing.

It is possible to take screen prints of the edits before and after but it would be easier for you to save the movie project with a different filename to show the interim stage after each edit.

If you need to learn how to take screen prints refer to the section **Producing screen prints** in Chapter 4, Assessment Objective 4, pages 74–75.

You will need to export your final clip in a suitable file format. Ideally, this final clip should also be available electronically for the moderator to view.

An introduction to Windows Movie Maker

To start Windows Movie Maker: Click **Start** → **All Programs** → **Windows Movie Maker** (in Windows XP Professional). At the top of the Windows Movie Maker screen you will see the menu bar and the **Toolbar** – they are similar to those in other Microsoft programs. On the left of the screen, you will either see the **Collections** pane or the **Movie Tasks** pane (Figure 12.2). If neither pane is visible, click the **Collections** [Collections] or the **Tasks** [Tasks] button on the Toolbar.

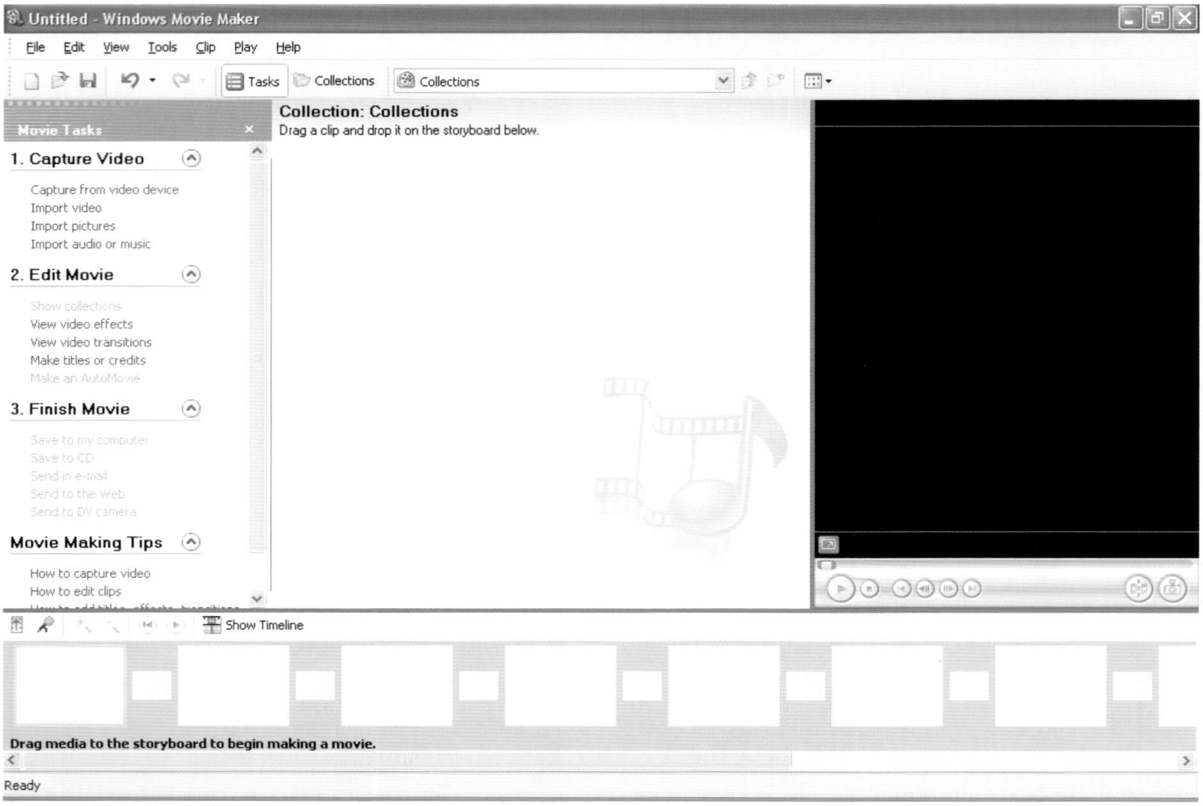

Figure 12.2: The Windows Movie Maker window.

Movie Tasks pane

In the **Movie Tasks** pane, you will find a number of different shortcuts to perform different functions within Windows Movie Maker. Figure 12.2 shows all the shortcuts for **Capture Video**, **Edit Movie**, etc., because each arrow is pointing upwards. To display the shortcuts for other options, click the downward pointing arrow.

Collections pane

If you click the Collections button on the Toolbar, the **Collections** pane will display on the left of the screen. There are three main Collections that come with Windows Movie Maker: **Video Effects**, **Video Transitions** and **Collections**. You cannot rename, move or delete any of these three preset options.

- **Video Effects**: when you select this option the available effects will display in the **Contents** pane in the centre of the screen. To see how the effect will display in your movie, you must select the effect in the **Contents** pane, then click the **Play** button at the bottom of the **Preview** window on the right of the screen.
- **Video Transitions**: select this option to see the different transitions available in Windows Movie Maker. Thumbnails will display in the Contents pane. To see how the transition will display in your movie, you must select the transition in the **Contents** pane, then click the **Play** button at the bottom of the **Preview** window.
- **Collections**: this section will be empty when you first start Windows Movie Maker. You can add additional Collections (folders) to help you organise your source clips.

To resize any panes on your screen, simply click and drag the dividing bar between the panes.

Storyboard and timeline views

At the bottom of the screen, there are two different views available for your movie project: **Storyboard** view (Figure 12.3) or **Timeline** view (Figure 12.4).

Figure 12.3: *The Windows Movie Maker Storyboard view.*

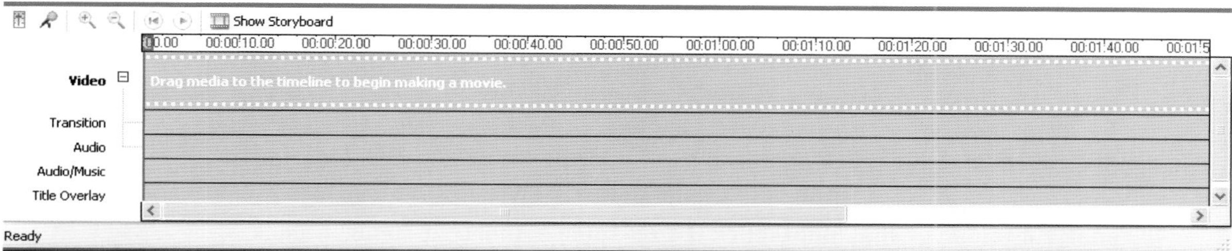

Figure 12.4: *The Windows Movie Maker Timeline view.*

To switch between views, click the **Show Timeline** Show Timeline or **Show Storyboard** Show Storyboard button in the bottom pane.

Storyboard view is the default view in Windows Movie Maker. This view displays the sequence of video clips and any video transitions or effects that you apply. Audio clips are not displayed in this view. Storyboard view is different to the storyboard that you create when planning your video clip!

Timeline view displays the video clips as well as audio clips and transitions and effects. Time is displayed as hours:minutes:seconds:hundreths of a second (h:m:s:hs, e.g. 00:00:40.00). In Timeline view, you can modify the duration of audio and video clips, volume of audio clips and record narration.

Also in Timeline view, if a plus symbol displays to the right of **Video** **Video** ⊞, click the plus to display the **Transition** and **Audio** options for the video clip.

Organising your collections

Collections are containers for your clips. They work like folders that you use in other Microsoft programs and in Windows.

It is a good idea to create a folder in the **Collections** pane for your project and subfolders (within the project folder) for your source files (digital images, downloaded or captured video clips and sound (audio) files) that you will use to create your video clip.

Creating folders

Figure 12.5: *Preparing folders for your collection.*

To create a new folder for your collections: Ensure the Collections pane is displayed → right-click on **Collections** to display a shortcut menu → Click **New Collection** New Collection → Delete the text **New Collection** and type a suitable name for your project folder → Press **Enter** (refer to Figure 12.5). Alternatively, click the **Tools** menu → Select **New Collection Folder** → Type a folder name → Press **Enter**.

To create a subfolder within this folder: Right-click on the folder name you have just created → Select **New Collection** from the shortcut menu and type a suitable subfolder name. You should create one subfolder each for **images**, **videos** and **sounds**.

The option or folder currently selected in the **Collections** pane will also display on the Toolbar to the right of the **Collections** button.

> **TIP**
>
> To move a folder or a file, click and drag the folder or file to the new location in the Collections pane.
>
> To rename a folder or file: Right-click it to display a shortcut menu → Click Rename → type a new name → Press Enter.

Activity 13: Start Windows Movie Maker and create folders...

In this activity you will:

- familiarise yourself with the Windows Movie Maker window
- create folders for your collections.

1. Start Windows Movie Maker and select the **Tasks** pane. View the options below the three sections, **Capture Video**, **Edit Movie** and **Finish Movie**.
2. Display the Collections pane. View the **Video Effects** available. Click the scroll bar to the right of the Contents pane to see all the different video effects available. Select different effects to view it in the Preview window.
3. Select **Video Transitions** and view the different transitions available.
4. Create a folder for your project. For the examples in this chapter the folder name is **Project1_ScubaDiving**.
5. In your project folder, create three subfolders called **images**, **sounds** and **videos**.
6. View the **Storyboard** and **Timeline** views. In Timeline view, click on the plus symbol to the right of Video **Video** ⊞ to expand the options for Video.

Understanding projects, movies and source files in Windows Movie Maker

Key terms

Movie

The term used by Windows Movie Maker for a video clip.

Project

A project is not the same as a movie (or video clip). Within a project, you import different types of media (e.g. source video files, images and sound files) into your collections. You then decide how you will use the collections in your project to create your movie and what transitions, effects, etc. you will apply.

When you save a project, it is saved with a .mswmm file extension. You can close your project at any time and when you re-open it, it will be in the same state as when you last used it.

Although you can work on several projects at the same time, we will work on just one in this chapter.

It is important to understand that a project does **not** contain your source files nor does it contain a copy of your finished movie. Your source files are the files you saved in your working area on the computer. Any editing you carry out in Windows Movie Maker does **not** change your source files. Windows Movie Maker must have access to these files in your working area. You must **not** move or delete any of your source files because Windows Movie Maker will not be able to find the file when you create your final video clip. Even though you will import your source files into Windows Movie Maker, the program makes reference to the source files in your user area. If you move or delete a file from your working area, when you open that project in Windows Movie Maker, the file will be represented by a cross as shown in Figure 12.6.

Figure 12.6: *Windows Movie Maker cannot make reference to a source file deleted in the working area.*

Files for your project

You can add content to your Windows Movie Maker project either by capturing content directly in Windows Movie Maker or by importing existing digital media files (i.e. source video clips, digital images and sound (audio) files) that were created in other programs. In this chapter, we will import existing files that you have already saved in your working area.

Windows Movie Maker supported image file types

The following table describes image file types that can be imported into Windows Movie Maker.

File extension	Definition	Description
.bmp	bitmap image	A common file format used for print-quality images.
.dib	device independent bitmap image	A generic Windows bitmap graphic, similar to a .bmp file.

File extension	Definition	Description
.emf	enhanced Windows metafile format	A generic vector graphic
.gif	graphics interchange format	A common format that can be used in most programs. It Is used for Web graphics and screen presentations.
.jfif	jpeg file interchange format	A bitmap graphic using a jpeg compression method.
.jpe, .jpg or .jpeg	joint photographic experts group	A common format that can be used in most programs. It is an ideal format for photographs, images for the Web and screen presentations.
.png	portable network graphics	A compressed file format similar to .jpg format.
tiff or tif	tagged image file format	A file format that supports transparency and can store layers.
.wmf	windows metafile	A graphic format developed by Microsoft. It has been mostly replaced by standard formats such as .gif and .jpg.

Windows Movie Maker supported video file types

The following table describes video file types that can be imported into Windows Movie Maker.

File extension	Definition	Description
.asf	advanced systems format	A media file format developed by Microsoft for streaming media.
.avi	audio video interleave	A video container or wrapper format created by Microsoft. It often uses less compression than other similar formats (e.g. .mpeg and .mov).
.m1v	mpeg-1 video	Video file based on the mpeg format.
.m2v	mpeg-2 video	Video only, without audio, encoded using mpeg-2 compression.
.mpe	mpeg movie	Video encoded in mpeg format.
.mpeg	mpeg video	A common video format standardised by the Moving Picture Experts Group (mpeg). Often used for creating movies that are distributed over the Internet.
.mpg	mpeg video	Similar to .mpeg format.
.mpv2	mpeg-2 video stream	Video clip with audio and video compression.

File extension	Definition	Description
.wm	windows media	Windows Media audio or video file. May contain audio, video or both, formatted for Windows Media Player.
.wmv	windows media video	Video or audio file compressed with Windows Media compression.

Windows Movie Maker supported sound file types

The following table describes sound (audio) file types that can be imported into Windows Movie Maker.

File extension	Definition	Description
.aif or .aiff	audio interchange file format	Uncompressed audio format on Apple Macintosh computers. It is supported by most computer systems, but is not as common as .wav format.
.aifc	compressed audio interchange file	CD-quality audio file, similar to .wav.
.au	audio file	Audio file created on a Sun Microsystems or Unix-based machine.
.mp2	mpeg layer ii compressed audio file	Audio File using mpeg Layer II compression.
.mp3	mpeg1 layer 3	MP3 is an acronym for MPEG audio layer 3. MPEG: Motion (or moving) picture experts group. A compressed audio format that is a popular way to store music. It can compress audio with little degradation in quality.
.mpa	mpeg audio	A compressed audio file using MPEG Layer I, II or III compression.
.snd	sound file	A generic sound format used by a variety of programs.
.wav	windows wave format	The default uncompressed audio format on Windows. This format is supported on almost all computer systems.
.wma	windows media audio	A compressed audio file format developed by Microsoft. It is similar to .mp3 format and is often used for playing music downloaded from the Internet.

Importing your source video files

Splitting a video clip during importing

When importing video clips, you can choose to have a video file separated into smaller, more manageable clips – smaller clips are created in an existing video file through a process called 'clip detection'.

1 In Windows Movie Maker, select **Tasks** [Tasks] on the Toolbar to display the **Movie Tasks** pane.
2 Below the section **1. Capture Video**, click **Import video** → Locate the folder containing your source video files. (To import more than one file, hold down the **Ctrl** key while you select the files you want to import.)
3 In the **Import File** dialogue box, untick or tick, as required, the check box for **Create clips for video files**. (To keep each clip as one continuous clip, the check box should be blank.)

TIP

If you untick the option to split (see Step 3), the importing will be much quicker and you can auto-split the file after importing if you wish to do so. You can also split the file yourself during the editing.

4 Click the **Import** button (refer to Figure 12.7).

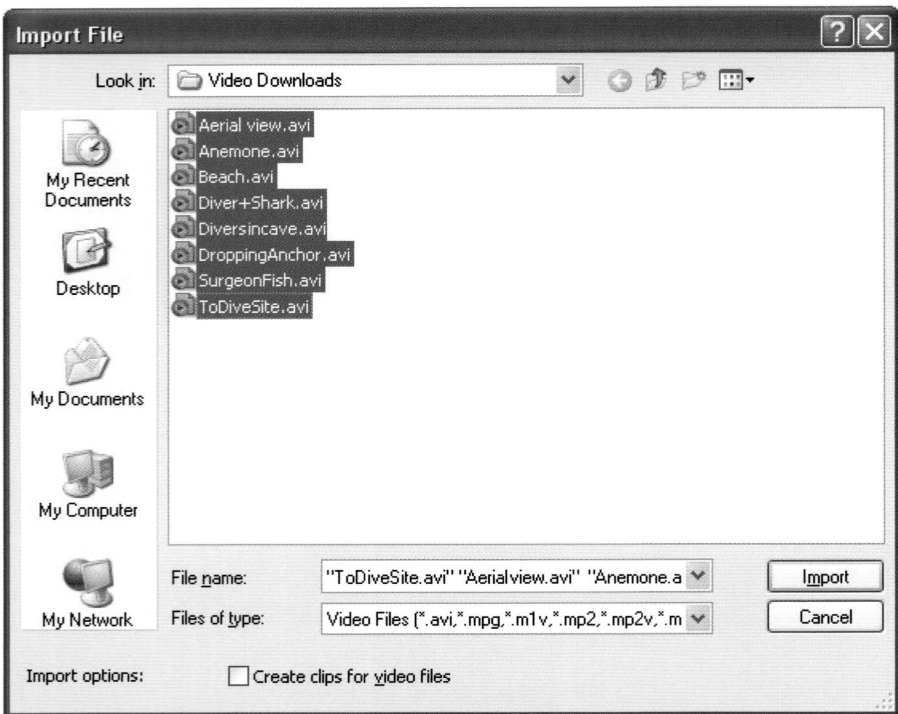

Figure 12.7: *Importing video files – the option to* ***Create clips for video files*** *is not selected.*

Auto-splitting clips during importing

If the option to **Create clips for video files** was ticked, the importing will take a little longer as Windows Movie Maker will go through each file deciding where to split it. While the clips are being imported, an **Import** window will display (refer to Figure 12.8).

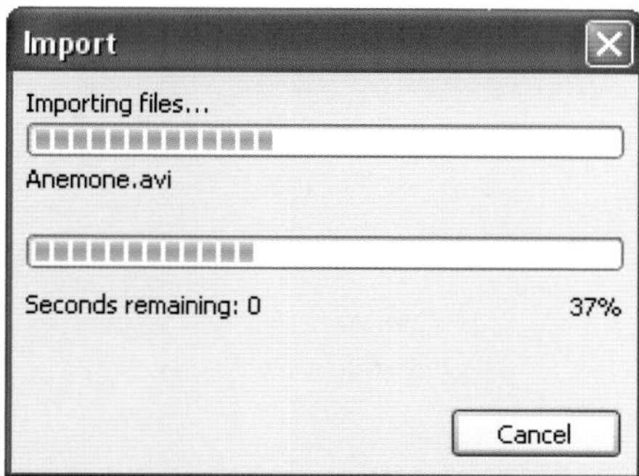

Figure 12.8: *A file being split during importing (optional).*

Windows Movie Maker will divide clips into separate clips within a collection. This does not change the source file in any way – it remains as one clip. When Windows Movie Maker splits an imported clip within your collections, it is simply referencing different parts of the source clip. Note that shorter clips will not be split.

Splitting clips after importing

If you want Windows Movie Maker to auto-split a video file once you have imported it into your Collections: Display the **Collections** pane → Select the file in the Collections pane → Right-click the file in the Contents pane to display a shortcut menu → Click **Create Clips**. Note that shorter clips will not be split. Refer to Figure 12.9.

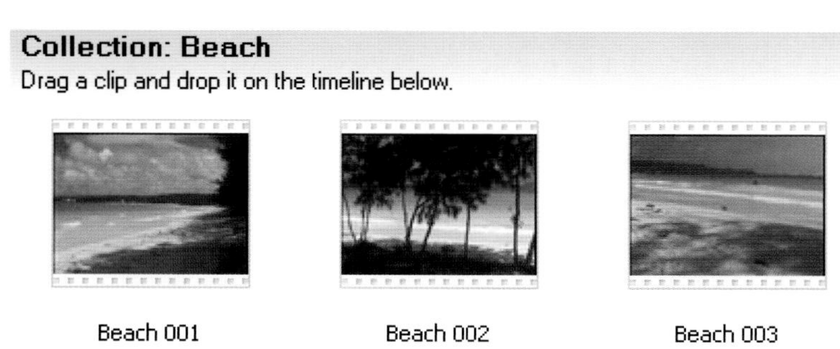

Figure 12.9: *A video file auto-split into smaller clips by Windows Movie Maker.*

Once you have split your clips, you can play the shorter clips and decide which of the split clips you will use in your final movie. You can also split clips at specific points manually. This is covered on page 216.

Organising your imported video files in your Collections

Imported video files will be placed in the **Collections** folder, *not* in the subfolder you created earlier. Display the **Collections** pane and click and drag the files individually from the **Collections** folder into the **videos** subfolder in your project folder. Refer to Figure 12.10.

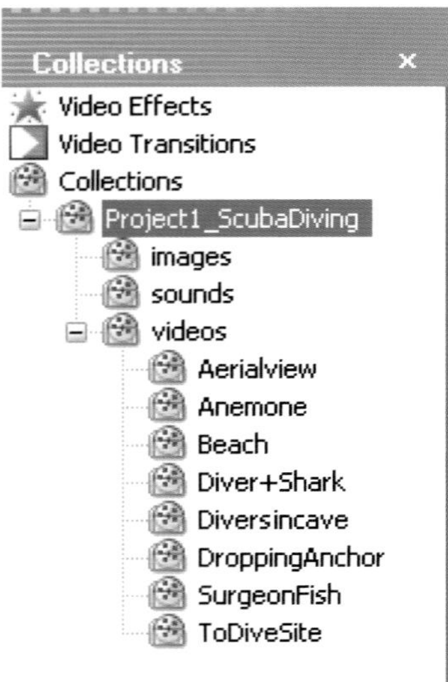

Figure 12.10: *Video files moved into the videos subfolder within the project folder.*

Importing your sound files

1. Display the **Collections** pane and select the subfolder in your project folder in which you want to import your sound files (i.e. the **sounds** subfolder). Unlike video files, sound files will be placed in the selected folder.
2. Select **Tasks** to display the **Movie Tasks** pane.
3. Below the section **1. Capture Video**, click **Import audio or music** → Locate your source files folder in your working area → Click to select the required file → Click the **Import** button. (To import more than one file, hold down the **Ctrl** key while you select the files you want to import.)
4. The sound files will be placed in the selected folder (i.e. the **sounds** subfolder). Refer to Figure 12.11.

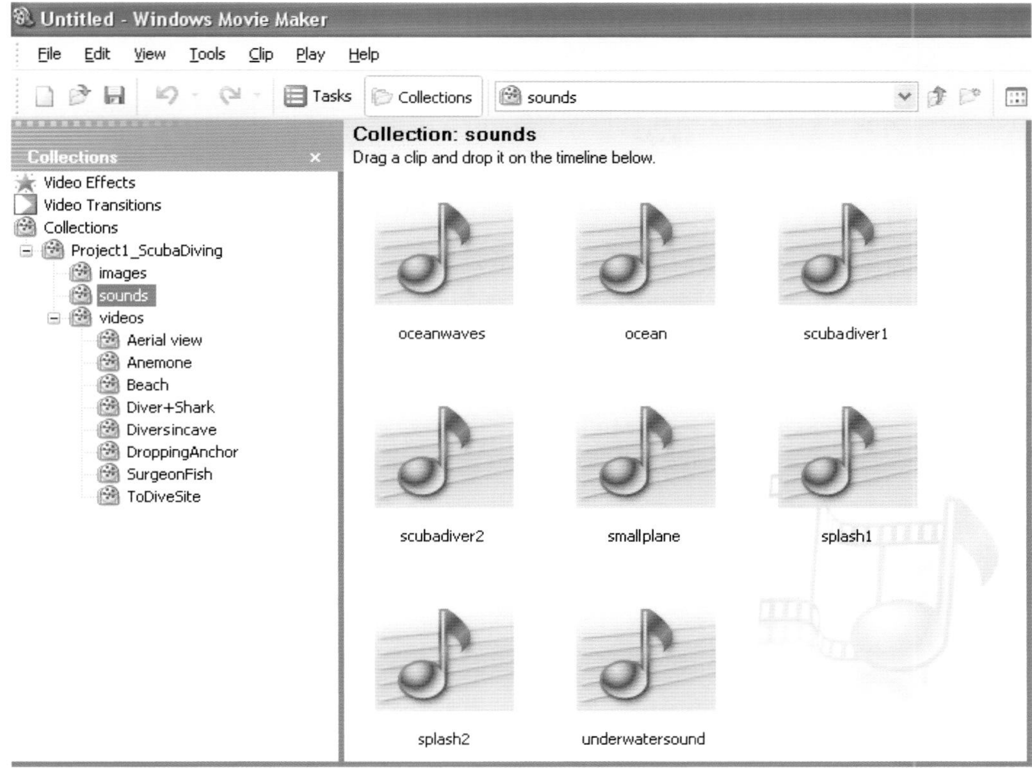

Figure 12.11: *Imported sound files.*

Activity 14: Import your source video and sound files...

In this activity you will import the video files and sound files that you sourced in Chapter 11.

Grading: Candidates working towards all grades must import video and sound components. ***Merit*** *and* ***Distinction*** *grade candidates must make good use of importing components and should therefore import video and sound clips as well as images and animations (this is covered in the next activity).*

- Reminder: in your working area, check the file formats of your source video and sound files. Refer to the list of Windows Movie Maker supported file types on pages 203–205 to ensure that they are suitable.
- Import your source video files into Windows Movie Maker. Do **not** select the option to create clips during importing.
- Display the Collections pane and move the imported video files into the **videos** subfolder within your project folder.
- Select the **sounds** subfolder in the Collections pane.
- Import your source sound files into your **sounds** subfolder within your project folder.
- If you wish to save your project now, refer to **Saving your project** on page 211. Otherwise, keep Windows Movie Maker open to import your images and animations.

Importing your source images and animations

Animations should be imported as pictures (images) into Windows Movie Maker. Before you begin, check your source files in your working area – ensure that your animation file(s) are in the same folder as your images.

1 Display the **Collections** pane and select the subfolder in your project folder into which you want to import the images and animations. Images will be placed in the selected folder.
2 Select **Tasks** to display the **Movie Tasks** pane.
3 Below the section **1. Capture Video**, click **Import pictures** → Locate your source files folder in your working area → Click to select the required file → Click **Import**. (To import more than one file, hold down the **Ctrl** key while you select the files you want to import.) Refer to Figure 12.12.

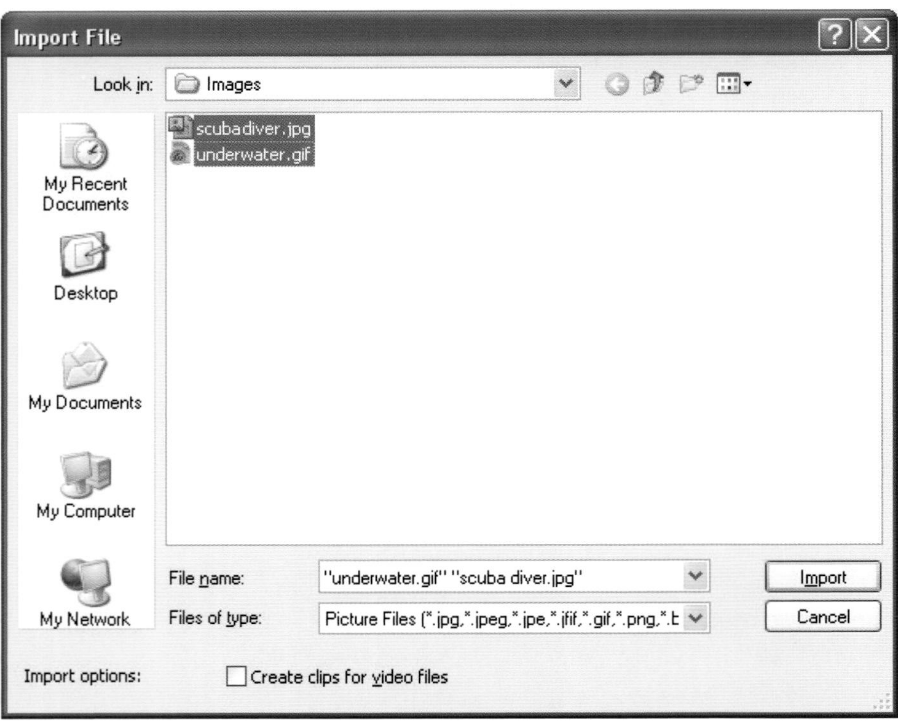

Figure 12.12: *Importing images and animations.*

TIP

If you import or move the same file(s) a second time into any of your folders, Windows Movie Maker will simply import the copy/copies into the folder. If you have any unwanted or duplicate files, you can delete the files easily.

To delete a clip or file from your Collections: Display the Collections pane → Click the file in the Contents pane → Press Delete. The file will be deleted from your project folder in Windows Movie Maker. It is not deleted from your source files folder.

Saving your project

Once you have imported all your source files, you should save your work as a project. Saving your project allows you to keep your current work as it is. You can open the file in Windows Movie Maker to make further changes. A Windows Movie Maker project file is saved with a **.mswmm** file extension.

If you have begun your editing, you can continue editing your project from where you left off when you last saved the project. When you save a partly-completed project, all your edits are retained.

It is important to understand that saving a project is different to saving a movie. Once you have completed all your editing, you will save your final video clip as a movie.

- **To save a project for the first time: File** → **Save Project** → Navigate to the folder in which you want to save your project → In the **File name** box, type a suitable name for the project → **Save**.
- **To save an updated project: File** → **Save Project**. The original project file is updated.
- **To save an updated project using a different file name: File** → **Save Project As...** → Navigate to the folder in which you want to save your project → In the **File name** text box, type a different name → **Save**.

TIP

If you close Windows Movie Maker and re-open it, although your collections will still be visible in the Collections pane, you must re-open your saved project (refer to the section 'Opening a saved project').

Closing Windows Movie Maker and opening a saved project

Closing Windows Movie Maker

File → **Exit** *or* click the red **Close** icon at the top right of the window.

Opening a saved project

File → **Open Project** or click the **Open Project** icon on the Toolbar to display the **Open Project** dialogue box → Navigate to the folder containing your project → Select the file → **Open**. The project name will display on the title bar.

Activity 15: Import your images and animations, and save your project...

In this activity you will:

- import the images and animations that you sourced in Chapter 11
- save your project.

Grading: **Pass** *grade candidates are not required to import all four types of components.* **Merit** *and* **Distinction** *grade candidates should import video, sound, at least one image and at least one animation.*

- Reminder: in your working area, check the file formats of your source image and animation files. Refer to the tables of Windows Movie Maker supported file types on pages 203–204 to ensure that they are suitable.
- Select the **images** subfolder within your project folder in the Collections pane.
- Import your source image(s) and animation(s) into your **images** subfolder.
- As you will need to show evidence of your editing, it is a good idea to use **Save as** to save different stages (e.g. xxxV1 with xxx being your project name).
- Save your project using a suitable name followed by **V1**.
- For practice, close Windows Movie Maker. Start it again and open your project.

TIP

Remember that Windows Movie Maker makes reference to the source files in your working area, therefore if you move or delete files, it is no longer able to read these files. (Refer to the section Understanding projects, movies and source files on page 203.)

In your centre, if you normally save your source files in a folder on a network drive (e.g. in a school or college you may be allocated your own folder on the H: or G: drive, or similar), then Windows Movie Maker will usually be able to read the source files from that drive even if you log on to a different computer or from a different room. However, if your source files are saved on a local drive (e.g. on the C: drive of a specific computer) then you will need to import your source files into Windows Movie Maker at the beginning of each new lesson. Similarly, if your source files are saved on an external drive (e.g. a memory stick), you should import these source files at the start of each lesson.

Viewing video and sound clip properties

Before you begin putting together your movie, it is helpful to know the duration of each of your video and sound clips. Remember, your final video clip (movie) should be at least 45 seconds long. You will learn how to edit your video and sound files so the duration is not too long, but the important thing is that your video clips should not be too short.

To view a clip's properties: Select the clip in the Collections pane → Right-click each clip in the Contents pane to show a shortcut menu → Click Properties and note down the duration.

Alternatively, change the display in the Contents pane to show the full details. On the right of the Toolbar, click the arrow to the right of **Views** → select **Details**.

In the Collections pane, select the **sounds** folder. You will see the duration of all the sound files (refer to Figure 12.13). To see the duration of the video clips: Click each clip in the **videos** subfolder (refer to Figure 12.14).

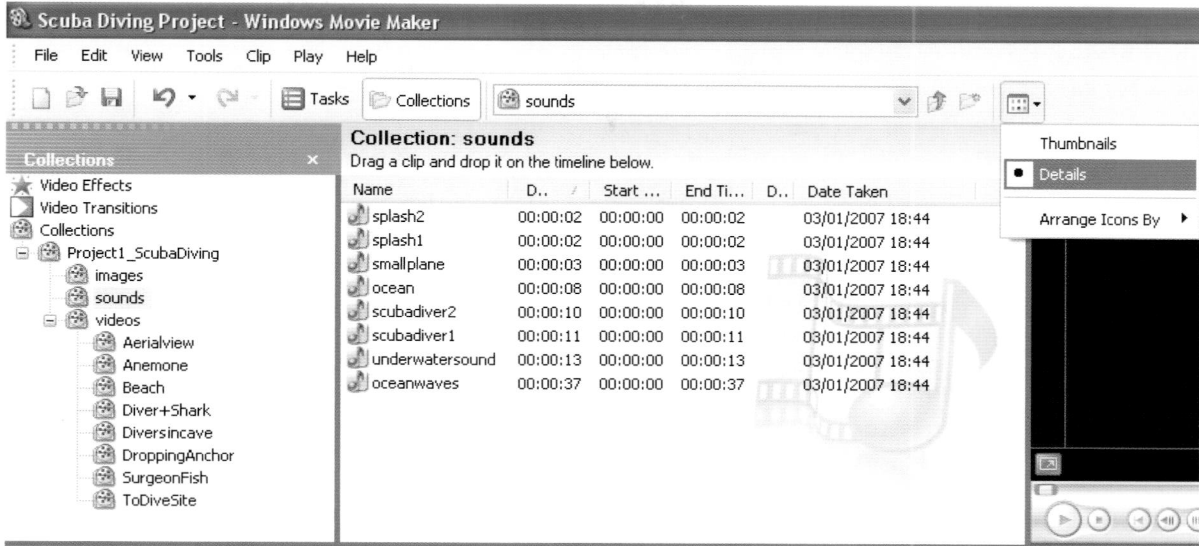

***Figure 12.13:** Displaying the properties of all sound files.*

Collection: Divers in cave

Drag a clip and drop it on the storyboard below.

Name	Duration	Start Time	End Time	Dimensi...	Date Taken
Diversincave	00:00:21	00:00:00	00:00:21	384 x 288	03/01/2007 17:54

***Figure 12.14:** Displaying the properties of a video file.*

Activity 16: View your clip properties...

In this activity you will check the duration of your clips. Remember your final clip should be at least 45 seconds in length.

- Open your saved project xxxV1.
- Display the details and view the duration of your video and sound clips.
- Make a note of the total duration of your video clips and the total duration of your sound clips.

TIP

To play each individual video or sound clip before you begin the editing process: Display the Collections pane → Select the clip in the Collections pane → Select it in the Contents pane → Press the Play button in the Preview monitor.

Creating the movie

Adding your video clips

Now you can begin the fun part of compiling your own video clip.

There are two ways you can look at and edit your project: **Storyboard** view or **Timeline** view. We will use both but we will start with the Storyboard view.

Adding video clips to the Storyboard

1 Click on the **Show Storyboard** button [Show Storyboard] to display the Storyboard view if it is not already displayed.
2 Display the Collections pane → Ensure all the contents of your project folder and videos subfolder are displayed → Click the plus symbol to the left of the folder name [+ videos] to expand the folder if necessary.
3 To add clips to your storyboard: Click and drag a clip from the Collections pane or from the Contents pane onto a blank box on the Storyboard.
4 Start with the clip you want to display first in your final movie, then the second and so on.

It does not matter where you drop a clip, it will always fill to the left-hand side. You can drag the same clip more than once if you wish but consider how it will look when the final movie is played.

5 Repeat this process to place all the clips you want to use in your final movie clip (refer to Figure 12.15).
6 Save your updated project.
7 To play the entire clip, select the first clip and press the Play button in the Preview monitor. You can also start playing from any point by selecting a clip in the Storyboard.

Figure 12.15: *Video clips positioned in Storyboard view.*

TIPS

- **To undo an action, click the Undo icon on the Toolbar.**
- **To delete a clip from the Storyboard, click on it and press the Delete key.**
- **To insert a clip between two clips, click and drag the clip to a position in between two thumbnails on the Storyboard.**
- **To move a clip on the Storyboard, click and drag the clip to the new position.**
- **To resize the Storyboard area, click and drag the blue dividing bar. As you decrease the size of the Storyboard pane, the size of the thumbnails is decreased and you can see more thumbnails. As you increase the size of the Storyboard pane, the thumbnail size increases and you can see fewer thumbnails.**

Adding images and animations

Add your images and animations in Storyboard view in the same way as you added video clips.

You can move and delete images and animations in Storyboard view in the same way as video clips.

Animations can be played in the Preview monitor by selecting the animation clip in **Storyboard** or **Timeline** view and pressing the **Play** button in the **Preview** monitor.

Viewing clip and video lengths

Before you begin any editing, it is helpful to know the total video length.

In Windows Movie Maker, time is displayed in hours, minutes, seconds and hundredths of a second. Here are some examples of video times in Windows Movie Maker:

00:00:30:00	30 seconds
00:00:50:00	50 seconds
00:01:10:00	1 minute, 10 seconds
00:01:30:00	1 minute, 30 seconds (1½ minutes)

A quick way to see the length of the combined clips is to look at the bottom right of the Preview monitor (refer to Figure 12.16).

Figure 12.16: *Total video length in the Preview monitor.*

When you hover your mouse cursor over an individual clip in Storyboard view, the clip name and duration will display.

Timeline view gives you more detail about the times associated with the various components of your project and gives you a graphic representation of the audio (when you add your sound files).

Display the Timeline view to see the total time as well as the individual clip times. You may need to click the **Zoom Timeline Out** button  to see all the clips.

TIP

To clear the Storyboard or Timeline: Edit → Clear Timeline or Clear Storyboard (depending on which view you are working in).

Activity 17: Compile your video clips and check total time...

In this activity you will:

- begin creating your video clip – you ***must*** refer to your storyboard that you created in Chapter 11
- position your video clips, image(s) and animation(s) on the Storyboard.

Grading: All candidates will need to edit the video clips. Pass grade candidates are not required to use images and animations in the final clip but must use videos and sound.

➔ Open your saved project xxxV1.

➔ Place your individual video clips in the correct sequence on the Storyboard.

➔ Add your image(s) and animation(s) in the appropriate position on the Storyboard.

➔ You will be editing your clips so will need to know what editing to carry out. Play the entire video clip from the beginning in the Preview monitor. Make a note of any clips that are too long or have unwanted content.

➔ Check your total video length at this stage.

➔ Save the updated project using a different filename (e.g. xxxV2).

Splitting clips manually

Video clips can be split manually in Timeline view or in the Collections contents pane.

1. Select the clip in Timeline view or in the Contents pane.
2. Play the clip in the Preview monitor.
3. Drag the play head to the point you want to split the clip.
4. Use the **Previous Frame** and **Next Frame** buttons to go to the exact place you want to create a split and click the Split button. When you hover the mouse cursor over the button, a tooltip displays the full name (i.e. **Split the clips into two clips at the current frame**). The clips will be split in the view that you selected (e.g. if you selected the clip in Timeline view, the split clips will display in Timeline view; the clip in the Contents pane will not be split).

If you have split a clip in Timeline view, you can delete part of the split clip if you wish by selecting the clip and pressing the **Delete** key. This will not change the clip in your Collections.

Combining clips

You can combine two or more video clips that were split. Combining clips is useful if you have several short clips and you want to view them as one clip.

In the Contents pane or on the Storyboard or Timeline, hold down the **Ctrl** key and select the clips you want to combine. On the **Clip** menu → click **Combine**.

Note that you cannot combine two separate clips or animations or images.

Trimming clips

Audio and video clips can be trimmed quickly in Timeline view.

Use the **Zoom Timeline In** button  to zoom in if you need to before trimming any video clips.

Position your mouse cursor at the end of the clip in the Timeline (the cursor changes to a red double-headed arrow → Click and drag the mouse to the left to trim the clip → Play the trimmed clip to ensure that you are satisfied with the result. Click **Undo** to undo the trim if required.

Repeat to trim any other clips. Keep a check on the total clip time as you trim clips. Remember, your video length must be at least 45 seconds.

Adding transitions

Key term

Transition

A visual change between two separate scenes. It is a feature that is added between source video clips, images or titles (e.g. page curl up, bars, circle). It provides a smooth change between clips in a movie – a transition plays when one clip ends and before another starts. Windows Movie Maker has 60 different transitions to choose from.

TIP

Add transitions before you add your sound clips to avoid the need to adjust sounds after adding transitions.

1 Display the Collections pane → select **Video Transitions**.
2 Before you add a transition to the Storyboard, you should preview it in the Preview monitor. Click on a transition in the Contents pane → Click the Play button in the Preview monitor.
3 To add a transition to your movie clip: Display the Storyboard view → Click and drag a transition from the Contents pane to the transition cell in front of the video clip (refer to Figure 12.17).

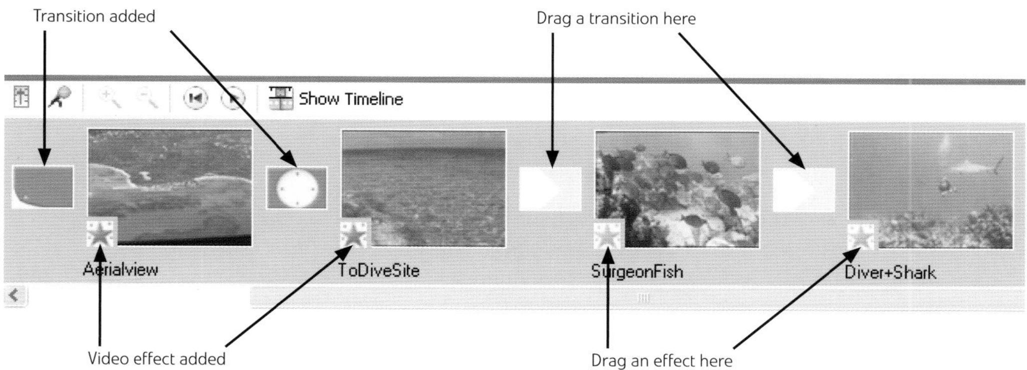

Figure 12.17: *Adding transitions and effects in Storyboard view.*

Adding effects

Key term

Video effect

Video effects let you add special filters to your movie clip (e.g. blur, ease in or ease out, fade in or fade out). A video effect changes how a video clip, image or title displays on the screen. It is applied for the entire duration that the video clip, image or title displays in your movie.

You can add any of the video effects from the **Video Effects** folder in the Collections pane.

1 Display the Collections pane → select **Video Effects**.
2 Select an effect in the Contents pane and preview it in the Preview monitor by clicking **Play**.
3 To add an effect: Display the Storyboard view → Click and drag an effect from the Contents pane to the video effect cell at the bottom left corner of the clip (refer to Figure 12.17).

TIP

You do not need to add a transition or effect to every clip. Play the entire clip from the beginning once you have applied transitions and effects to view the result. Make any changes as needed.

To delete a transition or effect: Click on it and press the Delete key.

To move a transition or effect: Click and drag it to the new position.

Activity 18: Split and trim clips, add transitions and effects...

In this activity you will:

- continue working on your movie project
- split and trim your clips
- add transitions and effects to your clips.

Grading: All candidates must edit clips. **Distinction** *grade candidates must also split and/or trim clips. Splitting and/or trimming a clip can be classified as an edit so* [illegible] *and* **Merit** *grade candidates are also advised to practise splitting and trimming.*

All candidates must add transition. **Merit** *and* **Distinction** *candidates must also add effects. A specific number of transitions and effects is not defined in the syllabus but as the plural is used, you are advised to add a minimum of two transitions and two effects.*

➔ Open your saved project xxxV2.

➔ Play your video clips and select at least one clip that needs splitting. Split the clip then play the split clips.

- If you have split a clip in Timeline or Storyboard view, you may need to delete any unwanted clip portions from the Storyboard or Timeline. If you split a clip in the Contents pane, you will need to drag the split portion of the clip that you want to include in your movie into the Timeline or Storyboard view.
- Play your entire movie and identify at least one clip that needs to be trimmed. Trim the video clip that needs trimming.
- Add at least two transitions in between your clips.
- Add at least two effects to the clips.
- Play your video clip from the start before you add sounds.
- You must not overwrite the original project file so that you can retain evidence of the clips before splitting and trimming.
- Save the project using the filename xxxV3.

Adding sound clips to your movie

To save editing time, ensure that you have split and/or trimmed clips, and added transitions before adding the sound clips to the Timeline.

1. Display the Timeline view. If your video clips do not have associated sound, you can click the minus symbol to the right of **Video** to contract this view **Video** ⊟ (refer to Figure 12.18).
2. Display the Collections pane and open your **sounds** subfolder.
3. Click and drag a sound file to the **Audio/Music** row in the Timeline. Unlike adding video clips, you can add a sound clip anywhere in the Timeline.
4. The length of a sound clip can be trimmed in the same way as trimming a video clip – use the **Zoom Timeline In** button to zoom in before trimming the sounds.

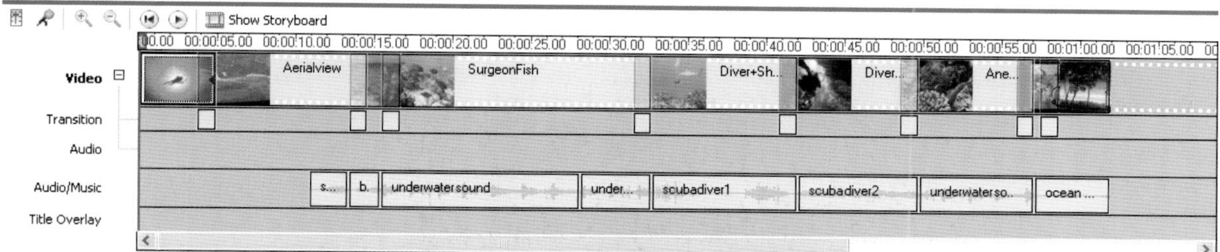

Figure 12.18: *Timeline view showing transitions added, total video length and trimmed video and sound clips.*

TIP

To move a sound clip on the Timeline: Click and drag it to a new position.

You can add the same clip more than once if you want to repeat a sound.

To move a video or audio clip fractionally to the left or right, you can nudge the clip: Select the clip → Click the Clip menu → Nudge Left or Nudge Right.

Adjusting the volume of sound clips

Display the Timeline view → Right-click an audio track to display a shortcut menu → Select **Volume...** to display the **Audio Clip Volume** dialogue box → Drag the slider to adjust the volume. If you want to switch the volume off completely tick the **Mute clip** check box. Refer to Figure 12.19.

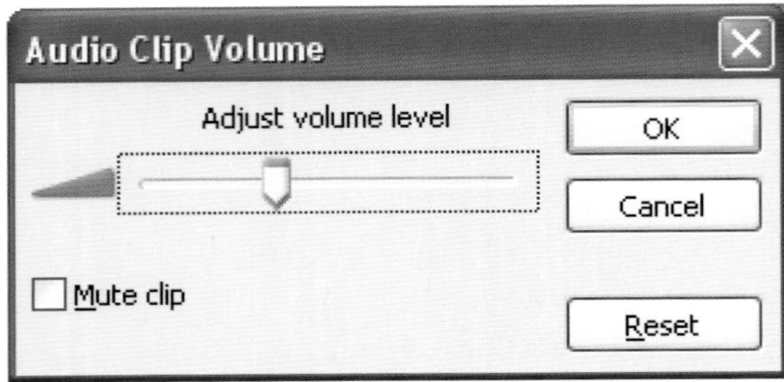

Figure 12.19: *Adjusting the volume of sound clips.*

Adjusting audio levels for video clips with captured sound

Note that some video clips will have sounds that were captured as part of the clip. These will display on the Audio track in Timeline view and can, of course, be heard when you play the clip. You can still add your own sound clips to the Audio/Music track to these clips. Refer to Figure 12.20 which shows the Timeline view – video clips one and three have background sound that was captured with the video clip and video clip two has no sound with the clip. Audio clips have been added to all three clips.

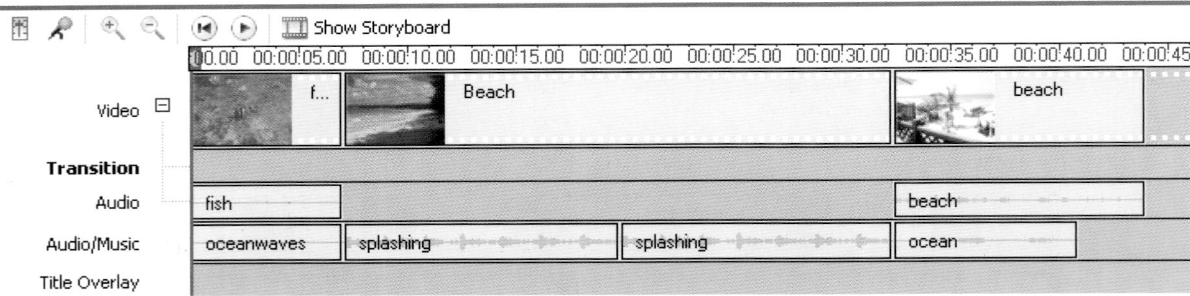

Figure 12.20: *Timeline view showing video clips with and without captured background sound.*

The default setting plays both the audio in both tracks at equal levels, but you can decide which sound should play louder than the other by adjusting the audio levels – the audio level you select will play throughout your movie.

To adjust audio levels:

1 **Tools** menu → **Audio Levels**. The **Audio Levels** dialogue box displays (refer to Figure 12.21).
2 To increase the audio level on the Audio/Music track, drag the slider bar towards **Audio/ Music**.
3 To increase the audio level on the Audio track that is part of a video clip, drag the slider bar towards **Audio from video**.
4 Click the red **Close window** cross to close the **Audio Levels** dialogue box.

Figure 12.21: *Adjusting the audio levels.*

Adding narration

You can record narration for all of your final video clip or for only part of the clip from within Windows Movie Maker.

To add narration, you will need a microphone attached to your computer. Your narration will be saved as a **.wma** file and is imported directly into your Collections as soon as you record it. You can then add the **.wma** file (your narration) on the Audio/Music bar in the Timeline in the same way as you add a sound clip.

Before you start recording, it is a good idea to write down what you intend to say and practise speaking the narration a few times.

Tips for recording narration:

- Make sure the room is quiet: switch off your mobile phone, remove any clocks or other similar objects. Switch off any noisy printers.
- Use a microphone stand (if possible) and do not handle the microphone cable. Sit/stand still whilst you are recording.
- If your microphone has volume controls, set the recording volume.

1 In the Collections pane, select the **sounds** subfolder within your project folder.
2 Display the **Timeline** view.
3 Click the **Tools** menu → Click **Narrate Timeline...** to display a control panel → Click **Show more options**.
4 You will see the screen as shown in Figure 12.22, in which you will need to set a number of options before you start recording your narration:
   - Drag the slider to adjust the **Input level**.
   - Below **Audio input source:**, set the option to Microphone.
   - If you want to limit the length of the narrated clip and have already added sound clips, then tick the box for **Limit narration to available free space on Audio/ Music track**.

Narrate Timeline

Drag the playback indicator on the timeline to an empty point on the Audio/Music track, click Start Narration, and begin your narration.

Steps:

1. Start Narration
2. Stop Narration

Done

Input level

Microphone

Learn more about narrating the timeline

Narration captured: 00:00:00

Time available: --:--:--

Limit narration to available free space on Audio/Music track

Mute speakers

Show fewer options

Audio device:

SoundMAX Digital Audio

Audio input source:

Microphone

Figure 12.22: *Beginning to record a narration (Timeline view).*

5 Check the position of the play head in the Timeline and adjust this by dragging if necessary – the narration will begin at the point where your play head is placed.

6 Before you begin speaking, check how much time you have available for your narration – check the point at which the next sound clip starts. Move your mouse pointer to the white bar in the timeline that displays the times. A tooltip will display the exact time. Refer to Figure 12.23.

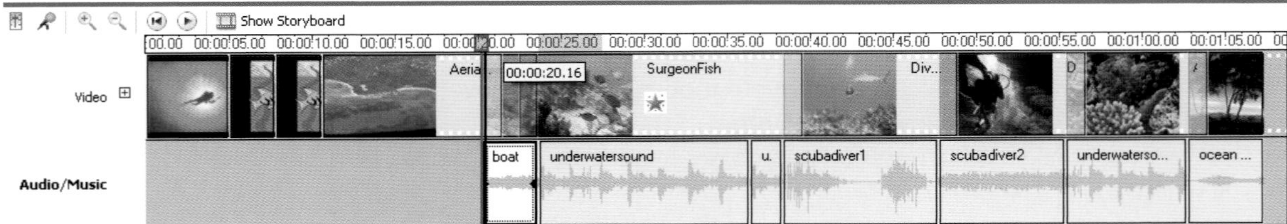

Figure 12.23: *Checking the time available for the narration in Timeline view.*

7 Click the **Start Narration** button and start speaking clearly into microphone. Keep an eye on the time to the right of **Narration captured**. Click **Stop Narration** when you have finished recording.

8 The **Save Windows Media File** dialogue box displays → Navigate to the folder in your working area where you want to save the file → Type a suitable filename (the file will be saved in **.wma** format) → Click **Save**.

9 The sound file will be imported automatically into your **sounds** subfolder (because you selected the sounds subfolder in Step 1).

10 The clip should appear in your Timeline. If it does not, click and drag this sound file to the **Audio/Music** row in the Timeline.

11 Play your entire clip and make any adjustments needed to the position and volume of the sound clip. Adjust the position of video clips as needed.

TIP

If you are or will be doing Unit 22 Creating Sound Using ICT, you could insert your sound clip from that unit into your movie project.

Activity 19: Add your sound clips and add narration...

In this activity you will add your sound clips.

Grading: All candidates must add a soundtrack. **Distinction** *grade candidates may add a soundtrack and/or narration.*

- Open your saved project xxxV3.
- Place your individual sound clips in the Timeline.
- If you are working towards a **Distinction** grade, record a narration and add the narrated clip to the Timeline.
- Ensure that all sounds are appropriate for the video.
- Zoom into Timeline view to ensure that your sound clips start and end at appropriate places.
- Play your entire video clip from the start to ensure that the sounds correspond appropriately to the video clip content and are of the correct duration. Make any adjustments as needed.
- You may need to 'fine tune' the duration of both your audio and video clips at this stage.
- Now that you have almost completed your final clip, you can move any image, animation, video or audio clips as needed.
- Check that the final clip is at least 45 seconds in length. There is no maximum length but try not to make your clip too long.
- Save the updated project using the filename xxxV4.

Adding titles and credits

Titles and credits let you enhance your movie by adding text-based information.

Key terms

Title

Text that appears on a screen at the beginning of a movie or in between clips. A title can be displayed on its own screen or can be overlaid on an existing clip. It plays for a specified amount of time, then the scene, video clip or image displays in your movie.

Credit

Text that displays at the end of a movie. In a longer movie, credits can provide information about those involved in the movie production. In shorter clips, such as your video clip or in cartoons, a credit can simply be 'The End'.

Adding a title and credits

1 Select the required video clip in Storyboard or Timeline view. Display the **Tasks** pane. In the section **2. Edit Movie**, click **Make titles or credits**. A screen asking you what you what you want to add and where is displayed (refer to Figure 12.24).

Figure 12.24: *Adding titles and credits.*

2 Select an option from the list.

3 Another window displays (refer to Figure 12.25 for adding title text). Type your text in one or more rows.

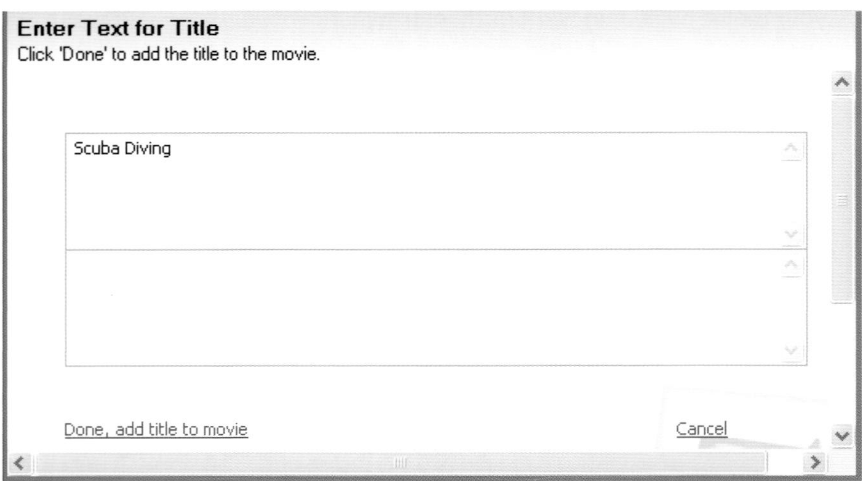

Figure 12.25: *Inserting title text.*

4 To format the text: Click on **Change the text font and color** (you may need to scroll down to see this option).

5 Select a font type from the **Font:** drop-down list → Select Bold, Underline or Italic, as needed. To change the text colour click A below **Color:** and select a colour. To change the background colour, click ■.
6 To change the animation effect (the way the text displays on the screen), click **Change the title animation** and select an option from the dialogue box.
7 When you have finished setting the text options, click **Done, add title to movie**.

Saving your final movie clip (exporting in a suitable file format)

When you have finished all the editing for your video clip (movie) project, you should save it as a computer file which can be played in other programs (e.g. Windows Media Player) and can be inserted into other applications (e.g. into a Microsoft PowerPoint presentation or a web page).

Before you save, you will need to consider the file size of the video clip. You will also need to decide how you need to make the video clip available to others (e.g. do you need to send it via email?) and where you are going to save the movie to (e.g. to a CD). *Before you begin saving the final video clip, you are advised to have a discussion with your teacher or tutor about the best file format to save it in your particular centre.*

1 Display the **Tasks** pane.
2 In the section **3. Finish Movie**, click **Save to my computer**.
3 A **Save Movie Wizard** dialogue box displays (refer to Figure 12.26) → Type a name for your final video clip and select the correct location where the file is to be saved (click **Browse** to change the default location) → Click **Next**.

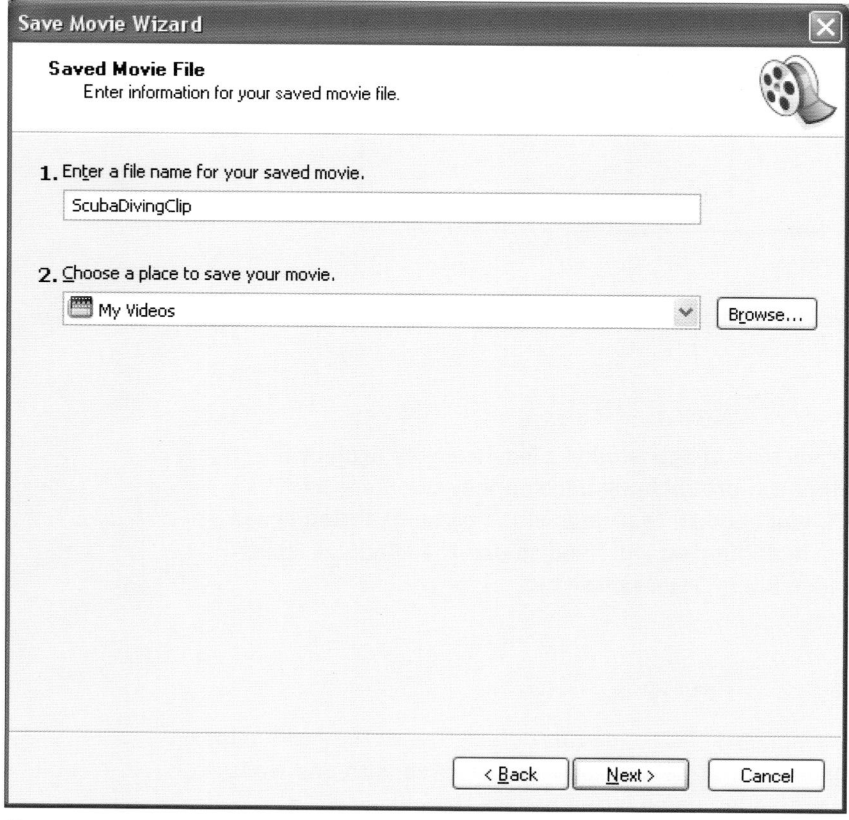

Figure 12.26: *Saving a completed movie.*

4 Another dialogue box displays. At this stage, you need to decide on the quality and file size of your saved movie. The default setting is **Best quality for playback on my computer**. You may keep this default setting, however this will produce quite a large file size. Below this radio button, click **Show more choices...**, then click the radio button for **Other settings**. Click the arrow to the right of the **Other settings:** drop-down list box and select an option. To save your video in a small size and ensure good quality choose the option for **Video for Broadband (150 kbs)**. Refer to Figure 12.27.

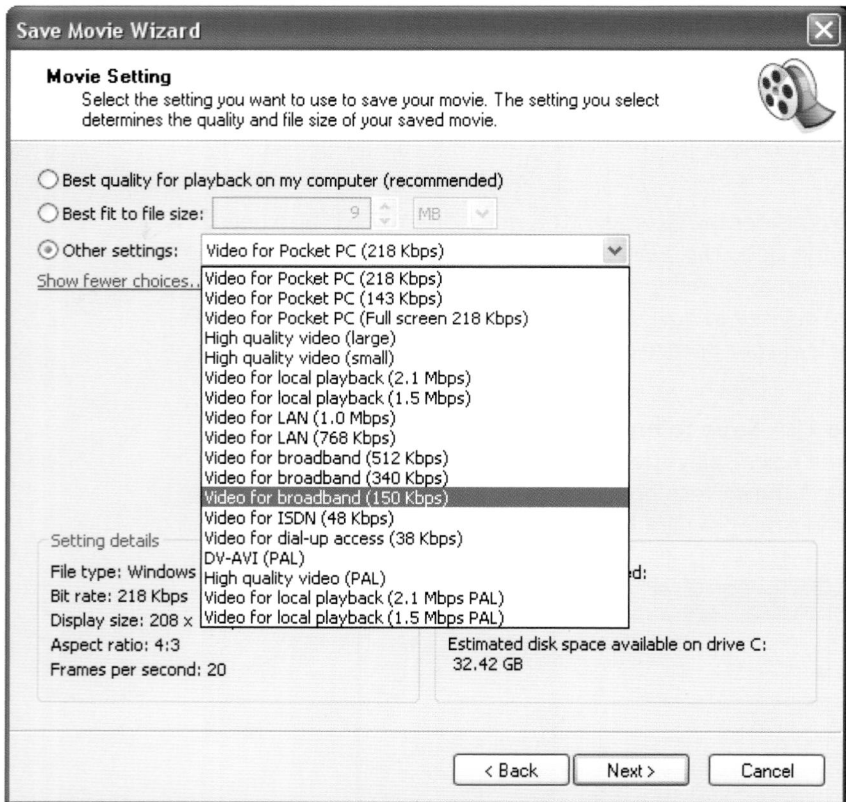

Figure 12.27: *Selecting the movie save setting.*

5 Click **Next**. The movie may take a few minutes to save. Your clip will be saved as a **.wmv** (Windows Media Video) file.

WARNING!

Do not delete your latest version of the Windows Movie Maker project file from your working area (this will probably be version 4 of the file – xxxV4). For Assessment Objective 4, you need to test your video clip and action areas identified for improvement. To do so, you will need to use the Windows Movie Maker file in **.mswmm** format.

TIP

Keep your original source components saved, do not delete these. They will help the moderator and your teacher/tutor to see what you started with and what video editing techniques you used to create the clip.

Activity 20: Add titles and/or credits, save movie in suitable file format...

In this activity you will:

- add titles to your movie project
- save your project as a movie file in a format that can be played in most media players.

Grading: All candidates must export the final video clip in a suitable file format. Adding titles is required for **Merit** *and* **Distinction** *grade candidates.*

➔ Open your saved project xxxV4.

➔ Add at least one title to your video clip. You may add more than one title and/or a credit if you wish.

➔ Play the clip to ensure that all elements work correctly and that the timings are correct.

➔ Save your updated project.

➔ Save your project as a .wmv file in a small to medium file size.

TIP

You could insert your created video clip in an interactive multimedia presentation or on a web page (e.g. if you are working towards Units 2 and/or 4).

Portfolio builder

In this chapter you have learned how to use Windows Movie Maker to create a video clip for a project scenario. You will now use the practical skills you have learned to create your own video clip for your portfolio. This is the creative, fun part of this unit!

Your video clip for your portfolio must be based on the design documentation (the plan and storyboard) that you should already have created for your portfolio. You must NOT start creating your video clip for your portfolio until you have created the plan and storyboard – as tempting as that might be! You must not 'go off on a tangent' and produce a product that you have not planned!

Your video clip must be at least 45 seconds in length and you must import a range of components (i.e. images, animation, video, sound). You should already have sourced, organised and checked these components, so importing them into Windows Movie Maker should be straightforward.

Before you begin creating the clip, read the 'How this assessment objective will be assessed...' and 'How to achieve...' sections of this chapter and discuss with your teacher/tutor what grade you could aim for.

Once you have imported the components you will need to edit them, use transitions and add a soundtrack. Higher level candidates should also split and trim clips, use transitions and apply effects. If you are working towards the higher grades, you will also need to add titles and narration. It is very important that you have evidence of the editing, therefore you are advised to use **Save as** to save the project with different filenames in order to show the files before and after editing.

When you have finished creating the clip, you must save it in .wmv format. Check the completed clip to make sure that it is appropriate and that it meets its identified aims. You must NOT delete the saved project files as you will need these during the testing which is the next stage.

Good luck!

Assessment Objective 4

Test the Video Clip

Overview

In this chapter you will learn how to produce a suitable test plan so that you can test your video clip. When you were creating the clip, you were taught to carry out some testing at various stages to ensure all elements worked as intended, but now you need to identify specific areas for testing and carry out specific tests to test your completed video clip more thoroughly. You will also learn how to suggest improvements as a result of the testing and how to action these suggestions.

Testing forms

To help you carry out and record your testing, example test tables can be downloaded from the Student Resources page on the Payne-Gallway website: **www.payne-gallway.co.uk**. The example test tables and checklists for Unit 23 are contained in the **Unit23StudentResources** folder, in the subfolder **Unit23Forms**.

How this assessment objective will be assessed...

This assessment objective will be graded by the number of tests you carry out on your video clip. Grading will also depend on whether or not you test the main areas of your video clip and how many of these main areas your tests cover. Another factor that will be assessed is how many of your tests are appropriate.

You will need to identify areas for improvement. If you action one of these you can achieve a **Merit** grade, and if you can action most of the areas for improvement you can achieve a **Distinction** grade.

The evidence you provide of your testing is crucial. There is no point carrying out numerous tests without clear evidence to prove you have done so. You need to be methodical in your testing and to ensure that you record details of each test as you go along. The first thing to do is to produce a good test plan.

Key term

Test plan

Also called a **test table**. It is a table showing all the elements in a product that should be tested, how they should be tested and what the expected outcome is.

Skills to use...

You will need to:

- produce a **test plan** to include specific areas for testing (given in the syllabus)
- test the content of the video clip for **suitability**
- test the clip to check that the correct **message** is conveyed
- test the **timing** of each component in the video clip to make sure that the time for each component is suitable
- play the entire clip to test that it runs for at least **45 seconds**
- test that **effects** and **transitions** have been included and that these are suitable
- test that the final clip has been saved in a **file format** that is suitable for a media player
- identify areas for **improvement** for each of the tests listed above
- **action** one of the identified areas for improvement (**Merit** level candidates only), or action most of the identified areas for improvement (**Distinction** level candidates only).

How to achieve...

Pass requirements

P1 You will test your video clip using a test table containing at least **four** tests.

P2 Some of your tests should be appropriate.

P3 You will identify areas for improvement.

Merit requirements

M1 You will test your video clip using a test table containing at least **five** tests covering the main areas of your video clip.

M2 Most of your tests should be appropriate.

M3 You will identify areas for improvement and action at least one of these.

Distinction requirements

D1 You will test your video clip using a test table containing at least **six** tests covering the main areas of your video clip.

D2 All your tests should be appropriate.

D3 You will identify areas for improvement and action most of these.

Key terms

Testing

The process of trying to find every possible problem, error or weakness in a product. A product is tested in order to be absolutely certain that it does what it is supposed to.

Your product is your video clip. You will need to test your video clip to ensure that you have actually done what you think you have done and what you had planned to do.

Criteria

The word 'criteria' is the plural of 'criterion'. A **criterion** is a standard by which something can be judged.

Testing

Before you begin the process of testing, you should understand what testing is and why testing is necessary. You may be asking yourself why you need to test your video clip now that you have created it and have already saved it as movie file (.wmv format). You may also think that you have already tested your video clip many times whilst you were creating it.

Why testing is necessary

Testing, following a methodical approach (i.e. to a defined list of test criteria, using a well-designed test plan, and recording the result of each test), will help identify any problems, errors, omissions and weaknesses. Testing your video clip is necessary so that you can make sure that:

- there are no problems when the clip is played
- you have not made any unintentional mistakes when you created the clip
- you have not left out any components (images, animations, source video clips, sound clips) or features during the creation
- that there are no unforeseen weaknesses.

Here are examples of issues that can be identified when testing a video clip like the one you created:

- **Problem:** The animation component is not animated (it does not move).
- **Error:** The wrong sound clip was used.
- **Omission:** You forgot to include a title.
- **Weakness:** The quality of the exported movie clip is poor.

If you are going to include your video clip in a presentation or on a website, it is very important that there are no such problems. Testing will help identify any such issues.

Professionals in the film industry use a much more stringent approach to testing and use independent testers to identify every conceivable problem or weakness before releasing a film or trailer.

In the syllabus, you are given an example list of criteria that you could include in your test plan – you may also be able to think of additional and/or alternative criteria.

Approaches to testing

There are a number of approaches that can be taken to testing and actioning any errors, problems or omissions identified.

- One approach is to:
  1. create the test plan
  2. carry out the tests
  3. select which problems/omissions to action
  4. action the solution(s).
- A second approach is to create the test plan, then carry out the tests and at the same time rectify any problems.
- Another approach is to create the test plan and at the same time test each criteria and action any solutions.

This chapter will follow the first approach. This will encourage you to work methodically and to concentrate on one thing at a time – i.e. firstly create the plan, secondly carry out the tests needed (depending on what grade you are working towards), and then, if you are working towards a **Merit** grade, you can action one identified area of improvement and, if you are working towards a **Distinction** grade, you can action most identified problems, omissions or weaknesses.

Following the second approach can become confusing – if you start to rectify areas identified for improvement whilst you are testing, you may find you correct another problem before you have had the chance to test it and record the testing.

Following the third approach is not recommended as you will be attempting to do three things at the same time. This can become very confusing as you can easily get sidetracked with the testing and correcting and forget to create a good plan, leading to a lack of evidence of the testing.

Test criteria

The test criteria are simply what needs to be tested. The syllabus identifies the following areas to be tested:

- suitable content
- whether the correct message is conveyed (put across)
- suitable time allowed for each component
- runs for the correct length of time (at least 45 seconds)
- suitable effects or transitions
- suitable file format.

How to test a video clip

The best way to test your video clip is to produce a good test plan which should ideally include the above test criteria given in the syllabus and any other criteria that you may think of. You should also refer to your design documents created for Assessment Objective 2 (in Chapter 11) to see *what* you had intended to include in your clip, *who* you had intended to produce it for and what the original *aim* of your clip was.

Creating a test plan (test table)

As a minimum, your test plan should show:

- all the **elements** that need to be tested
- **how** each element will be tested
- what **should happen** when the element is tested
- what **actually happened** when the element was tested.

Merit and **Distinction** grade candidates should also show:

- what **action** was taken to solve the problem, weakness or omission.

The first three items are what you plan to test and the last two will show the results of the tests. Each of these criteria is discussed in more detail in the section 'Understanding the test criteria and how to test them' (pages 235 and 236).

Starting to create the test plan

For this assessment objective, you are required to produce a test plan. You could create a test checklist instead. This is very similar to creating a test plan – the differences are explained on page 234 in the section titled 'Creating a test checklist'.

When producing your test plan, it would be a good idea to use the above list of test criteria (as suggested by the syllabus) as headings in your test table. You can then add extra tests that you can think of, as well as add details of how to test the element and the expected outcome.

Two slightly different examples of the first stage of creating a test plan are shown in the following tables.

Element to be tested	How to test this element	Expected outcome	Actual outcome	Action taken
Suitability of content for aim				
Suitability of content for audience				
Message communicated				
Time allocated to video clips				
Time allocated to sounds				
Time allocated to image				
Time allocated to animation				

Element to be tested	How to test this element	Expected outcome	Actual outcome	Action taken
Length of time of clip				
Suitability of effects				
Suitability of transitions				
Suitability of file format				

***Example 1** of the first stage of creating a test plan for your video clip.*
(Note: the actual test plan would have more room in each cell to enter data.)

Element to be tested	How to test this element	What should happen	What actually happened	Action taken
Suitable content				
for aim				
for audience				
Correct message communicated				
message				
Suitable time allocation for each component				
video clips				
sounds				
image				
animation				
Video clip runs for correct length of time				
clip duration				
Suitability of effects and transitions				
effects				
transitions				
Suitability of file format				
file format				

***Example 2** of the first stage of creating a test plan for your video clip.*

Creating a test checklist

If you want to create a checklist instead of a test table, you can do this in a very similar way, except that the column heading for column four would be different. Instead of the heading **Actual outcome** or **What actually happened**, the heading would be something like:

Expected result produced? or **Did the test produce the expected result?**

If you used this method, when you carry out the test, you could simply enter a ✓ if the actual result is the same as the expected result or a ✗ if it is not.

Creating a table in Microsoft Word

You can create a table using any word-processing program or even draw it by hand. The advantage of using a word processor is that the table will be neater and you can correct mistakes and add rows and columns more easily.

In Microsoft Word: Open a new blank document → Click the **Table** menu → **Insert** → **Table...** to display the **Insert Table** dialogue box → Enter the number of rows and columns required → Select the button for **AutoFit to window** → **OK**.

You can set the page orientation to **Portrait** or **Landscape**, but selecting **Landscape** will give you more width in each column, which is preferable. If you change the orientation the table width will automatically adjust because you selected **AutoFit to window** when you created the table.

The table in Example 1 (on pages 232 and 233) has five columns and thirteen rows. If you think of additional test criteria, you can add extra rows and/or columns to your test table.

To add more rows below an existing row: Click in the row above where you want the new row to be inserted (this will be the last row if you want to add a new row at the bottom of the table) → **Table** menu → **Insert** → **Rows Below**. Rows above an existing row, and columns can be added in a similar way.

The table in Example 2 has five columns and 18 rows. The cells in some rows have been merged and shaded.

To merge cells: Highlight the cells in the row to be merged → **Table** menu → **Merge Cells**.

To shade cells: Click in the cell → **Format** menu → **Borders and Shading...** → Select the **Shading** tab → Select the required colour → Click the arrow on the **Apply to:** list box and select **Cell** → **OK**. Refer to Figure 9.1 on page 148.

Activity 21: Create your test plan...

In this activity you will start creating a test plan for your video clip.

- Refer to your planning documents.
- Identify what tests you will need to carry out. You are advised to use the test criteria given on pages 232 and 233 as a basis.
- Enter the column headings in row one and the elements to be tested (i.e. the test criteria) in column one.
- Save your test plan using a suitable filename (e.g. Video Clip Test Table) – you will update this in the next activity.

Adding other test criteria to your test plan

Look at your design documents created for Assessment Objective 2 and the 'How to achieve...' requirements for Assessment Objective 2 (Chapter 11, page 178) and Assessment Objective 3 (Chapter 12, page 196). These will remind you of what you included in your planning documentation and storyboard, and what you included in the actual clip. Looking at this documentation may give you some ideas of more tests that you could carry out. Here are some additional criteria you could add in the **Element to be tested** column of your test plan:

- software used
- editing clips: splitting, trimming, combining clips
- adding titles
- volume of soundtrack (volume of different components)
- adding a narration.

Activity 22: Identify other elements to be tested...

In this activity you will add a few more test criteria to your test plan.

- Refer to your planning documents and storyboard.
- Identify other additional elements in your storyboard that you had planned to include in your clip.
- Add extra rows to your table and details of all the other elements that should be tested.
- Save your updated test plan.

Understanding the test criteria and how to test them

1 Suitability of content?

At the beginning of this unit, you reviewed two existing video clips. During your review you identified the aim and target audience, and commented on whether the aims were met.

When you planned your video clip, you decided on the aim of your clip and who your target audience would be. You then went on to create your video clip. Now, as part of your testing, you need to ensure that it meets your original stated aim and that the content is suitable for your stated target audience.

Your work during your reviews should make you realise how important it is for the aim and audience of your clip to be clear to the viewer, how important it is for your aim to be met and how important it is for your clip to be suitable for your intended audience.

Testing that the content meets the stated aim

To test that the aim has been met, you should refer to your planning documents, read the stated aim, then play your video clip to make sure that it does indeed meet your stated aim. Use the **Pause** button if you need to pause the clip in order to make notes, or the **Rewind** button if you need to review part of the clip again. You need to consider if **every** feature (title, source video clips, sounds, images, animations, timings, etc.) in the clip is suitable for your aim. If any aspect or component is not suitable for your aim, you need to record this fact in your test plan.

Testing that the content is suitable for the target audience

Testing that your video clip is suitable for your target audience is very similar to testing whether it meets your stated aim. Look at your planning documents and remind yourself of your stated audience. Play your clip to make sure that all the components in it are suitable for your target audience. If any components are not suitable, you need to record this in your test plan. The importance of recording every aspect of your testing in the test plan is repeated here because it is so crucial. Without evidence of the stages of your testing, there is no evidence that you have tested your video clip.

It could be possible that you have included the content according to your storyboard, but that your original planning and/or storyboard were incorrect. Testing will identify this and you should note this in your test plan. You are not required to change your plan or story-board.

Updating the test plan

Once you have understood how to test a test criterion (in this case, test for suitable content and what the expected outcome should be), you should update your test plan. You need to enter details in the columns headed **How to test this element** and **Expected outcome**. (Note: your column headings may be slightly different.)

Refer to the example of part of a test plan below. The text in italics has now been added so that it explains how this particular criteria (i.e. suitability of content) will be tested and what should happen.

Element to be tested	How to test this element	Expected outcome	Actual outcome	Action taken
Suitability of content for aim	*Read stated aim in planning document and watch entire clip.*	*Should promote scuba diving.*		
Suitability of content for audience	*Read stated audience in planning document and watch entire clip.*	*Should be suitable for teenagers aged 12–17.*		

Activity 23: Add details of testing for suitable content...

In this activity you will add details in your test plan of how to test for suitability of content and details of the expected result.

- Read your planning document to remind yourself of your stated aim and audience.
- Add brief details in your test plan of **how** you will test for suitability of content and what the **expected result** should be.
- Save your updated table.

2 Correct message conveyed?

You may be wondering how a video clip that may contains no or very little text, and mostly images, can convey a message. However a message can be put across quite effectively using spoken words, pictures, sounds and actions. You must have heard the saying 'a picture is worth a thousand words' – that is because pictures, especially moving pictures, can be very powerful in providing information without the need for any explanatory text, speech or sounds.

Your video clip was created for a specific purpose and you now need to test whether the message given to viewers of your clip meets that purpose. You should make sure the message being given is realistic, not exaggerated or overly-dramatised. For example, if the video clip shows the hostel where teenagers would be staying, it should show the actual hostel, not another one which has much better rooms and facilities.

You also need to think about whether the message being put across in your video clip is appropriate for your target audience. For example, if the target audience is young children aged 5 to 10, it would be inappropriate to show activities such as bungee jumping.

Testing that the correct message is communicated

To test that the correct message is put across, you should read the stated aim and target audience in your planning document again. You may think by now that you know what the aim and audience are and don't need to read it but it is surprising how sometimes what you have actually written is not what you think you have written.

Next, play your video clip, keeping a clear idea of the aim and audience in your head, and decide if your video clip delivers the message that meets your stated aim and is also appropriate for your stated target audience. This is important and also easy to test incorrectly. For example, you may be concentrating on how impressive the views or locations are, how impressive the transitions and effects are, or what a cheerful animation you have included – however, these are not what you are supposed to be testing!

As with testing for suitable content, it may be possible that the message being communicated in your video clip does not match the project scenario because your plans or storyboard were incorrect. Testing will identify this and you should note this in your test plan.

Updating the test plan to add details of testing for correct message

You should update your test plan to add details of how to test for the correct message and what the expected outcome is.

Activity 24: Add details of testing for correct message...

In this activity you will add details in your test plan of how to test that the correct message is communicated and of the expected result.

- Read the project scenario and your planning documents to remind yourself of your stated aim and audience.
- Add brief details in your test plan of how you will test whether the correct message is conveyed and what the expected result should be.
- Save your updated table.

3 Suitable time allocation for each component?

For this test you need to check the time of the individual components (i.e. the time of each source video clip, image, animation and of all the sound clips). This is easy to check by opening the latest version of your project file in Windows Movie Maker (the .mswmm file not the .wmv file). Make sure that you open the final version.

Whilst testing the time allocated to each component, you should also test that you have used the correct component. For example, you may have inserted a 'temporary' video or sound clip, while you were waiting for permission from the copyright holder to use another. Testing each element of the video clip will help you to identify any such forgotten 'elements'.

Testing the time of each component

1. Import the final project file into Windows Movie Maker (**File** menu → **Open Project** → Select the project file from your working area → **Open**).
2. Display the Timeline view by clicking on **Show Timeline** Show Timeline.
3. On the Timeline, click on a component (an image, animation or video clip), the duration of that component will display as a tooltip and will also display at the bottom right of the Preview monitor. Refer to Figure 13.1. Remember time is displayed as hours: minutes: seconds: hundredths of a second.

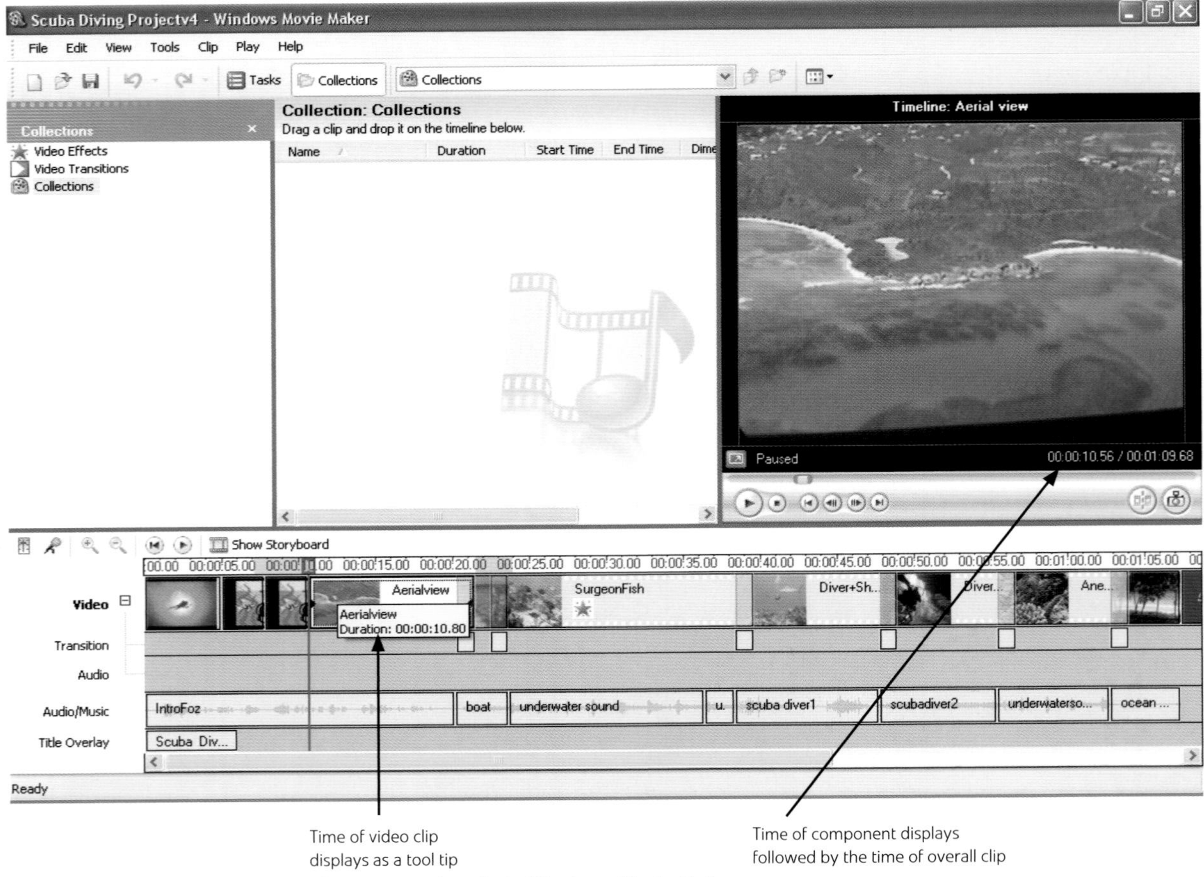

__Figure 13.1:__ Testing the timing of a source video clip in Windows Movie Maker.

Repeat the testing for each of the other source video clips, image(s) and animation(s) – one at a time.

To test the duration of sound clips, click on the clip in the **Audio/Music** row in Timeline view. The duration will display as a tooltip. Refer to Figure 13.2.

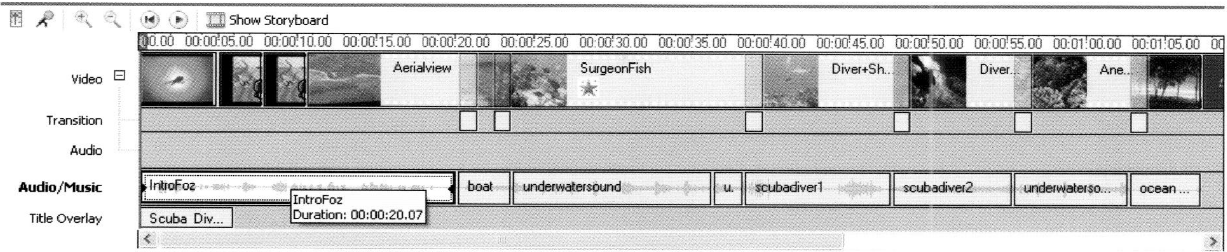

Figure 13.2: *Testing the timing of a source video clip in Windows Movie Maker.*

As you test the duration of a component, write down its duration on your test plan.

You must make sure you check the duration of every component: video clips, images, animations as well as sound clips.

Activity 25: Add details of testing the timing of each component...

In this activity you will add details in your test plan of how to test the timing of each component and the expected result.

- Add brief details in your test plan of what the duration of each component is expected to be and how you will test it.

If you want the durations to be tested in a particular way (e.g. in Windows Movie Maker), then you should state this in your test plan. You may also find it useful to list the name of each component.

- At this point you may find it useful to add extra rows to your table so that you have a separate row for each component (this is optional).
- Save your updated table.

4 Runs for correct length of time?

This is a straightforward test. Remember your video clip should be at least 45 seconds long.

Testing the total running time

Open the clip in a media player, e.g. Windows Media Player, or in Windows Movie Maker → Click **Play** and check the overall duration. You can drag the play head or click the **Forward** button to go to the end quickly.

In Windows Media Player, the overall time will display somewhere on the screen (where it displays will depend on the version of your Media Player). In Windows Movie Maker, the overall time will display at the bottom right of the Preview monitor. The clip duration will also display if you position your mouse cursor over the clip in your working area. Refer to Figure 13.3.

Figure 13.3: *Testing the clip duration in Windows Media Player and in the working area.*

Activity 26: Add details of testing of total clip time...

In this activity you will add details in your test plan of how to test the total running clip of the clip.

- Add brief details in your test plan of what you expect the duration of the clip to be and how you will test it.

If you want the total time to be tested in a particular way (e.g. in Windows Media Player), then you should state this in your test plan.

- Save your updated test plan.

5 Suitable effects or transitions?

A video effect changes how a video clip, image or title displays on the screen. A transition is a feature added in between components. The syllabus requires all candidates to use transitions and **Merit** and **Distinction** grade candidates to use effects. You were advised in Chapter 12 to use a minimum of two transitions and two effects.

Testing effects and transitions

You can test effects and transitions by playing the clip in a media player or opening the final project file in Windows Movie Maker. It is very easy to see how many transitions and effects have been added, and where, in the Storyboard view of Windows Movie Maker.

Transitions can be easily identified if the clip is played in Windows Media Player but effects are not as clear to make out. You are therefore advised to test for effects and transitions in Windows Movie Maker.

Another important test is to make sure that the transitions and effects are suitable. When creating the clip, it is easy to get carried away and add too many transitions and/or effects.

You should check the applied effects very carefully. Effects can spoil the picture quality, so if an inappropriate effect has been applied (e.g. **Fade Out, To Black** or **Watercolour**), this can ruin the picture quality.

Activity 27: Add details of how to test for effects and transitions...

In this activity you will add details in your test plan of how to test the effects and transitions.

- Add details in your test plan of how you will test the transitions and the expected result.
- If you have added effects to your video clip, add details of how you will test the effects and the expected result.
- Save your updated table.

6 Suitable file format?

Windows Movie Maker allows you to save a completed video clip (movie) in many different formats. Refer to Chapter 12 (page 225) for how to save a clip in some of the many ways available in Windows Movie Maker.

Some options produce very large file sizes. Therefore not only is it important to check that you have saved your final video clip in a suitable file format and to a suitable medium, but also that you have selected a suitable file size.

Testing for suitable file format

The file format can be tested by checking the file format in your working area. You will need to display the file extensions (if they are not already displayed). To display file extensions: Open the folder in your working area → **Tools** → **Folder Options...** → Select the **View** tab → Make sure there is no tick in the box for **Hide extensions for known file types** → **Apply** → **OK**.

Check that the file type is a **Windows Media Audio/Video file** with a **.wmv** file extension. The file size can also be checked in this view (refer to Figure 13.4). Another way of testing the file format is to play the clip in a player other than the program in which you created the clip.

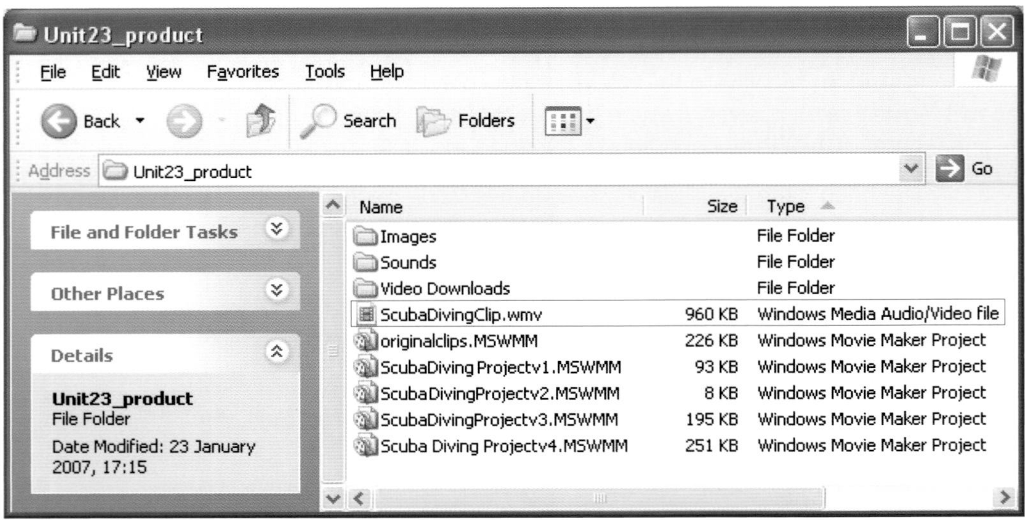

Figure 13.4: *Checking the file format and file size.*

Activity 28: Check the file format...

In this activity you will add details in your test plan of how to test the file format.

- Add details in your test plan of how you will check the file format and the expected result.
- You may add details of how to check the file size as well (optional).
- Save your updated table.

Now that you have created your own test plan, you may wish to compare it with the two example test tables **AO4_VideoTestTable** v1 and v2 provided with this book. Also provided are the same test tables with examples of 'What should happen' when the test is carried out. These files are titled **AO4_VideoTestTablev1_WithExamples** and **AO4_VideoTestTablev2_WithExamples**. The example forms contain sufficient detail for **Distinction** level.

- You may use the ideas in the example forms to make changes to your plan.
- You should now be familiar with how to test the various elements in your video clip. You may add other criteria to your plan if you wish (remember the minimum number of tests for **Distinction** level candidates is six). Additional criteria you could add are 'software used' and 'editing techniques'.
- Save your completed test plan. Next, you will begin the tests themselves.

Carrying out the tests

Once you have produced your test plan, and included details of how to test each element, and what should happen when each element tested, you will find the actual testing quite straightforward.

To do the testing, you will need:

- your completed video clip (movie) in .wmv format (Windows Movie File)
- your final project file in .mswmm format (Microsoft Windows Movie Maker format)
- access to a computer with a media player, e.g. Windows Media Player, and Windows Movie Maker
- your test plan.

You can handwrite or type comments in your test plan as you carry out each test. The advantage of using a computer to update your test plan is that you can copy and paste during the testing. You are not required to produce any screenshots to prove that you have carried out the tests – the evidence of the testing in the test plan is sufficient.

You should now look at your test plan and decide how many, and which, tests you will carry out: at least four tests for **Pass** level; at least five for **Merit** level; and at least six tests for **Distinction** level. If you want to carry out all the tests you have identified in your plan, that's good practice and absolutely fine! **Merit** and **Distinction** level candidates are required to test the *main areas* of the video clip.

The main areas of the video clip are the moving images (videos), the soundtrack, image(s) and animation(s) – these are the parts of the video clip that viewers see and hear. **Distinction** level candidates will have added narration – this is considered to be a main area of the clip as it forms part of the soundtrack. Features such as transitions and titles are not considered to be the main areas of the clip. Note: titles need to be included only by candidates working towards the higher grades.

Recording evidence of testing

When carrying out the tests, you should complete one test at a time and make sure you make notes in the **Actual Outcome** (or equivalent) column of your test plan as you perform each test. Record the outcome immediately – it is easy to record details inaccurately or even forget them altogether if you leave it till later! If you do not have evidence of a test, you cannot prove that you have actually carried it out.

1 Carry out the first test.
2 Record the actual result in your test plan.
3 Then carry out the second test, record the result, and so on.

If the actual outcome is the same as the expected outcome, you can record it in any of the following ways:

- Write (or type) details of what happened during the test.
- Copy and paste the detail from the **Expected Outcome** column into the **Actual Outcome** column.
- Write (or type) 'As expected' in the **Actual Outcome** column.

If you have created a test checklist, you could simply enter a ✓ if the actual result is as expected.

You can copy and paste 'As expected' from one cell to another too.

If you carefully followed the instructions when creating the clip, and checked your work at each stage, you should find that the actual result is the same as the expected result. But mistakes can happen, so even if you think you were very careful as you created your clip, testing carefully is important.

If, as a result of testing an element, you find that the result is different to what is expected, or that you have forgotten to do something, enter a comment in the **Actual Outcome** column. You have identified an area of improvement.

TIP

Remember to save your test plan frequently (if you are using a word processor).

Activity 29: Carry out the testing...

In this activity you will carry out various tests on your video clip.

*Grading: Pass level candidates must carry out at least four tests; **Merit** level candidates must carry out at least five tests; **Distinction** level candidates must carry out at least six tests. **Merit** and **Distinction** level candidates **must** test the main areas of the clip.*

- Refer to your test plan and decide how many and which tests you will carry out on your video clip.
- Carry out the first test and record the result in your test plan. Then carry out the second test, record the result and so on.
- Save your updated test plan.

Identifying and actioning areas for improvement

In your test plan, look at the areas where the actual outcome and the expected outcome differ. Decide what improvement you need to make (if any) and add it to your test plan for each area.

Pass level candidates are not required to action any areas identified for improvement. **Merit** level candidates must action at least one area and **Distinction** level candidates should action most areas identified for improvement. This is not as difficult you may think – you already know how to do this! The skills required to correct any errors or omissions found are the same as the skills you learned for creating the video clip.

To action any problems or omissions, you will need:

- your final project file in .mswmm format (Microsoft Windows Movie Maker format)
- access to a computer with Windows Movie Maker
- your test plan.

Action each area, one at a time, and record details of each change as you make it. Be careful not to get so involved with making changes to your video clip that you forget to record details of the changes. Providing evidence of the changes is very important at this stage. Your evidence will be:

- the notes you make in your test plan
- your amended movie project file in .mswmm (Microsoft Windows Movie Maker) format
- the final amended, exported movie clip in .wmv (Windows Movie) file format.

Correcting areas identified for improvement

1 Changing the content to make it suitable for the aim, audience and message conveyed

If, during your testing, you find that the content of your video clip is not suitable for your audience, that it does not meet your stated aim or that it does not convey the right message, then the content will need to be changed. If the actual source video clips, images, animations or sounds are not appropriate, then you will need to do one or more of the following:

- Delete the inappropriate part(s) of the clip by trimming the unwanted part(s).
- Replace the inappropriate components with more suitable clips.
- Move clips to another position.

If you need to trim clips refer to the section 'Reducing timing of individual components' below. To increase the timing of a component refer to the sections 'Increasing timing of images and animations' below and 'Increasing timing of source video clips and sounds' on page 246.

To delete a clip: Display the Timeline view by clicking the **Show Timeline** button Show Timeline → Select the clip → Press the **Delete** key.

To move a clip: Display the **Timeline** view → Click and drag the clip to the new position.

When you have finished making any changes, check the running time of the whole clip to make sure that it is still at least 45 seconds long.

2 Changing the time allocated to individual components

Reducing timing of individual components

If the timing for a component (source video clip, sound clip, narration, image or animation) is too long, the timing should be trimmed in Timeline view as follows:

1. Zoom in using the **Zoom Timeline In** button .
2. Position your mouse cursor at the end of the clip in the Timeline (the cursor changes to a red double-headed arrow) → Click and drag the mouse to the left to trim the item.
3. Play the trimmed clip(s) again to ensure that the new timing is correct.

Increasing timing of images and animations

To increase the duration of images and animations: Position your mouse cursor at the end of the clip in the Timeline (the cursor changes to a red double-headed arrow) → Click and drag the mouse to the right to increase the timing of the image or animation → Check the new timing by positioning your mouse cursor on the component in the Timeline view (a tooltip will display the new duration).

Increasing timing of source video clips and sounds

To increase the timing of the source video clips and sound clips (including narrations), click the right side of the clip in the Timeline and drag to the right. Note that you can only increase the timing to the length of the original source clip. For example, if the source clip was 15 seconds, you cannot drag it to increase the length beyond 15 seconds.

If you want the particular images in a video clip to play for longer, or a particular sound to play for longer, then drag the source clip from the Collections folder into the Timeline so that the clip appears twice in the Timeline. You can trim the timing of one or both clips so that the combined duration is as you want it.

Alternatively, you can drag a new clip into the Timeline from your Collections to include a different clip altogether. If you do not have a suitable clip in your Collections, you will need to find a suitable clip and import it into Windows Movie Maker.

3 Changing the duration of the whole video clip

Reducing timing of the whole clip

If the length of the video clip is more than 45 seconds, it is not essential that you reduce the timing as there is no prescribed maximum time. However, if you think that your clip is far too long, you can reduce its length by reducing the timing of individual components as described above in the section titled '2 Changing the time allocated to individual components'.

The running time of individual images and animations within your video clip are likely to be much shorter than the running time of the individual video clips. The sound clips are likely to synchronise with the video clips. Therefore if you want to reduce the total running time, it is likely that it is the duration of individual video clips that needs to be trimmed. Refer to the section above.

Increasing timing of the whole clip

If the length of the video clip is less than 45 seconds, you will need to increase the length. To increase the total running time you could:

- add new components (e.g. images, animation or source video clips)
- increase the length of the time of individual components (see' Changing the time allocated to individual components')
- add titles and or credits or increase the duration of titles and/or credits. To add titles and credits refer to the section 'Adding titles and credits' on page 223 of Chapter 12.

Once you have made any changes, check the running time of the whole clip again.

4 Changing or adding effects and transitions

Changes or additions to effects and transitions should be made in Storyboard view. Click the **Show Storyboard** button Show Timeline .

- To delete an existing effect or transition: Click once on an effect or transition → Press the **Delete** key.
- To move an effect or transition: Click and drag it to the new position on the Storyboard.
- To insert a new effect: display the Collections pane → select **Video Effects** → Select an effect in the Contents pane → Press **Play** to preview it → Click and drag the effect to the video effect cell at the bottom left of a video clip on the Storyboard.
- To insert a new effect: Display the Collections pane → Select **Video Transition** → Select a transition in the Contents pane → Press **Play** to preview it → Click and drag the transition to the transition cell between the video clips on the Storyboard.

5 Saving an amended project as a movie file

Display the **Tasks** pane → Below **Finish Movie**, click **Save to my computer** to display the **Save Movie Wizard** dialogue box → Type a suitable filename – use a different filename from the one used for the original movie file before testing → Select the file location → **Next** → **Finish** (a dialogue box displays) → Select **Show more choices** → Click **Other settings** → Select an option (e.g. **Video for Broadband (150 kbs)** → **Next**. Your clip will be saved as a **.wmv** file (Windows Media Video).

6 Saving an amended project in a suitable file format

If you find during testing that you have not saved your video clip in a suitable file format, then import the final version of the project file into Windows Movie Maker and follow the instructions in Chapter 12 (page 225) in the section titled 'Saving your final movie clip (exporting in a suitable file format').

7 Adding a soundtrack

If you find during testing that you have not added a soundtrack (i.e. sound files) to your movie clip then follow the instructions in Chapter 12 (pages 219–221) under the sections titled 'Adding sound clips to your movie' and 'Adjusting audio levels for video clips with captured sound'.

8 Adding narration

If you find during testing that you have not added a narration and would like to do so, follow the instructions in Chapter 12 (page 221) in the section 'Adding narration'. Note that adding narration is only required by **Distinction** level candidates.

If you need to make changes to the actual content of your narrated clip, it is best to delete that sound clip from the Timeline view and record the narration again. If you need to reduce the length of the clip, follow the instructions for 'Reducing timing of individual components' on page 245 in this chapter.

Activity 30: Identify area(s) for improvement and action improvements...

In this activity you will make change(s) to your video clip as a result of the testing.

*Grading: **Pass** level candidates are not required to make any changes; **Merit** level candidates must correct at least one identified problem/omission; **Distinction** level candidates must correct most of the problems/omissions identified as a result of the testing.*

- Refer to your test plan, identify areas that could be improved and decide how many you will correct.
- Make the changes to your video clip as required.
- Save your amended movie project file using a different filename from the last saved version (e.g. if your final project file was xxxV4, this corrected version could be saved as xxxfinal).
- Export your amended video clip as a .wmv file in a suitable file size using a different filename to the movie file exported before testing.

Portfolio builder

By reading and understanding the guidelines in this chapter, and working through the activities, you have learned how to test a video clip and how to record your tests. For your own portfolio, you will need to create a test table or checklist and test the video clip that you created for your portfolio.

You should read the 'How this assessment objective will be assessed…' and 'How to achieve…' sections of this chapter – the number of tests you carry out, what you test and whether or not you action any identified areas of improvement will all affect your grading.

For your portfolio, you will need to produce a test plan, then test the clip and identify any areas for improvement. Depending on the grade you are working towards, you will also need to action one or most of the identified areas for improvement. You may use or adapt the test plans provided with this book. You must make sure you write down every aspect of your testing and correcting.

Good luck!

Index